Metacriticism

Metacriticism

Suresh Raval

The University of Georgia Press
Athens

Copyright © 1981 by the University of Georgia Press
Athens, Georgia 30602

Design by Sandra Strother
Set in 10 on 13 Palatino
PRINTED IN THE UNITED STATES OF AMERICA

Library of Congress Cataloging in Publication Data

Raval, Suresh.
Metacriticism.
Includes index.
1. Criticism.   I. Title.
PN81.R33   801'.95   81-4872
ISBN 0-8203-0587-1   AACR2

The publication of this work was made possible in part through a grant from the National Endowment for the Humanities, a federal agency whose mission is to award grants to support education, scholarship, media programming, libraries, and museums in order to bring the results of cultural activities to the general public.

FOR MY PARENTS

Oh! Blessed rage for order, pale Ramon,
The maker's rage to order words of the sea,
Words of the fragrant portals, dimly starred,
And of ourselves and of our origins,
In ghostlier demarcations, keener sounds.

Wallace Stevens

It might be imagined that some propositions, of the form of
empirical propositions, were hardened and functioned as
channels for such empirical propositions as were not hardened
but fluid; and that this relationship altered with time, in that
fluid propositions hardened, and hard ones became fluid.

Wittgenstein

Contents

PART ONE
Some Problems and Perspectives in Critical Theory

PART TWO
Logic, Rhetoric, and Value in Critical Theory

Preface

THIS BOOK IS A METACRITICAL ANALYSIS of the concept of criticism which shows that the fundamental concepts of criticism, though they can be logically developed and defended, have their ground in history. It attempts an account of the structure of several major concepts developed during the last two hundred years and develops a general theory of the nature of the reasoning that informs the practices of criticism. Following Wittgenstein, though I hope not programmatically, I have sought to counter any narrow and univocal view of the logic of critical concepts. And I have sought to counter the argument, underlying several forms of contemporary criticism, that because reason in its traditional forms tends to be objectivist it must be abandoned. This argument commits itself to a total rejection of the concepts of criticism and culture and proposes in effect a concept which is itself no less totalizing, reductionist, and self-defeating. Some proponents of this position seek to replace logic with rhetoric and reason with imagination, and end by reasserting the dualities that they initially seemed to oppose. This study argues that logic and rhetoric, reason and history, subsist in a relation of complex interdependence, that a failure to grasp this relation leads the theory and practice of criticism to paradox, quandary, and finally crisis.

A major guiding principle of this study is that the investigation of the nature, status, and significance of criticism has become the dominant concern of the most influential critical thinkers since the New Critics. And one of its main aims is to understand what each of these thinkers has told us about criticism, how it is to be adequately characterized, and what is the significance of criticism in the endeavor to understand the nature and status of humanistic inquiry. This mode of proceeding challenges the position of those who argue that after the New Criticism criticism has little of significance to say to us, just as it challenges the position of those who argue that liberating oneself from New Criticism (even if one naively considered it an easy task) necessarily means advancing to the new and unquestionable frontiers of critical understanding. Critical opponents often write as if their own point is the correct one and the others are confused or in serious error. When critical opposition isn't developed in such rigid terms, it leads at times to uncritical assimilation of the presumed great advances in other disciplines. In order to escape both from the intellectual skepticism entailed by the first position and from the weak-kneed pluralism entailed by the second, it is important to examine critical concepts and positions in their own terms, to probe them for internal weaknesses and difficulties. This, I believe, can help us to acquire a more adequate and comprehensive understanding of the concept of criticism. To bring out the insight underlying a given concept requires, as Hegel would put it, showing what is false and abstract in its various manifestations.

The diversity of critical positions and thinkers treated in this work may suggest to readers the ones that get left out. For instance, I don't discuss structuralism and Marxist criticism, though there are implications here for studying them. This work, however, does not seek to be exhaustive. Its principal mode of discussion is not historical exposition, extended summaries of different theories, or a programmatic defense of a particular theory of criticism, but rather conceptual analysis. In modern criticism there is a strong tradition stemming from Kant. The philosophical foundations of that tradition need to be more fully probed and established in relation to contemporary critical theories. This feeling prompted me to give a somewhat detailed expository account of Kant's aesthetics, though readers familiar with the contours of Kant's thought may want to skip those pages. Nevertheless, I would hope that my treatment of Kant's theory justifies the exposition. The interest in examining philosophical assumptions led me to deal with the vital issues raised by psychoanalysis, hermeneutics, and poststructuralism. In contemporary criticism, although critical theory and criticism have turned to Continental thought, modern aesthetics and recent criticism and theory have tended to shun one another. The reason for this mutual avoidance is twofold: many critics and critical theorists are skeptical of the power and value of analytical philosophy, and analytical philosophers are suspicious of critics excited by Continental thought. This attitude has continued to widen the gulf between literary criticism and analytical philosophy. This study attempts, in a modest way, to bridge the gulf and to show the value that may result from an interchange between these various disciplines. One of the benefits of such an interchange may be that none of the disciplines will be able to maintain its coterielike intellectual climate.

A BOOK LIKE THIS ONE owes a special debt to the many theorists and critics who have written directly or indirectly on the issues I deal with. I am glad to acknowledge here my debt to the work of those whose views have challenged me to confront the theoretical issues of criticism. Beyond these inevitable professional debts, I have over the years incurred a number of personal debts which I should like to acknowledge here. For advice, encouragement, and criticism I want to record my gratitude to the following teachers, colleagues, and friends: Malcolm Brown, Douglas Canfield, Edgar Dryden, Robert B. Heilman, Jerrold Hogle, Robert O. Payne, Herbert Schneidau, Frank Warnke, and Hayden White. Gerald McNiece read the final draft and gave shrewd rhetorical criticism and generous moral support for which I am deeply grateful. In the summer of 1976 I benefited from the lectures of René Girard, Frank Kermode, and Hayden White at the School of Criticism and Theory at the University of California, Irvine, instituted by Murray Krieger and Hazard Adams.

My deepest gratitude is to the two teachers at Bombay University, India, who, nearly fifteen years ago, introduced me to issues and interests whose importance I began to realize only after I had finished (and broken away from the aims of) my doctoral dissertation written in the United States. M. P. Rege introduced me to Kant and taught me how to struggle with the difficulties of his thought. R. B. Patankar introduced me to Wittgenstein and aesthetics, and reinforced my conviction that the philosophical understanding of literature must depend on a passionate interest in literature and its history, though this interest by itself can never be enough for sophisticated theoretical inquiry. His teaching was as greathearted as it was self-effacing; whatever insights of value this work may have would not be possible without the example of his teaching.

I owe a debt of gratitude also to Lee T. Lemon and René Wellek. Professor Lemon offered some acute criticism and advice, enabling me to make changes of substance and style in my manuscript. Professsor Wellek, with his characteristic generosity and toughminded-ness, pulled some loose threads, raised incisive questions, and offered criticism which made me rethink and sharpen what I had con-fidently assumed was already finished. That his criticism wasn't in-tended to force me to adopt his position on specific issues will remain for me an ideal of exemplary scholarly conduct. The errors of thought and expression are, like the views proposed and analyses developed here, mine.

I am grateful to the editors of the following two journals for per-mission to reprint material that first appeared in their publications. Chapter 3 is a slightly revised version of my essay "Intention and Contemporary Literary Theory," which appeared in the *Journal of Aes-thetics and Art Criticism*, March 1980. "Rational Inquiry in Literary Crit-icism" appeared in *Philosophy and Phenomenological Research*, March 1980; it is incorporated in an extensively revised and expanded form in Chapter 6.

I am grateful to Dean Paul Rosenblatt for a grant which enabled me to prepare the final version for the press. I am grateful to Ellen Harris for excellent copy editing, and to the editorial staff at the Uni-versity of Georgia Press and Robert Buffington, general editor, for being everything an author could wish.

Frances Raval, wife and friend, has brought the gift of literary sen-sibility and love for which gratitude can have no expression.

Introduction

WHEN PLATO DENOUNCED POETRY as twice removed from reality and exalted philosophy as giving rational knowledge of forms and therefore of reality, he began a major theoretical dispute about the nature of poetry. This dispute has cast a long shadow on the history of literary theory. Much of the subsequent theory from Aristotle through Sidney and Shelley to Richards and the New Critics is a defense of poetry. Aristotle, for instance, defended poetry for sharing in common with science and philosophy the concern for the "universal" and thus gave it a place of honor. This defense, with various modifications, held considerable sway until almost the end of the eighteenth century. With the advent of romanticism, however, there arose a new problematic of art which placed emphasis on individuality, originality, sincerity, and spontaneity. These romantic categories are radically opposed to the Aristotelian categories of probability and necessity as well as to the neoclassical concern with commonly shared truths. Yet the pervasively romantic mode of criticism did not altogether eliminate the objectivist bias among at least some critics, who sought to put literary criticism on a solid rational footing and to provide for it a scientific basis. These critics hoped to overcome the fluidity of terminology and concepts used in critical discourse and thus to rid criticism of subjectivist tendencies. For they argued that without an objectively conceived foundation the activity of criticism hampers dialogue and prevents methodological and cognitive advance in criticism.

The desire to put criticism on scientific grounds seemed for a while to triumph in our own time when structuralism emerged on the critical scene with an extraordinary arsenal of "scientific" instruments. The words of Claude Lévi-Strauss bear eloquent testimony to this desire and indeed to the belief that now the desire is about to be

1

fulfilled: "For centuries the humanities and the social sciences have resigned themselves to contemplating the world of the natural and exact sciences as a kind of paradise they will never enter. And all of a sudden there is a small door which is being opened between the two fields, and it is linguistics which has done it."[1] The pursuit of scientific objectivity was intended in part to put to rest the other, presumably subjective approaches to literature. And the argument for objectivity in criticism soon developed into a plea for the adoption of advanced scientific methods. For one thing it took its inspiration from the recent achievements in linguistics and anthropology, which partly owe their startling developments to the employment of methods of modern science. Insofar as this is true, the supporters of scientific methods in criticism insist, there is every reason for critics to use the means of success in one field for similar results in another field.

Contemporary criticism, however, has brought to the forefront of critical debate issues that no longer afford easy categorization or methodological certitude—and this is true despite the fact that the rhetoric of crisis is conducted in the mode of unquestionable authority and truth. By an ironic reversal perhaps endemic to the history of thought, some of the leading critics are no longer concerned with the problem of defending literature, a task traditionally reserved for poets and apologists for poetry. Some critics have sought to expose literature as a sham and have announced the death of literature. Some of these critics propose at interminable length the replacement of literature by silence, and some others propose a dissolution of all fundamental questions of traditional criticism. It cannot be denied, then, that the scene of criticism is one of crisis and that there would seem to be little hope of escaping to the comfortable certainties of philosophical and methodological abstractions. For the increase in theoretical speculation in criticism during the past decade or so would seem to suggest a rather ambiguous and questionable relation between the practice and theory of criticism. The rhetoric of crisis has given rise to a number of different suspicions: the privilege accorded in the past to literature was arbitrary, the product of a bourgeois culture incapable of reflecting on its own condition as a sham; literature has a complicity in the ambiguous and contradictory nature of culture; neither the practice nor the theory of criticism can acquire a coherence by which each might hope to make sense of literature; practical criticism and literary theory, far from having an integral relation, are inevitably

2

antithetical; and finally, the logic of theory or practice can be shown to be not just questionable at some moments but inherently suspect because it cannot disguise its arbitrary and rhetorical character. Whether the sense of crisis is genuine or a product of some serious conceptual confusions masked in the idiom of theoretical profundity, one senses crisis when not only is the distinction between literary and ordinary language challenged—since the distinction can never be supported by any straightforward and unquestionable set of criteria—but the whole categories of language, literature, and culture are repudiated.

It is in order to account for this crisis that Paul de Man has argued that "the notion of crisis and that of criticism are closely linked, so much so that one could state that all true criticism occurs in the mode of crisis."[2] Moreover, de Man has argued in a number of essays that all cultural endeavor in general and all critical endeavor in particular are predicated upon *error*, since they come into being by opposing previous answers and questions against which the historically later efforts "offer their own definitions and alternatives." De Man's concept of criticism implies that all criticism involves "a fundamental misreading of literature which is always, systematically a misreading performed by others."[3] Given this intrinsic element of misreading, itself necessitated by the nature of literary language, which is the source of mystification in the critic, though it is itself free from the duplicity and confusion of ordinary language, de Man would seem to propose a concept of interpretation which gives centrality to rhetoric.[4]

De Man's concept of criticism emerges from his engagement with the thought of Jacques Derrida, who has, following the radical potentialities of recent Continental thought, questioned the notions of language, being, center, and origin which are central to Western philosophy and put into question the presumed distinctions between literary and ordinary language, philosophy and literature, literature and criticism. Exposing a certain problematic inherent in the work of Lévi-Strauss and the concept of humanistic interpretation underlying it, Derrida offers the alternative of radical interpretation, which, he argues, "affirms free play and tries to pass beyond man and humanism . . . [and] does not seek in ethnography . . . the inspiration of a new humanism."[5] It is in order, as it were, to contain Derrida and to save the concept of art[6] that de Man seemed to have proposed his concept of literary language in *Blindness and Insight*. Yet in his essays since 1971 de Man has moved to a position not simply closer to Derrida's but complementary to it. This position, known as "deconstruction," questions the concepts of literature and criticism, and problematizes the philosophical conceptions of knowledge, language, and understanding. If this mode of questioning is something more than just one more manifestation of the contemporary urge for comprehensive theoretical or antitheoretical models—and the influence of Derrida's work is already considerable—then we have a deepening and unalterable crisis for criticism and finally for all cultural endeavor. Deconstruction, then, has become important both because of the implications of its stance and because of the kind of interpretations it has inspired of literary, philosophical, and psychological texts. I want to discuss this position and examine its value in order to determine its significance for the concept of criticism. My intention is not to conduct a full-fledged philosophical inquiry into poststructuralist thought, but to raise the questions pertinent to criticism and its theory: What is the relation of a presumed philosophical or metaphysical insight into the nature of things or language or culture as a whole to understanding, and talking about, literature and criticism? I discuss this in Chapter 7.

If deconstructionist criticism has developed a rhetoric of the inevitability of crisis and located it in the very nature of language, there is a group of critical theorists among whom there prevails an altogether different mood. E. D. Hirsch, who is a major theoretician of interpretation, may safely be considered a spokesman for this group. A proponent of objectivist interpretation who would both overcome the conflict among different critical theories and show a way of reaching the most probable, objective interpretations of literary works, Hirsch has said:

> How important are the theoretical disagreements that now divide serious students of interpretation? How true is the resigned opinion that our various schools and approaches are like a multitude of warring sects, each with its own uncompromising theology? Is it the destiny of those who practice interpretation never to achieve an ecumenical harmony of theoretical principles? If that is our destiny, so much the worse for theory, which is then only an ideology of a sect, and so much the better for the common sense of a practitioner who disdains theory to get on with his work.[7]

Hirsch does not mean to repudiate the importance of theory for criticism. Rather he contends that the logic of inquiry in criticism is the

4

same as in the sciences. Objectivist theorists, then, are worried that unless criticism is founded on a principle of rational inquiry that would enable critics to refute some interpretations and to establish the most probable as the proper one, criticism is open to radical skepticism. It is not simply the proliferation of self-indulgent and bizarre interpretations that worries the objectivists. They fear the very dissolution of rational discourse in criticism. If critics cannot eliminate certain interpretations on objectively defensible grounds, if they cannot justify certain procedures as valid for the proper conduct of critical inquiry, they are then faced with the anomalous conclusion that anything goes, that all interpretations are equally correct. Deconstructionist critics, then, would be right in claiming that language contains within itself a ceaseless process of sign-substitutions, making it impossible for us to say and mean anything in particular.

The scene of conflict in critical theory thus confronts us with the fundamental question of the logic of inquiry in criticism: What is the nature of inquiry in literary interpretations? If criticism and its theories are subject to serious scrutiny, can we still say that critical theories can be neither true nor false? And if we can, when and on what grounds? What is the nature of disputes that arise in criticism? I attempt to deal with these questions in Chapter 6. I shall argue that though different critics and critical theorists, holding different and conflicting concepts of art and criticism, often talk at cross-purposes, they nevertheless do at times engage in genuine critical debate, and that their debate often turns on such questions as: "What is literature?" "Why is a work called a work of art?" "What reasons can we give for calling it art?" Moreover, as we examine their answers, we can show where and how difficulties arise in specific theories, where these theories do go wrong, and what their difficulties and errors imply about both critical theory and the concept of criticism.

SINCE MY CONCERN is with critical theory as it has been variously formulated and defended in modern criticism, I shall not be giving many illustrations of practical criticism. But to anchor the problem of the nature of literary works and its relation to the concept of interpretation in the practice of criticism, I shall attempt here a brief discussion of two major readings of a famous short poem by Wordsworth, and offer a sketch of a rival reading. My discussion will imply the following points: different insights or categories lead critics to constitute the poem differently; incompatible interpretations cannot be reconciled, though a specific reading may be criticized as being obvious, weak, confused, or inadequate; yet even incompatible readings in principle claim to be valid readings; and, finally, one cannot eliminate one of the incompatible readings as conclusively wrong. I develop and defend these points more fully in Chapter 6. We can now turn to Wordsworth's Lucy poem:

> A slumber did my spirit seal;
>   I had no human fears:
> She seemed a thing that could not feel
>   The touch of earthly years.
>
> No motion has she now, no force;
>   She neither hears nor sees,
> Rolled round in earth's diurnal course,
>   With rocks, and stones, and trees.

As Cleanth Brooks interprets the poem, Wordsworth has developed "a context calculated to pull 'human fears' in opposed directions," so that an attentive reading generates an ironic effect. Yet irony in the first stanza is latent and manifests itself more directly in the second stanza when we realize that the "slumber" that had sealed his spirit has now sealed hers. The speaker's slumber is revealed as a delusion because her death has shown that she was not beyond mortality. The complexity of the second stanza, moreover, derives from the subtle opposition built into its language. Though Lucy has no motion normal to human beings, she has become absorbed into the processes of nature: she rolls round in the earth's movement with other objects of nature. His former assurance that Lucy was beyond "the touch of earthly years" makes it shocking for him to accept the reality of Lucy's death. She is deprived of all human sensuous properties: "No motion has she now, no force; / She neither hears nor sees." The final two lines powerfully suggest a "dead lifelessness." "The statement of the first stanza," Brooks concludes, "has been literally realized in the second, but its meaning has been ironically reversed." If the first stanza evoked a confident sense of Lucy's reality as a being of nature and hence beyond mortality, the second has completely reversed that sense: Lucy is dead, whirling in the earth's daily course. For Brooks the poem holds together its contradictory movement through a subtle use of irony.[8]

F. W. Bateson proposes an interpretation that is fundamentally incompatible with Brooks's. Bateson finds the poem moving to a "climax in the pantheistic magnificence of the last two lines." No doubt, he would agree, the Lucy of the first stanza is opposed to the "grander dead-Lucy" since the latter has become involved in the sublime processes of nature. The poem achieves a reconciliation between the two philosophies because Lucy, though now dead, is "part of the life of Nature" and has transcended her merely human condition. The poem thus embodies Wordsworth's major philosophical attitude and, though there are some internal contrasts within the poem, achieves its unity without recourse to dramatic irony. Its unity derives from the views Wordsworth held. Consequently, the poem is a significant representative of Wordsworth's personality.[9]

Let me now sketch another reading of the poem which is in large part my own. The poem dramatizes a complex interplay of feelings in the speaker's mind, and it is the gradual and almost unselfconscious disclosure of these feelings that constitutes the poem's power. The speaker's slumber is, of course, a delusion, since he had invested a finite being with the property of infinity. His awakening from the slumber at first returns his deluded perception to a stunned recognition of Lucy's finitude. Thus the second stanza registers the speaker's sense of shock: "No motion has she now, no force; / She neither hears nor sees." Yet the stanza moves toward and culminates in a rich paradox. The lifelessness of Lucy has now become a permanent part of "earth's diurnal course" in which "rocks, and stones, and trees" are in a motion beyond the "touch of earthly years." The negatives of the first stanza seemed to operate as the metaphor of permanence or eternity, whereas the negatives of the second stanza first introduce a metonymic perception of loss and fragmentation and thus seem to contradict the movement of the first stanza. Nevertheless, to an attentive reading, the negatives soon appear compatible with those of the first stanza, although with a difference. The metaphor of permanence that opens the poem has, as it were, discovered its deficiency and, by passing through the metonymy of death and fragmentation, discovered the language (or metaphor) that expresses the speaker's deeper feelings. It seems to me that the important moment for the speaker lies here in a re-cognition of his feelings. The metonymy of loss has led to the metaphor of insight. A delusion has been removed from the speaker's perception: though Lucy is dead, she has only passed from a finitude to a mode of permanence. For Wordsworth this movement of mind bridges the distance between his response to

7

the living and the dead Lucy in a spontaneous feeling of comprehension. Through this feeling the poet acquires a deeper understanding of his own feelings. It is this complication of feelings which, brought to the level of awareness, makes the poem "meditative beyond irony." [10]

Now, all of these interpretations rest on how Wordsworth's poem is to be properly interpreted. Bateson seeks to reconstruct the author's stance, which he thinks determines the poem's meaning. Brooks interprets the poem as an autonomous work animated by a principle of irony which makes for a powerful experience of the poem. The third reading interprets the poem by characterizing the feelings that pervade the Wordsworthian consciousness in the poem. If Bateson, following a method of historical scholarship, argues for an affirmation of life implicit in the poem, Brooks emphasizes the poem's bitter irony. Contrary to both, the third reading argues for the poem's meditative mood, which operates beyond either irony or affirmation. It is possible to say that the last reading seeks to characterize the interplay of irony and affirmation in phenomenological terms.

Bateson could give at least three arguments for his interpretation: Wordsworth, as a historical human being, is central to the understanding of the poem; his attitude, construed on the best possible evidence, ought to be taken into account; and finally, internal evidence alone is not sufficient for proper criticism. [11] All three arguments are logically connected, and insist on the value of biographical and historical scholarship. Brooks could argue in response that Bateson's recourse to external evidence is questionable, because the success of the poem depends on whether the poem has freed itself from dependence on historical or biographical contexts. Yet he would not deny that these contexts may be skillfully embodied within the structure of the poem. For the last reading one could argue that it is important to grasp the nature of consciousness that is central to Wordsworth's mode of writing poetry. And, one could add, it is indispensable to relate the poem to the other Lucy poems and to the ligatures of Wordsworth's inward feelings. Unlike Brooks, whose organicist premises commit him to respond to poems as self-contained objects, this reading considers the poem to belong in a matrix of Wordsworthian moods and questionings that hold a constant communion with nature and his own self.

Bateson could take exception to both readings. Against the last reading he might argue that, however complex the feelings aroused by the poem, it nevertheless represents a determinate pantheistic attitude, an attitude which any satisfactory reading of the poem must articulate. Against Brooks's reading he might say that if one begins to look for irony one can find it almost anywhere. Recent deconstructionist criticism, he could add, is nothing but a culmination of the logical implications of the New Critical doctrine of poems.[12] Bateson would even admit that someone may prove his specific reading wrong or inadequate (only if it could be shown that Wordsworth in fact did not hold the philosophy that Bateson ascribes to him), but he would still insist that his method is not wrong.[13] This, however, is an argument available to all three critics: each one could in principle allow for the possibility of error in his reading, yet each would defend the critical principle that he holds for realizing poems.

All three interpretations are coherent. Bateson does not clarify many of the structural details that Brooks nicely elucidates. Yet Brooks, by an exclusive emphasis on the organicist doctrine of poetry, fails to account for the poem's voice. The voice, especially in the second stanza, though it registers a sense of shock, is nevertheless meditative and does not operate strictly in terms of the ironic reversals stressed by Brooks. Brooks, however, given his conception of poems, is not required to ask questions that otherwise seem inescapable: Who is Lucy? Why isn't she described in more specific detail? What is the significance of the fact that the poem is predominantly an exploration of the state of the poet's mind, or his feelings? Bateson's reading implies an awareness of these questions, though his answer depends on biographical facts. Someone will no doubt find the third reading inadequate or deficient and propose a rival or complementary reading. In short, there will be other reappropriations of Wordsworth's poem, and they will spring in part from a small shift in sensibility. When there occurs a large and fundamental shift in sensibility there will undoubtedly be interpretations that will be radically different from the ones we have known so far. Thus the plurality of interpretations that art invites is a testimony to its great power to fascinate us and compel us to reinterpret it.

Thus if literary works could be interpreted in different ways, and if literary interpretations could be coherent and more or less compelling even if divergent, immediately there arises the question about the identity of literary works: Given differences in the interpretations of a poem, are different critics talking about the same work? If they are or are not, how are we to talk about the identity of literary works? And there are a number of related questions which must be dealt with in order to answer the question of identity satisfactorily: Could different interpretations be harmonized into a single comprehensive reading by some unified theory of criticism? What are the implications of the possibility or impossibility of such a theory for the concept of criticism? In other terms, does criticism have a logic such that it can prescribe the conditions of what is and is not proper in responding to literary works? If it does or does not, what is a satisfactory account of the concept of criticism? A thorough investigation of these questions is necessary for confronting the sense of crisis in contemporary criticism and for exposing what might be the result of wrong, confused, or misplaced expectations from criticism.

This book attempts to deal with the questions I have outlined above. Part One deals with several major theories of criticism, and Part Two deals with the questions already raised. My discussion, however, of the aesthetic theories of Kant and the philosophical idealists, in Chapter 1, requires some justification. The reasons for considering them are several. First, Kant provided what is perhaps an unparalleled demonstration of the internal dynamics of our statements about beauty and implicitly set the central questions for our statements about art. He construed the classic problem of aesthetic theory to be that of accounting for the extremely problematical situation that occurs in our discussions of beauty. This situation may be roughly characterized in the following manner: although we all agree that beauty is ineffable and therefore beyond analysis, we argue as if it is a question of right and wrong, as if our judgments are objective or cognitive, as if our disputes can be unequivocally resolved in favor of a correct answer.

Second, Kant significantly influenced the aesthetic theories of philosophical idealists, and both have had enormous influence on one of the most powerful movements of criticism in this century, the New Criticism. Third, the history of modern criticism since Kant can be viewed as a series of responses to the doctrine of aesthetic autonomy; most theories of criticism accept, reject, or assimilate this doctrine. Fourth, even if we complacently believe that both the New Criticism and idealism are dead, a close scrutiny of other methods will show how both continue to exert some influence. Fifth, our analysis of the concept of poetic autonomy will show that some of its difficulties derive from its idealist conceptual structure and that critics have had eventually to face these difficulties and at some moment in their criticism to abandon the constraints imposed by that structure. Sixth, all these point up an interesting feature about the scene of criticism: that it is changing or unstable, though proponents of different theories often seem to argue that their theories are rationally grounded or systematically arrived at and allow for progressive increase in our knowledge of literature. And, finally, the Kantian and idealist aesthetics have some radical consequences for criticism owing to their metaphysical doctrines. This feature of their aesthetic theories has an interesting relationship with the criticism of those who follow Derrida, since this criticism also owes allegiance to some metaphysical doctrines. A close scrutiny of the Kantian and idealist aesthetics and deconstructionist criticism will help us better understand the nature of both criticism and critical theory.

My purpose is to examine the logic of various critical theories, and to show the strategies by which they defend their respective positions, and, if they break down or seem inadequate, to explain where and why. I do this by firmly keeping in view the history and theory of criticism. It is part of my argument that concepts of criticism are not exactly logical because they acquire their significance in the history of a literary culture. Nor are they exactly empirical matters, since once some of them have emerged, they continue to exert pressure in later periods in one way or another. Yet they are amenable to a metacritical scrutiny which seeks to examine the logic of a specific critical concept and its relation to other concepts. I try to clarify the concept of metacriticism in Chapter 8.

Given the concept of metacriticism as I hold it, this book does not attempt to prove or defend a particular theory of criticism. Its main points, however, can be stated here. (1) All concepts of criticism are offered as both necessary and sufficient. (2) Some of these concepts (or theories), insofar as they show genuine insights into literature, are individually sufficient for experiencing some aspects of literature, but none by itself is a necessary one for criticism to function vitally. (3) The interesting thing about disputes in criticism, however, is that proponents of each mode of criticism claim to provide valid interpretations of literature. (4) If this leads to honest confrontation among different modes of criticism, it can lead to a general deepening of our understanding of literature. But if this claim about necessary validity leads merely to sophistry and partisan rhetoric of arbitrary praise and condemnation, then to that extent the contending critic detracts from the complexity and vitality of critical discourse. (5) Any method that makes intelligent and sensitive criticism possible can never be logically refuted or disproved, though it may eventually cease to attract attention. It can even find a more sophisticated expression and defense in a later articulation. But its claim for universal validity can certainly be disproved; to do this is to show that it is inadequate, though not to falsify all of its insights. (6) All conceptual structures of criticism are necessarily partial, and yet it is in their nature to claim value and validity for their own specific proposals by denying rival conceptual structures and their proposals. (7) And, finally, this denial takes a complex form so that an adversary conceptual structure assimilates the valuable insights of the structures it rejects by subordinating them under its own premises. Thus the history of criticism is a changing scene of criticism; it reveals a dialectical process of assimilation and exclusion by which different concepts engage in mutual contest, a contest which is in principle endless and yet involves elements that are amenable to logical scrutiny. Such a scrutiny would reveal the structure of rationality by means of which different critical concepts exhibit and defend the logic of their respective positions, and this structure would show that logic and rhetoric, reason and imagination are deeply intertwined and cannot be conceived as oppositions without simplifying these concepts as well as the discourse in which they are proposed as oppositions.

PART I

Some Problems and Perspectives in Critical Theory

Concepts, like individuals, have their histories, and are just as incapable of withstanding the ravages of time as individuals.

Kierkegaard

CHAPTER ONE
Immanuel Kant and Aesthetic Theory

It is a peculiarity of modern philosophical discussions of Kant's aesthetic theory that they have offered a rather puzzling and uncertain assessment of its importance for concepts of aesthetics and criticism. Harold Osborne, for instance, has said that Kant "was . . . the most powerful mind to have written on aesthetics in modern times," but he considerably qualifies his statement thus: "Kant's own contribution lay chiefly in his ability to give a logically articulated form to the attitudes which were prevalent and to mold them into a coherent system." On this view, Kant's aesthetic theories, despite their "singular acuity in pinpointing the questions whose existence has persisted into the twentieth century,"[1] amount to little more than a rigorous formalization of the central insights of contemporary thought. R. K. Elliott, too, has argued, in an important essay on Kant, that the "Analytic of the Beautiful" "cannot account for the demand for positive agreement or withstand skeptical criticism of its assumption of a common sense." Elliott, moreover, argues that the connection that Kant establishes between the beautiful and the moral in part 2 of the *Critique of Aesthetic Judgment* "does not destroy the autonomy of Taste but ensures its possibility." "Taste, like Morality, can be saved from contradiction only by the employment of metaphysical Ideas."[2]

Elliott's statement implies a more fundamental assumption that aesthetic theories can be proved or disproved, an assumption which Kant seems to have shared. For Kant, however, the assumption becomes complicated and problematical because he also rightly assumed that the aesthetic world is impossible without certain a priori principles. Given this latter assumption, skeptical criticism leveled against any aesthetic theory, including Kant's, does not necessarily disqualify that theory. For if we grant that skeptical criticism does indeed disqualify Kant's theory in the "Analytic" then we have accepted for aesthetic theories a structure of reasoning that can conclusively refute some theories and confirm others, without having established the validity of such a structure of reasoning. Kant's doctrine, whether conceived in terms of the "Analytic" or in terms of the entire third *Critique*, can certainly be questioned on one of two grounds. It can be questioned on internal logical grounds, or it can be rejected on more fundamental conceptual grounds. But this questioning doesn't stem simply from Kant's failure to overcome aesthetic skepticism.[3] For though Kant's project in the third *Critique* was in part to overcome this skepticism, we need to discuss the nature of aesthetic theories and to ask whether they can be proved or disproved. I shall discuss this problem, throughout the present work, in terms of the nature of theories of criticism.

If we say that Kant's aesthetic theories are simply a formalization of contemporary eighteenth-century aesthetic discussions, we cannot account for the enormous impact of Kant's formalist aesthetics on the idealist aesthetics of Hegel, Bosanquet, and Croce, among others; nor can we account for its impact on the history and theory of criticism, on critics and critical theorists such as Poe, A. C. Bradley, Pater, and many others who employ the conceptual vocabulary for art that is distinctively Kantian. In our own times some modern philosophers, such as Stuart Hampshire, have expressed views about art which, if carefully examined, will seem to be essentially Kantian. Moreover, the central assumptions of modern aesthetics are distinctively Kantian, assumptions that characterize art as autonomous, the aesthetic attitude as one of detached contemplation, and aesthetic pleasure as disinterested. On the other hand, Kant's aesthetic theories, if placed in their historical context, seem radically at odds with the contemporary discussions on art and art objects. For contemporary neoclassical criticism held that works of art are classifiable into kinds, whereas Kant argued that every work of art is unique and therefore unclassifiable. His contemporaries took art to be subservient to morality and, following Aristotle, attributed cognitive value to art, whereas Kant attempted a sustained argument that art is autonomous, that aesthetic judgments are singular, and that aesthetic experience is radically different from moral and cognitive experiences. His contemporaries also believed that for aesthetic objects there are universal objective standards by means of which critics can claim objective validity for critical appreciations and judgments, whereas Kant avoids what René Wellek calls the "two extremes which have at different times paralyzed criticism: anarchic subjectivity and frozen absolutism."[4]

No doubt the contemporary critical scene was ridden with controversies on the nature of beautiful objects. But it is no exaggeration to say that Kant seems to have almost entirely ignored them. He was, of course, aware of the empirical mode of discussions of beauty and aesthetic pleasure by Addison, Hutcheson, and Burke, and he regarded Burke as the most important exponent of that mode.[5] But he considered the empirical mode to be simply "psychological" and "physiological" and therefore inadequate to elucidate the form of the aesthetic judgment "this rose is beautiful"; for it claims a subjective but universal validity. Kant thus construed the philosophical question for aesthetic theory to be the elucidation and discovery of an a priori principle which is the condition of the possibility of aesthetic experience. Conceived in these terms, Kant's philosophical stance on aesthetic theory would seem to involve a radical rejection of contemporary aesthetic theory and critical practice. This is a remarkable fact, for the relationship of the third *Critique* to the first *Critique* would now seem to be a peculiar one. In the first *Critique* Kant has given the most formidable analytical validation of the conceptual structure underlying Newtonian physics. It is natural that we should expect him to provide a metacritical validation of the contemporary critical thought in the third *Critique*. Instead, Kant has given us a metacritical validation for a mode of critical practice that would dominate Western criticism almost a century later.

The enormous significance of Kant's aesthetics, from a metacritical view, lies in his exploration of the form of the concept of beauty. For even if we say that the question of beauty is no longer relevant to the understanding of concepts of aesthetic and critical theories, Kant's resolute analysis of the form of the concept of beauty may contribute to our thinking about the *form* of the concepts of criticism. The concept of beauty or art is nothing other than a concept of criticism; consequently a modern critic or theorist can plausibly espouse what may be characterized as a Kantian concept of art appreciation. By raising the question of the nature of aesthetic judgments, whether there can be universal aesthetic judgments, Kant has set some of modern aesthetics' "central questions."[6] In this chapter, then, I shall attempt to elucidate and assess Kant's aesthetic theories, relate those theories to his philosophical system, and discuss their importance for aesthetic and critical theories, especially those of the philosophical idealists.

Kant's Aesthetic Theory

KANT DIVIDES PURE CONCEPTS into two kinds: theoretical concepts such as cause and substance, which are natural concepts; and practical concepts, which are concepts of freedom because they are used to prescribe conduct and to tell us what we ought to do. From the first we can have practical precepts which tell us how to control human behavior and manipulate human desires; these precepts are technically practical. Moral laws, on the other hand, are practical in a different sense, since they confront man as a moral agent. Moral laws are therefore unconditionally prescribed. Moreover, moral concepts such as duty, right, and obligation are called concepts of freedom, since it is the presupposition of their application that the human will can freely choose to do what ought to be done. In other words, for Kant *ought* implies *can*.

Now, since moral concepts do not result in propositions which describe what exists but in commands which prescribe right courses of conduct, they do not give us knowledge of the objects to which they are applied. Kant therefore considers the realm to which moral concepts are applied to be suprasensible. If, for instance, a moral law is applied to a person it is supposed that the person is an agent who can freely choose to obey moral laws and that his choice to do what is right is an uncaused cause of the moral action. If, on the other hand, his choice is looked at as an event occurring in nature it can no longer be construed as an uncaused cause. We are therefore required to suppose that the agent to whom a moral law can be prescribed is a suprasensible being. We can validly suppose this because the *Critique of Pure Reason* has established that sensible objects, given to us in intuition, are not all that there is; they are only phenomena or appearances of things-in-themselves which cannot be given to us in intuition.

The pure concepts of the understanding legislate for and give us a priori knowledge of the realms of phenomena, whereas the pure concepts of reason legislate for the suprasensible realm but do not give us knowledge of it; the pure concepts of reason only prescribe the moral law to this realm. However, the moral law prescribed to a suprasensible agent must be realized in actions which occur in the sensible realm. The realm of phenomena must therefore be such as to permit the possibility of fulfillment of the moral law which is addressed to the suprasensible realm. There must then be some common ground or unity which reconciles these two otherwise separate realms and makes the transition from one realm to the other possible.

Kant conceives of this transition by postulating both between the faculty of reason and the faculty of understanding the faculty of judgment and between the faculty of knowledge and the faculty of desire, the faculty of feeling. Understanding legislates for knowledge of phenomena by producing a priori concepts such as the concepts of unconditioned moral law that prescribe right courses of conduct to the agent endowed with sensuous desires. The faculty of judgment contains "a principle peculiar to itself," which is "subjective *a priori*" (*Aesthetic Judgment*, p. 15).

The peculiar a priori principle of judgment Kant formulates in terms of the concepts of purpose and purposiveness (or finality). It is an essential precondition of there being nature that any event which occurs in nature should happen according to causal laws. Thus, given an event the judgment that it is causally conditioned is a determinate judgment. Moreover, if every event in nature occurs according to a causal law the condition of the possibility of experience is satisfied, and we can therefore say that the a priori demand that our understanding makes on nature is satisfied. But the understanding makes a further demand that the causal laws form a coherent system; it is thus passing toward subsuming particular causal laws and these under still more general laws, and so on. This demand is made on the principle that the laws of nature must be conceived as if they were furnished by "an Understanding" (not our understanding) in order to make possible a system of particular laws of nature. "Accordingly the principle of judgment, in respect of the form of the things of nature under empirical laws generally, is the *finality of nature* in its multiplicity. In other words, by this concept nature is represented as if an understanding contained the ground of the unity of the manifold of its empirical laws" (*Aesthetic Judgment*, pp. 19–20). This is a principle of reflective judgment, a principle which is a priori, not empirical;

subjective, not objective. It only determines our way of thinking about nature, not the general character of nature. It is by means of this concept of purpose which the faculty of judgment employs reflectively that the transition from the realm of freedom to that of necessity and from necessity to freedom is made possible (pp. 36–39). Kant has now prepared the stage for the analysis of the concept of beauty which he attempts in the four moments of the "Analytic of the Beautiful."

A JUDGMENT OF TASTE is of the form "*x* is beautiful" or "*x* is ugly." Such a judgment is not cognitive or logical; it is aesthetic. A cognitive judgment is one which ascribes a certain character to an object. The judgment "*x* is beautiful" does not ascribe a certain character, the one denoted by the word *beauty* to *x*, for there is no such character; it only states that the subject has a feeling of pleasure or satisfaction in connection with *x*.

Why does Kant say that the word *beauty* does not stand for any character, quality, or attribute? What kind of quality must beauty be, then? Either it is an empirical quality given as the content of a sensation (like "green") or it is a categorial feature of the objects of knowledge such as "substance," "cause," which are a priori ascribed to them. According to Kant these categorial features are a priori concepts—categories—which are not derived from the contents given in sensations by a process of abstraction. If we did not think of the objects of knowledge as substances, causes, and so on, there would be no objects of experience for us at all; the contents of our experience will in effect be dispersed into disconnected, momentary sensations, and even the judgment that these sensations are there will not be possible. Thus a judgment like "this is red" is a cognitive, logical judgment because it ascribes the feature redness to "this" and this feature is given to us as the content of our sensation, a content directly apprehended by us. A judgment "a flower is a substance" is a logical, cognitive judgment because it ascribes the character of substantiality to "flower." Although this character is not abstracted from sense-experience and is an a priori concept, it is a meaningful concept and we have a right to predicate it of objects of our experience. For unless we thought of objects of our experience as substances, no knowledge of objects would be possible for us at all, and consequently judgments like "this flower is red" could not be asserted at all. However, the word *beauty* does not stand for an empirically given feature, nor does it stand for an a priori concept. For Kant "*x* is beautiful" is an aesthetic judgment asserting that the subject contemplating *x* has a feeling of pleasure in regard to *x*. It follows that there is no concept of beauty.

The feeling of pleasure or satisfaction to which a judgment of taste refers is a peculiar kind of pleasure and is to be distinguished from other kinds of pleasure. Ordinary pleasure is connected with interest, whereas aesthetic pleasure is disinterested. An aesthetic judgment is based not on the ground that it gratifies certain desires which are universal but on the ground that as an object of contemplation it is necessarily pleasant. It is because of its claim to universal acceptance that it can be challenged. However, the form of the aesthetic judgment resembles the form of the cognitive judgment such as "*x* is green" which ascribes a certain character to *x* and is therefore objective. It might therefore seem as if there is a feature of things called beauty just as there is a feature of things called green. But the last move involves a serious confusion, because the philosophical problem involved in the judgment "*x* is beautiful" is to elucidate the nature of its claim to universality and to give a philosophical justification of it.

Cognition of any object involves, according to Kant, two distinct mental faculties: imagination, which gathers together the manifold of intuitions, and the understanding, which unites these intuitions with the help of a concept. If the play of the faculties of imagination and understanding in the cognition of any object is such as to carry with it the feeling of pleasure, the object will necessarily appear to be pleasant to all who cognize it. The play of the faculties must be felt to be such as to be essentially pleasant, not conceptually grasped so as to have a necessary connection with pleasure. If it is not essentially pleasant but is instead conceptually connected with pleasure, it will turn out to be a psychological state and therefore reducible to the matter of interest, and then it will be a subjectively, but not universally, pleasant cognition. In Kant's words:

> The cognitive powers brought into play by this representation are here engaged in a free play, since no definite concept restricts them to a particular rule of cognition. Hence the mental state in this representation must be one of a feeling of the free play of the powers of representation in a given representation for a cognition in general. Now a

21

representation, whereby an object is given, involves, in order that it may become a source of cognition at all, *imagination* for bringing together the manifold of intuition, and *understanding* for the unity of the concept uniting the representations. This state of *free play* of the cognitive faculties attending a representation by which an object is given must admit of universal communication: because cognition, as a definition of the Object with which given representations (in any Subject whatever) are to accord, is the one and only representation which is valid for every one. [*Aesthetic Judgment*, p. 58]

Kant compares the judgment of taste with the practical judgment of the form "*x* is good." The predicate "good" can be ascribed to *x* on the basis of the character of *x*. But the ascription of the predicate "beautiful" to *x* is immediate; it is not dependent on any character which *x* has. We can ask meaningfully why *x* is good, and the answer is of the form "*x* is good because it has such and such a character." Moreover, "good" is something to be realized; one has therefore an interest in it. But the judgment "*x* is beautiful" makes no reference to the ontological status of *x*; it only asserts that the contemplation of *x* is intrinsically pleasant; whether *x* is an actual existent or an imaginary object makes no difference to the beauty of *x*. Aesthetic satisfaction is therefore disinterested satisfaction. To say that aesthetic satisfaction is disinterested is to say that it is free satisfaction; it is not dependent on any private inclination of the subject but must be judged to be universal (*Aesthetic Judgment*, pp. 50–60).

Kant then develops what is perhaps the most crucial feature of his aesthetic theory: an analysis of the concept of purpose (pp. 61–80). Anything that comes to exist because someone thought of it as desirable and brought it into existence is purposive. But there may be things which cannot be characterized as purposive in that sense because we have no reason to believe that someone has desired and therefore produced them. And yet they are such that we find that we can best understand and explain their existence and character only by assuming that they are purposive, that they owe their existence and nature to a will, that some purpose has been realized in and through them. Such things are purposive without there being an actual purpose behind them; they therefore represent purposiveness without purpose. It is a methodological principle that the human eye or heart · has been constructed for a certain purpose, though we have no real grounds to believe that it has been constructed for that purpose. By adopting this principle we can control our thinking about the organism and carry out further research about it in order to produce coherent explanations of its structure. We thus methodologically attribute to the organism a formal purposiveness, a purposiveness without purpose.

A beautiful object is pleasant, but not because it satisfies a specific purpose of the subject who judges that object to be pleasant. Nor is it objectively purposive like a knife or a church. We can judge a knife or a church to be good if it satisfies such and such criteria, but we cannot say in the same way that an object is beautiful if it satisfies such and such criteria. For if we did the judgment would be cognitive, consisting in the application of a concept to a particular object, but not aesthetic, which consists in reporting an immediately felt feeling in connection with the object.

Since the aesthetic judgment is neither objective nor subjective, it must rest on a priori grounds. This feeling of pleasure must be grounded in some character of the subject which is necessarily shared by all subjects. And this shared attribute can only be their character of being a subject, for the subject is someone who entertains, synthesizes, and contemplates representations; and these representations (which constitute a beautiful object) must be such as to be adapted to the act of contemplation. Although we have no real grounds to believe that they have been deliberately so designed as to be adapted to contemplation by us, we must assume that they have been so designed. This is the purposiveness of a beautiful object without a purpose. Thus a beautiful object is one the contemplation of which is intrinsically pleasant, but not pleasant because it answers to our conception of what a thing of that kind ought to be.

> The consciousness of mere formal finality in the play of the cognitive faculties of the Subject attending a representation whereby an object is given, is the pleasure itself, because it involves a determining ground of the Subject's activity in respect of the quickening of its cognitive powers, and thus an internal causality (which is final) in respect of cognition generally, but without being limited to a definite cognition, and consequently a mere form of the subjective finality of a representation in an aesthetic judgment. [*Aesthetic Judgment*, p. 64]

If the contemplated object possesses features that appeal to our subjective inclinations or sentiments, then the object is charming. We must therefore distinguish, Kant argues, between charm and beauty. The contemplation of a charming object is pleasant, but we know that

23

pleasure varies from person to person since it is derived from sentiments which all subjects need not possess. The contemplation of a
beautiful object, on the other hand, is pleasant because this pleasure
is derived from a relation between the essential character of the subject as a subject contemplating the representation and the essential
character of the representations as objects to be contemplated by the
subject. "A judgment of taste which is uninfluenced by charm or emotion (though these may be associated with the delight in the beautiful), and whose determining ground, therefore, is simply finality of
form, is *a pure judgment of taste*" (*Aesthetic Judgment*, p. 65). A pure
judgment of taste is a formal judgment, a judgment concerned not
with the matter of representations, with colors, tones, and so on, which
may be pleasant or unpleasant, but with the form of representations.

Our contemplation of an object involves both contemplating the
variety of representations by means of the imagination which constitutes that object, and synthesizing these representations into a unity
elaborated by the understanding. A beautiful object is therefore a unity
of multiplicity. Kant realized, however, that this description would be
true of any object whatsoever and therefore argued that whatever distinguishes a beautiful object is the peculiar adjustment of this unity
and multiplicity to each other and to our faculties of cognition such
that a contemplation of the object will be intrinsically pleasant.

Kant finally introduces his important distinction between free and
dependent beauty. A pure judgment of taste issues in a judgment of
free beauty. The unity of an object of free beauty in our contemplation
is not derived from any specific purposes; it is merely formal, and
thus the aesthetic judgment is entirely independent of the concept
of perfection (*Aesthetic Judgment*, p. 69). If, on the other hand, an object is judged to be perfect, the beauty attributed to it is dependent
beauty; it "adheres to a concept." A beautiful church is judged to
be beautiful because it is what a church ought to be. However, the
beauty attributed to a flower is free beauty because we have no notion
of what a flower ought to be. We cannot judge whether a flower is
perfect, or judge its degree of perfection, by applying to it the concept
of an ideal flower. We judge it to be beautiful because the contemplation of it is intrinsically pleasant. Kant mentions the parrot, the
hummingbird, the bird of paradise, foliage for framework or on wall-
papers, designs à la grecque, and music without words as examples
of free beauty, for they are "self-subsisting beauties which are not ap-
purtenant to any object defined with respect to its end, but please

freely and on their own account" (p. 72). But the beauty of a man, a house, or a bridge "presupposes a concept of the end that defines what the thing has to be, and consequently a concept of its perfection" (p. 73). Thus once the concept of perfection is introduced it will be possible to prescribe rules for achieving certain ends even in the context of beautiful objects. Kant nevertheless insists that "perfection neither gains by beauty, nor beauty by perfection" (p. 74). Yet the distinction is useful for settling critical disputes insofar as it enables one to show that critical confrontations are often not genuine since the opponents in an aesthetic dispute may be concerned with the two different forms of judgments: a pure aesthetic judgment is responsive to free beauty, whereas an impure one is responsive to the dependent.

Since the determining ground of an aesthetic judgment is the feeling of the subject, there can be no objective rule for it. Yet, because this feeling of the subject with regard to the beautiful can be ascribed to all judging subjects, "we have the empirical criterion, weak indeed and scarce sufficient to raise a presumption, of the derivation of a taste, thus confirmed by examples, from grounds deep-seated and shared alike by all men, underlying their agreement in estimating the forms under which objects are given to them" (p. 75). Thus, although "some products of taste" are "exemplary," they need not and must not encourage imitation, because taste must be an original faculty. It follows then that "the highest model, the architect of taste is a mere idea which each person must beget in his own consciousness, and according to which he must form his estimate of everything that is an Object of taste, or that is an example of critical taste, and even of universal taste itself" (pp. 75–76). Since this archetype of taste, resting as it does upon "reason's indeterminate idea of a maximum" (p. 76), is not capable of being represented by means of concepts, it is called the ideal of the beautiful. However, the beauty involving such an ideal cannot be free beauty, nor can its judgment be pure, but is determined by a concept of objective finality.

What is "agreeable" actually causes pleasure in a person, and such pleasure can be brought under some conceptual categories. Pleasure in the agreeable is a "theoretical objective necessity," but pleasure in the beautiful, though necessary, is of a special kind. Kant calls it "exemplary," which he defines as "a necessity of the assent of *all* to a judgment regarded as exemplifying a universal rule incapable of formulation" (p. 81).

Kant's attempt throughout the "Analytic" is to safeguard aesthetic judgments from lapsing into absolute objectivity or absolute subjectivity. If aesthetic judgments are subsumable, like the cognitive, under a definite objective principle, the agent would be able to claim unconditioned necessity for them. If, on the other hand, they were completely devoid of any principle, as with judgments of mere likes and dislikes, necessity would have no meaning whatever. Being thus subjective and yet demanding universal validity and being objective yet not subsumable under any definite objective principle, aesthetic judgments possess a logic characterized as subjective universality, which Kant calls "a common sense." In making an aesthetic judgment one presupposes a common sense in all human beings such that it allows them to experience an accord between their cognitive faculties at the moment of aesthetic apprehension. Aesthetic judgments therefore exact agreement from everyone. "We are suitors for agreement from every one else, because we are fortified with a ground common to all" (p. 82). Thus although there is an *ought* implied in the form of this judgment, it is different from the *ought* implied in ethical judgments. The *ought* in aesthetic judgments is pronounced only conditionally because we cannot bring an object under that ground common to all human beings unless the object is properly discriminated as an aesthetic representation. Kant is thus cautioning us against the conflation of aesthetic representations with nonaesthetic representations and objects.

Assessment of Kant's Aesthetic Theory

MOST AESTHETICIANS would seem to agree that it is Kant's distinction between free and dependent beauty that seems to involve a radical shift in his aesthetic theory from its rigorous and pure formalism to what may be construed as an expressionist theory. In free beauty no concepts are involved, whereas dependent beauty involves the concept of the end, which can no longer be construed as purposiveness without a purpose. For the judgment of both manmade objects, such as a church or a palace, and creatures of nature (or natural objects), such as a horse, the freedom of the imagination is circumscribed by the concept of the end, and as a result these objects cannot be conceived to induce free play of the cognitive faculties without the intrusion of a concept. Thus the difference between free and dependent beauty would seem to be a radical one. If this is true it should then follow that Kant would no longer insist on the withdrawal of the ontological claim from the judgment of dependent beauty, though this withdrawal is necessary for the judgment of free beauty. Thus since the concept of an end now circumscribes the freedom of our imagination, we cannot cut off cognitive and moral judgments from the aesthetic judgment of dependent beauty. In other words, to talk about the beauty of a church is also to imply the ontological claim that the church exists, but to talk of the beauty of a rose does not involve such a claim unless one wants to make an enumerative and therefore cognitive statement about the rose.

However, Kant has told us earlier that the concept of an end is not a constitutive concept but a reflective one, and it would not therefore confer objectivity on the sensory manifold supplied to the mind. It is important to bear in mind that Kant gave the concept of purpose a place of centrality in his analysis of beauty because he wanted to show that the realm of aesthetic experience establishes a connection between the cognitive and ethical realms. By accommodating the concept of purpose in the realm of sense experience Kant is able to show that the concept of ethical end too has a place in the phenomenal world. Thus although the concept of purpose is introduced in his aesthetic theories, Kant's introduction of it is by gradual stages: in free beauty we have purposiveness without purpose, in dependent beauty we have purposiveness with the consciousness of purpose, and in the ideal of beauty it is the ethical end in human beings as suprarational beings capable of self-determination. Yet, to repeat, throughout the *Critique of Aesthetic Judgment* Kant does not regard the concept of purpose as a legitimate cognitive concept. According to the concept of purpose in nature, our understanding operates on the assumption that the great number of empirical laws can be derived from a few principles, perhaps one supreme principle, since without such an assumption we should not be able to connect these laws with each other in the coherent system of a science. But this principle cannot be empirically verified and is therefore a reflective principle of the judgment. It is not a condition of the possibility of nature but a necessary need of our understanding to comprehend nature as a closely integrated and organic system.

If the foregoing explanation is correct we can validly say that even in the context of dependent beauty Kant argues for the withdrawal of the ontological claim, for it is a logical necessity of his philosophical system, which, while establishing connections among his three faculties of mind (reason, understanding, and judgment), must nevertheless maintain differences among them. Kant's claim, moreover, that the aesthetic judgment does not involve an ontological claim about the aesthetic object is part of his general theory of aesthetic experience. It is in his four moments of the "Analytic of the Beautiful" that Kant resolutely defines the autonomy of aesthetic experience. In order to establish this autonomy conclusively he must show its radical difference from the experiences of the cognitive, the practical, and the agreeable, since they involve an ontological claim with regard to the object of experience. We cannot, in other words, validly claim to have a perception unless the object which one claims to have perceived is an actual existent, nor can we validly claim to judge something as pleasant or agreeable unless it is also claimed that it actually exists. Thus if Kant could prove that the aesthetic experience does not involve an ontological claim while insisting at the same time on the necessity of the ontological claim for the cognitive and practical experiences, he would then be able to argue conclusively that the aesthetic experience is a radically autonomous one. If my account here is correct we can see why, even after a change of emphasis from the predominantly formalist theory of sections 1–23 to the predominantly expressionist theory of sections 43–60, Kant conducts his later discussions "as if he has been discussing the Natural Beauty he had been discussing in the earlier sections."[7]

Kant does not regard beauty as a natural property existing in the world. Nor does the question of the existence of an aesthetic object during aesthetic experience arise for him. Consequently, Kant radically differs from both the naturalists and the nonnaturalists. He differs, for instance, from Plato, who conceived of beauty as an Idea; from G. E. Moore, who will give it the status of a nonnatural, indefinable property; and from I. A. Richards, a naturalist, who will analyze it in terms of a complex psychological state amenable to empirical inquiry. For all of these thinkers aesthetic judgments are cognitive. For Kant, on the other hand, they are expressive of a feeling of the accord or harmony experienced in the mind of the contemplator. Kant would reject the notion of existence of beauty that is not contemplated, since the idea of unexperienced beauty is for him logically absurd.

IN PROPOSING universal assent for aesthetic judgments Kant struggles with the formidable difficulty that aesthetic skepticism poses, for by denying universal validity aesthetic skepticism declares aesthetic judgments to be peculiar to specific observers, and thus it takes the course of radical subjectivism. What agreement may obtain between two observers is, according to aesthetic skepticism, entirely contingent, and aesthetic disagreements are therefore matters of individual preferences and not genuine disagreements amendable to rational resolution. For Kant, however, the aesthetic skeptic confuses judgments about the agreeable with aesthetic judgments and has therefore no criterion for distinguishing the beautiful from the merely agreeable. Kant would say further that if something merely pleases the agent he must not consider it beautiful. Whether or not he answered the skeptic, it is important to note that Kant is here preoccupied not simply with terminological discriminations but rather with the central question of rationally grounding our aesthetic judgments without collapsing them with the cognitive. Kant's effort is important inasmuch as he found repellent the whole idea of saying that everything is as it appears to specific percipients and that each of us carries his own standards of aesthetic goodness. If aesthetic disagreements are to be meaningful and if criticism is to be possible at all, Kant thinks that aesthetic judgments should not be reduced to radical subjectivism. Thus although aesthetic judgments are not objective like cognitive and moral judgments, but subjective, they nevertheless demand universal validity which cognitive and moral judgments possess.

Kant's solution to the problem of giving rational structure to aesthetic judgments without denying their subjectivity lies in proposing that they are singular. Since they do not involve concepts, a priori or a posteriori, the subject term of an aesthetic judgment is an individual which cannot be subsumed under a class. If the subject term could be subsumed under a class we would obtain a criterion of the beautiful, and aesthetic judgment would be like cognitive and moral judgments. However, for Kant, all that beautiful objects have in common is their being beautiful, and there is no criterion by which to identify the beautiful. "We want to get a look at the Object with our own eyes, just as if our delight depended on sensation. And yet, if upon so doing, we call the object beautiful, we believe ourselves to be speaking with a universal voice, and lay claim to the concurrence of every one" (*Aesthetic Judgment*, p. 56).

In cognition proper, we remember, the harmony between different mental faculties is achieved through a determinate concept of the understanding. If, for instance, anything is to be an experience at all, it must occur according to causal laws, and this is a determinate concept. An aesthetic judgment, on the other hand, depends on the subjective conditions of cognition in a harmony between imagination and the understanding. This peculiar form of cognition is without the help of a determinate concept and accounts for the uniqueness of aesthetic judgments (for which we "lay claim to the concurrence of every one") possible. Now, Kant seems to be talking here about the mental faculties as substantive entities, but his discussion makes sense only if we construe them in terms of logical forms of propositions. In other words, Kant characterizes the logical nature of aesthetic judgments as synthetic a priori statements which imply nothing less than necessity. Thus since aesthetic judgments are not objectively but subjectively universal, they are incapable of proof, for there are no objective criteria on which to build proof of validity. Unlike synthetic a priori statements, synthetic a posteriori statements are derived from experience and are only probably, not necessarily, true. Synthetic a priori judgments in the sciences, however, are verified by appeal to experience, but Kant would argue that in aesthetic judgments "the appeal is to feeling." Thus, synthetic a posteriori statements are empirical, whereas the synthetic a priori statements are indubitable intuitions of truth; hence the latter constitute the condition of the possibility of experience. In simple terms, propositions of experience are embedded in certain propositions or presuppositions which make both our experiences and our talk about them possible and meaningful. These presuppositions, or synthetic a priori propositions, are not derived and cannot be derived from experience. In Kantian terms, they are contributed by our understanding.

Now, if our propositions make sense because they are made possible by a priori propositions, how can the aesthetic experience be possible, as Kant suggests, without the use of such a priori propositions? Kant seems to suggest that aesthetic experience is prior to the application of these a priori propositions which are the conditions of the possibility of our moral and cognitive experiences. Though there is no concept of the understanding present in aesthetic experience, the manifold in a given representation appears to become synthesized as if in accordance with a rule. Thus the accord between imagination and the understanding in aesthetic experience is purposive in terms of cognition in general, for despite the absence of a rule of synthesis the sensory manifold allows for synthesis in our cognition as if it were deliberately adapted to our cognitive faculties by a will not our own. Yet Kant insists that we have no right to speak of any purpose in nature, for that would involve noumenal considerations which are out of the bounds of our sense.

The notion of purposiveness without purpose operating in aesthetic experience allows for a synthesis of a given sensory manifold by separating its properties from their cognitive framework. We must not forget, however, that these properties in the cognitive context are possible only within their categorial framework. When, for instance, we judge an object aesthetically we are not concerned with its actual existence; but when we are not responding aesthetically it can certainly be an object of cognition and also involve an ontological claim, without which it cannot be an object of cognition. Kant thus insists on the autonomy of aesthetic experience from the moral and cognitive experiences. In this austere context of aesthetic experience for which the withdrawal of the ontological claim is necessary, a property is contemplated in relation to other properties, but the cognitive question of the property being a property of something is considered strictly irrelevant.

Kant seeks to exemplify this peculiar sort of cognition in aesthetic experiences by his distinction between free and dependent beauty. Dependent beauty involves the concept of perfection, which does not operate in the apprehension of free beauty. Kant's distinction, as was noted earlier, brings about a radical shift from his formalist aesthetic theory to an expressionist theory. Yet Kant's original contribution to aesthetics lies in his remarkable working out of the formalist conception of aesthetic experience in the four moments of the "Analytic." The expressionist shift that he seems to signal remains undeveloped, for though the concept of perfection in dependent beauty enables him to see the importance of content in art, Kant has not given us a detailed working out of its underlying conceptual structure.

Thus Kant, though he seeks to keep cognitive and aesthetic experiences apart, wants at the same time to maintain a close relation between them. He links them together in order to argue that just as cognitive judgments are universally communicable, the state of mind during aesthetic experience, too, is universally communicable. By establishing this link Kant hopes to maintain, on the one hand, subjective universal validity of aesthetic experiences and the accord of the cognitive faculties with cognition generally and, on the other hand, their separation from cognitive experiences which claim objective universal validity. This is out of Kant's desire to overcome both aesthetic skepticism and radical subjectivism in aesthetic judgments. But if such communicability of the state of mind were to be truly universal, experts in the cognitive inquiries should also be the experts in aesthetic inquiry. The question of cultivating sensibility in order to experience works of art more fully would have no meaning, nor would the question of aesthetic education have any value, since expertise in the cognitive inquiries should ensure, in virtue of the universal communicability of cognition in general, mature response to beauty.

Kant's solution to the problem of settling controversies in aesthetic discussions is also very inadequate. For the scope he allows for aesthetic controversies is wholly negative insofar as he characterizes aesthetic judgments by contradistinguishing them from other kinds of judgments, by pointing out what they are not. The aesthetic judgment is not logical or ethical, hence it is not cognitive; therefore it is not objective or objectively universal; though it is propositional in its formal structure it is not actually so; yet it claims universality not objectively but subjectively; and thus it is singular. In other words, apprehension of beauty involves no rules of synthesis, nor does it allow for concepts. Though there is an important insight in Kant's theory, the theory itself, being a product of the coherence demanded by his philosophical system, is too austere to do justice to the complex patterns of response involved in aesthetic apprehension.

Kant and Idealist Aesthetics

I SHALL NOW DISCUSS idealist aesthetics of Hegel, Croce, and Bosanquet, confining my discussion strictly to the internal history of their thought on art in relation to Kant. Thus it will not deal with many German neo-Kantians who would be centrally relevant to a full historical study of idealist aesthetics. Moreover, a fuller critical discussion of even Hegel and Croce would have to examine many other issues that do not immediately concern us here. Hegel's seeming devaluation of art, for instance, does not imply a denigration of art but rather discloses the place art occupies in the life of modern man. Hegel obviously knew that there will always be artists, but the significance of his thought on art derives from his specific grasp of man's history. He conceived the value of the initial stages of art to inhere in its relation to truth and reality and believed that modern art has lost that connection. This view will not be examined here, though if probed carefully it can reveal his formidable insight into the nature of both art and history. I thus focus on certain general features of Hegel's aesthetic theory. My discussion of Croce deals with his youthful idealist thought, because there he embraces the logical consequences of the extremist idealist position. A treatment of Croce's mature thinking must take into account the modifications he made of his earlier position.

Idealist philosophers and aestheticians such as Hegel, Croce, Bosanquet, A. C. Bradley, and R. G. Collingwood accepted Kant's most important doctrine that aesthetic experience is autonomous, that it is different from moral and cognitive experiences. The following words of Hegel clearly illustrate this point:

> The interest of art . . . is distinguishable from the practical interest of desire in virtue of the fact that it suffers its object to remain in its free independence, whereas desire applies it, even to the point of destruction, to its own uses. The contemplation of art, on the other hand, differs from that of a scientific intelligence in an analogous way in virtue of the fact that it cherishes an interest for the object in its isolated existence, and is not concerned to transform the same into terms of universal thought and action.[8]

But idealists do not subscribe to the whole of Kantian aesthetic theory since that would involve acceptance of Kant's philosophical system, with which his aesthetic theory is closely bound up. More specifically, the metaphysical views of reality that idealists hold force them to revise Kantian aesthetics, especially the view that aesthetic judgments, though they claim necessity and universality, are in essence subjective. For idealists, on the other hand, necessity and universality are themselves predicates of objectivity; thus insofar as aesthetic judgments claim these two they cannot be subjective. Idealists therefore transform Kant's reflective principle of adaptedness of contingent nature to our cognitive faculties into a constitutive principle. For Kant, as we saw earlier, it is a reflective principle that nature is created by a nonhuman understanding for our convenience in order, as it were, to facilitate man's efforts to build a system. For Hegelian idealists, on the other hand, it is not just a postulate but a fact that the ground of the contingent nature is really identical with man's rationality, and nature is therefore really adapted to man's mind. This conception has its concise articulation in Hegel's notion of the Absolute, the Concrete Universal, of which nature and the mind of man are the differentiations.

It is important to note, however, that Hegel does not regard everything in the universe as equally significant, since for him there are degrees of reality which manifest the Idea at different levels of Being, the lowest of which is the unconscious nature and the highest, the self-conscious mind of man. The Idea finds its fullest sensuous expression in art because it is in art that the human mind, itself the highest manifestation of the Idea, manipulates mere sensuous material to make it expressive of spiritual significance. For Hegel, then, "The beautiful may . . . be defined as the sensuous semblance of the Idea." Like Kant, idealists insist upon order as the fundamental postulate of beauty. In Hegel's words, "The beauty of art has become recognized as one of the means which resolve and bring back to unity that antithesis and contradiction between the mind and Nature as they repose in abstract alienation from each other in themselves, whether this latter is regarded as external phenomena or the internal world of feeling and emotion." Here the mind is construed to mean reason or rationality, whereas Nature is construed to mean both the sensuous material yielded by perception and the chaos of passions and emotions within us. Both these forms of Nature must reveal order if beauty is to be realized. Beauty in effect is not the expression of emotions and passions but rather the expression of an ordered and structured emotion in a sensuous material that is itself structured and ordered. Consequently, Hegel regarded the emotion which overwhelms and overpowers man as not one which finds embodiment or expression in art.[9]

Hegel's most important contribution to idealist aesthetics is, of course, the relations he established between the beautiful and the merely sensuous and between the beautiful and ideal thought. The following passage perhaps best captures these relations:

> Though the sensuous must be present in a work of art, yet it must only appear as surface and *semblance* of the sensuous. For, in the sensuous aspect of a work of art the mind seeks neither the concrete framework of matter, that empirically thorough completeness and the development of the organism which desire demands, nor the universal and merely ideal thought. What it requires is sensuous presence, which, while not ceasing to be sensuous, is to be liberated from the apparatus of its merely material nature. And thus the sensuous in

works of art is exalted to the rank of a mere *semblance* in comparison with the immediate existence of things in nature, and the work of art occupies the mean between what is immediately sensuous and ideal thought. It is not as yet pure thought, but despite the sensuous it is also no longer simple material existence, like stones, plants, organic life. Rather the sensuous in the work of art is itself something ideal, not, however, the ideal of thought but as a thing still in an external way. This semblance of the sensuous presents itself to the mind externally as the shape, the visible look, and the sonorous vibration of things. . . . In art, these sensuous shapes and sounds present themselves not simply for their own sake and for that of their immediate structure, but with the purpose of affording in that shape satisfaction to higher spiritual interests, seeming that they are powerful to call forth a response and echo in the mind from all the depths of consciousness. It is thus that, in art, the sensuous is *spiritualized, i.e.* the *spiritual* appears in sensuous shape.[10]

Although Hegel defines art as "the sensuous semblance of the Idea" the Idea manifests itself in different forms of art in terms of different degrees of the presence of the sensuous. Thus the less sensuous the art, the less the extent of the sensuous material in art and the higher its value, since it is thereby able to embody the greater spiritual significance of the Idea in its relatively purer form. Hegel has thus defined the value of art strictly in terms of its expression of spiritual significance. He therefore concludes that classical art is higher than the symbolic, the romantic higher than the classical, painting higher than architecture, and poetry higher than painting. Hegel's characterization of the nature and value of art, however, already contains within it an ultimate deidealization of art, for he argues further that art would be transcended by the Absolute in its upward movement toward complete self-consciousness and that philosophy would finally replace art.[11]

Both Bosanquet and Croce accept the Hegelian thesis that beauty is the sensuous manifestation of the spirit, but they reject Hegel's relegation of art to a position inferior to that of philosophy. Hegel had argued that of the three manifestations of the spirit—thought, beauty, and moral goodness—thought is of the highest value. Bosanquet and Croce argue that all of them are equally significant, that all of them individually constitute different realms of experience, and that the question of qualitative comparison among them simply does not arise.[12] More specifically, Bosanquet rejects Hegel's elevation of art over nature. According to him, the order that man creates through art is not confined to man's rationality and to his creative products but also extends to nature. Nature too exhibits an order that is independent of the order that science discovers in it or imposes on it, an order that is felt and experienced by the sensibility of man. Nature thus accommodates itself to the spirituality of man.

Bosanquet takes over Hegel's notion of structured emotion that finds expression as art and develops it further. He argues that consciousness fully articulates and elaborates the emotion in sensuous form. And here Bosanquet seems to return to Kant's insistence on form, though there is a significant difference between them. What is organized is not important to Kant's principle of form, whereas for Bosanquet's principle of form, as mediated by his idealist metaphysics, what is organized is equally significant. For Kant the material is the contingent element and cannot in principle be universally shared, while for the absolute idealists the material is an organic and therefore necessary part of reality and cannot be excluded without violating interrelationships among parts of the organic whole of a work of art. Form, emotion, material are inextricably woven together in the organic totality of that work. Bosanquet can thus say:

> As the object reveals more form the feeling which is united to it has . . . 'more'; more to take hold of, to dwell upon, to communicate. Great objects of art contain myriads of elements of form on different levels, knit together in more and more complex systems, till the feeling which they demand is such as to occupy the whole powers of the greatest mind, and more than these if they were to be had.[13]

Bosanquet's attempt, however, to revise Hegel's aesthetic theories and to give art a proper place in the activities of the spirit is far more temperate than is the attempt by Croce, who develops the idealist aesthetics to its logical extreme. This can be seen by briefly examining the idealist discussions of Kant's important question about the status of beauty or aesthetic objects in relation to the human mind. For idealists a world from which human consciousness has been abolished cannot be said to have beauty or aesthetic objects. And this is entirely plausible to hold. But Croce goes further than this and conceives art to be strictly mental, for, he says, what are ordinarily recognized as works of art are simply aids to memory or means of communication and nothing more.[14] Bosanquet has criticized Croce's position as philosophically confused as well as untenable. He argues that besides making the fact of communication an insoluble enigma, it undermines the significance of the actual medium in the process of aesthetic creativity. Croce's defense of art derives from his generally plausible argument about the mind's capacity to work with imaginal material, but we cannot even conceive the possibility of such workings of the mind without first conceiving the mind's actual manipulation of sensuous medium. Bosanquet is thus able to make some fundamental revisions in what he considers as Croce's arbitrary and exaggerated idealism, "a profound error of principle, a false idealism." He thus concludes: "Things, it is true, are not complete without minds, but minds again are not complete without things. . . . Our resources in the way of sensation, and our experiences in the way of satisfactory and unsatisfactory feeling, are all of them won out of our intercourse with things, and are thought and imagined by us as qualities and properties of the things."[15] Bosanquet's recognition of the importance of the medium enables him to criticize Croce's indiscriminate collapsing of all the arts, inasmuch as Croce ignores all the differences among different arts as completely insignificant for aesthetic theory as well as for aesthetic apprehension. However, the question of the status of aesthetic objects has become a major issue in recent critical theory, and I shall return to it in Chapter 6.

Croce has made a comprehensive attempt to work out and develop further the implications of idealist aesthetics, and it is a courageous attempt because Croce does not hesitate to embrace the extremest implications of the theses that art objects are unique and that aesthetic experience is autonomous. For instance, Croce asserts an absolute identity between intuition and expression: "To intuit is to express; and nothing else (nothing more, but nothing less) than *to express*."[16] However, according to Croce, intuition is commonly available to all men, and since we are almost constantly intuiting, all of us are artists and all of us are aesthetic contemplators. Such a notion of aesthetic experience explicitly forbids any notion of effort and competence as necessary to experience aesthetic objects fully.[17] Yet Croce attempts to soften his theory somewhat by making a distinction between intuition and perception according to which intuition is a natural possession of all men, whereas perception involves effort and therefore considerations that move one away from aesthetic experience to criticism. It is clear that Croce does not believe that criticism can facilitate aesthetic experience, for he argues that criticism becomes necessary only when one is dealing with works that are flawed.

But how can Croce make this argument if we are constantly intuiting and if intuitions are necessarily acts of aesthetic contemplation and if any expression is by definition intuition?

KANT AND THE IDEALISTS theorize about art in order to place it within their philosophical systems, and they thus create insuperable difficulties for their theories, since they cannot give a full and satisfactory account of both aesthetic experience and the concerns of various modes of practical criticism. As soon as Kant gives recognition to what is organized in art his austere formalism gives way and turns into a kind of expressionism. He does not articulate, however, the conceptual structure involved in a recognition of content in art, since he has effectively established a bridge between his two philosophical systems by creating a third one. Idealists, on the other hand, claiming to possess a true insight into the nature of the ultimate reality, make a tripartite division of reality into truth, goodness, and beauty. Once they have made these divisions they proceed to mark them off by articulating fully the differences among them. Theorizing about art therefore becomes for them a matter of reflection on an aspect of ultimate reality. From their important Kantian insight that aesthetic experience is not reducible to moral and cognitive experiences they proceed to develop so-called aesthetic theories that are in fact the results of their metaphysical presuppositions. I shall attempt a critical scrutiny of both the uniqueness thesis about works of art and the question of aesthetic experience in Chapter 4, in the context of recent critical thought concerning them.

CHAPTER TWO

Creativity and Aesthetic Theory

Many aestheticians claim that in creativity there is a mental process involved, that this process reflects what is essential to the understanding of works of art, and that a proper understanding of creativity gives the most direct access to the central and characteristic features of the various products of creativity. Convinced that artworks are unique objects, they claim that the process responsible for their production must also share the features that make them unique: "The uniqueness inherent in the aesthetic object reflects the uniqueness of the activity in which the object was made."[1] They therefore attempt theoretical and practical inquiries into the process of artistic creativity. More specifically, the preoccupation with artistic creativity has an important theoretical interest. If one can argue that artistic creativity is uniquely creative as compared to the creation of all other objects, and if one can derive that thesis from the thesis that aesthetic objects are unique, then one can also argue that there is a conclusive means of rejecting Aristotle's theory of the making of poems.[2] There are, however, philosophers such as Monroe Beardsley who have separated the connection between artistic creativity and aesthetic objects on the ground that aesthetic objects are the objects of value inviting our lingering attention and interest, whereas artistic creativity does not and cannot help us apprehend the value of artworks.[3] Beardsley has sought to refute the romantic theory of art as self-expression, a theory that establishes too close a connection between the artist and his aesthetic products and opens the door to genetic criticism. Both positions on the question of artistic creativity are important, especially since they have received considerable theoretical support in modern aesthetic and critical theory, and the second claim has become well known as a refutation of the "intentional fallacy."[4]

In this chapter I attempt to explain both the conceptual difficulties in some important modern discussions of artistic creativity and the bearing of these difficulties on aesthetic theory. This will involve a consideration of the status of the concept of creativity. I will argue that the concept of creativity depends, not on the concept of artworks as unique entities, but on one's concept of art itself. If one holds artworks to be unique aesthetic objects, then there is no need for a theory of artistic creativity, and Beardsley is right. But if one holds the uniqueness of artworks to derive from a connection between art and the temperament or personality of its creators, then of course the concept of artistic creativity becomes important to critical inquiry. I will argue, moreover, that, regardless of whether one considers that the theory of artistic creativity is important in talking about artworks or that creativity is a highly complex process, the concept of creating is not radically different from the concept of making.[5]

I

SOME PHILOSOPHERS are interested in artistic creativity because they think a consideration of it enables them to defend a particular conception of mind. Eliseo Vivas, for instance, finds in artistic creativity a difficulty for any "naturalist" theory of mind. He argues that the burden of a naturalist is to explain what he cannot explain:

> The control that the new whole, which from the standpoint of consciousness has not yet been fully born, exercises over the artist's mind as he proceeds to bring it to birth . . . [we need to explain] the purposive thrust of the mind, the mind's ability to follow the lead of something that is not-yet-there. It is this fact, the control of the not-yet-there total situation over the present, that leads the idealist to insist that a factor is here at work of an essentially teleological nature.[6]

The aesthetic object, in other words, is not controlled by some clearly defined intention in the artist's mind, but rather becomes fully revealed in the process of its creation. Consequently, for Vivas, creation is also discovery. But all of this is not without difficulties. As Vincent Tomas shrewdly puts it, "that the artist's choices are controlled by a whole that is not-yet-there is not a fact but a theory."[7]

As it turns out, however, Tomas himself has an alternative theory

40

according to which "what the control consists of is in the making of the critical judgments about what so far has been done." The artist knows what is right and what is wrong "because there is something pushing from behind." "Whenever the artist goes wrong, he feels himself being kicked, and tries another way which, he surmises . . . will not be followed by a kick. What is kicking him is 'inspiration', which is already there. What he makes must be adequate to his inspiration. If it isn't, he feels a kick."[8] Though Tomas writes here in a way that seems to insist on the artist's feelings during the act of creation, his basic contention seems to be that artists make judgments of right and wrong. This is surely true. Yet his argument does not take into account certain difficulties.[9] For instance, why should one assume that what the artist does "must be adequate to his inspiration"? The empirical fact that the artist always wants to produce good artworks does not authorize the assumption that an artwork is adequate to inspiration. In fact, the desire to produce a good work makes it necessary for the artist to exercise control over his inspiration, or to make sure that the inspiration is good enough. The kicks of inspiration, then, are no evidence that what the artist is doing is necessarily good or bad. Moreover, if the artist, after he has completed his work, feels that his work is not adequate to what he really wanted to achieve, should we then take his judgment as necessarily a compelling one? For instance, Conrad, after the completion of *Lord Jim*, said: "I admit I stood [in *Lord Jim*] for a great triumph and I have only succeeded in giving myself utterly away. . . . I've been satanically ambitious but there's nothing of a devil in me, worse luck; the *Outcast* is a heap of sand, the *Nigger* a splash of water, *Jim* a lump of clay."[10] Postponing a consideration of the testimony of creative artists until later in this chapter, I should nevertheless state here that their testimony, though interesting, need not be necessarily compelling. For it may reflect their judgments or interpretations, and is no more than one more judgment or interpretation which is subject to the same scrutiny as the interpretations offered by others.

What both Vivas and Tomas are trying to do is give their supposedly indubitable versions of the nature of the creative process. And what both of them are ignoring is that all the factors they mention and many other indeterminate ones may be at work in artistic creativity and that none of them alone constitutes the differentia sufficient to characterize the nature of artistic creativity. This is to agree

41

with Haig Khatchadourian that artistic creativity cannot be characterized in a single, determinate manner since it embraces a variety of patterns.[11] Khatchadourian has therefore sought to refine and amplify the theory of artistic creativity proposed by Tomas and further developed by Beardsley. Yet he does not pause to reflect on the fundamental difference between Beardsley and Tomas. Acknowledging the fascination of the problem of artistic creativity, Beardsley nevertheless contends that the value of what the artist produces is "independent of the manner of production."[12] For Tomas, on the other hand, though works of art are unique aesthetic entities, they derive their value from a special process of creativity.

Tomas is right in saying that the artist makes critical judgments as well as relying on inspiration. Yet Beardsley's position is theoretically more consistent than Tomas's, since it is not generally clear to either the critic or the theorist when the artist's decision is a matter of critical judgment and where a matter of inspiration. To call a particular moment in a play or novel the result of either critical judgment or inspiration cannot reveal the numerous factors that may have contributed to its production, nor can it lead us to the single and indubitable theory of creativity that would conclusively put to rest our sense of awe about works of art. For in calling that moment by either label one succeeds at best in pointing attention to the moment. Moreover, labels like "inspiration" and "critical judgment" belong to the texture of critical language (criticism) and become meaningful only when they are transformed from mere intuitive hunches into fully discriminated critical response. They are indifferent to the vitality of a critical performance, since in themselves they do not provide us with a method of criticism.

The accounts of artistic creativity proposed by idealist and organicist theorists are motivated by a desire to replace the imitation theory of art, especially the Aristotelian theory of making, which, they think, does not do justice to the complex and organic nature of artworks. Vivas will readily admit, it is true, that the *Poetics* offers an organic theory of poetry and gives a conceptual validation of the value of poetry in man's life, against Plato's relegation of poetry to an inferior ontological status. Vivas, however, argues that Aristotle's "notion of likely impossibility is incompatible with the rest of the theory," since its adoption has forced Aristotle, unbeknownst to himself, to abandon his principle of imitation. Vivas therefore avers that "Aristotle gained a stranglehold on poetic theory until almost our own day." [13]

Now, Vivas is right in saying that Aristotle's theory "makes truth a component of poetry" because his concept of imitation logically entails the criteria of what is, and what is not, proper in an act of artistic imitation. In opposition to Aristotle, however, Vivas contends that "questions of possibility and impossibility are irrelevant . . . and the ordinary laws of reality have no authority" [14] in talking about either artistic creativity or aesthetic experience. Vivas's charge is serious. It is that Aristotle did not see that the *Poetics* involves a fundamental self-contradiction which, if Vivas is right, is open to simple observation. But this charge, I will now argue, radically miscontrues Aristotle's concept of imitation. Vivas can make his charge only if he could show that by "imitation" Aristotle meant "copying." Yet that is what Vivas cannot do, without greatly distorting Aristotle, for by "probable impossibility" Aristotle seems to imply empirical, not logical, impossibility. Consider for a moment Vivas's own example of Kafka's story "The Metamorphosis." If we could conceive that Gregor Samsa overnight turns into a monstrous beetle, we could also conceive what is in the realm of empirical, lived reality impossible: that the beetle should be able to suffer, like a human being, anguish over his condition, especially since his parents will soon knock at his door. It is also conceivable that he would be able to crawl on the walls and the ceiling of his parents' living room.

Aristotle's concept of poems is closely intertwined with his doctrine of probability that occurs in a passage quoted by Vivas: "In fact . . . the writing of poetry is a more philosophical activity, and one to be taken more seriously, than the writing of history; for poetry tells us rather the universals, history the particulars. 'Universal' means what kinds of things a certain person will say or do in accordance with probability or necessity, which is what poetic composition aims at, tacking on names afterward; while 'particular' is what Alcibiades did or had done to him." [15] Simply stated, Aristotle's contention is that literature, like philosophy, interprets life and does not simply present it. Furthermore, since all interpretation consists in bringing particulars in relation to universals, those particulars which cannot be subsumed under universals have no place in literature. Thus while history and biography attempt to document one or another event or life and must take into account the contingencies in that event or life, literature must be a closely integrated organic structure such that all elements of contingency are thoroughly eliminated. No doubt this is a highly rationalistic organic theory of poetry. If one holds another theory, one may certainly question and even reject it; one may also question and reject the contention that literature does not deal with the contingent. But there is no self-contradiction involved in the *Poetics* between its concept of poems and its doctrine of probability. It only needs to be mentioned that Vivas finds self-contradiction in the *Poetics* because he has attributed to Aristotle his own rather idealist notions of aesthetic experience and artistic creativity, with which the *Poetics* is certainly at odds.

II

WE CAN NOW TURN to a fuller discussion of the concepts of inspiration and creativity and see whether they give us a defensible theory of the creative process such that this theory could radically distinguish creating from making.

Consider first the question whether inspiration, critical judgment, or some other factor is at work in artistic creativity. Although some processes, but not necessarily the same processes, are necessary for one to be able to produce a work of art, it is not correct to assert that creativity is identical with any of those processes. After all, some of the processes that may have been operative in Shakespeare's mind when he wrote a play might have also operated when he was telling or enjoying a joke. But the play itself could not be a criterion of what had been going on in Shakespeare's mind when he wrote it; at best it would be only a symptom or evidence from which one could infer that the so-called creative process requisite for the writing of the play had presumably taken place in his mind. It is this inference which prompts creative-process theorists like Michael Mitias to insist that "to understand how the object is unique or valuable one should study the activity in which the object is produced." Mitias is, of course, right in saying that "the object presents evidence for the occurrence of creativity"; but he argues that it cannot be the locus for an explanation of "what it means for a thing to be creative." [16] He is thus defending a theory of the creative process that he considers necessary for artworks to be characterized as original, unrepeatable, and therefore valuable.

It may be admitted at once that to talk about the creative process of, say, a poem in terms of the ways in which words, sounds, and meaning become interrelated in one's realization of it is entirely appropriate. If the theorist, however, starts elucidating and defining the mental processes that the artist presumably goes through in order to arrive at the realized aesthetic entity, he is bound to ask questions that the materialist theories of mind find inescapable. The most crucial of these questions is one of locating the mind: Where is the mind? For the theorist of art concerned with the process of creativity in the artist's mind, there is still another question: How is the image called up in the mind? How does a sensation or feeling become transformed, in the recesses of the artist's mind, into an artistic metaphor? What is the subtle alchemy of changes involved in the mind that welds disparate materials into a realized aesthetic entity? By slow degrees, on these questions and assumptions implicit in them, mind becomes inaccessible, and the logical consequence is solipsism. The materialist theories of mind thus give rise to problems that are not simply insoluble but also conceptually erroneous. We can ask, for instance, where a particular building or man is, but we cannot ask similar questions involving mental concepts. They are not intelligibly employed in the ways we employ physical concepts; when they are, they become a mystery and render communication a dilemma. It is in order to overcome these difficulties that Wittgenstein abandoned the physicalist modes of investigating mental concepts since, as he put it, our head is bumping against the logical grammar of our language.[17] Viewed in this way, creativity is not to be construed as an occult element or a mental faculty, but as an ability realized through the production of artworks.

Theorists concerned with artistic creativity often assume that whatever is essential in producing a fully formed aesthetic object must be adequate to the particular process of knowing that leads to the phenomenon of achieving that object. They are therefore tempted to advance one or another "mental process" as the one that is essentially connected with the process of creativity. Wittgenstein's discussion of mental processes—a discussion that calls in question all accounts of a mental process or disposition—provides us a way of showing the impossibility of ever discovering any single criterion for the alleged mental process or disposition that could be distinguished from artworks themselves.[18] The impossibility does not of course denote the alleged complexity of artistic creativity but rather the conceptual confusion underlying the search for a special process of creativity.

45

Consider, for a moment, Wittgenstein's remarkable passage on the so-called process of understanding:

> We are trying to get hold of the mental process of understanding which seems to be hidden behind these coarse and therefore more readily visible accompaniments. But we do not succeed; or rather, it does not get as far as a real attempt. For even supposing that I had found something that happens in all these cases of understanding,— why should *it* be the understanding? And how can the process of understanding have been hidden, when I said, "Now I understand" *because* I understood?! And even if I say it is hidden—then how do I know what I have to look for? I am in a muddle.[19]

Wittgenstein therefore admonishes us to try "not to think of understanding as a 'mental process' at all—for that is the formula that confuses us."[20] The creative process that is presumably responsible for the production of aesthetic objects, too, is not a "process" which artists undergo in order to produce their works. It is here that W. E. Kennick's distinction between creative acts and creative processes provides a valuable clarification. As distinguished from creative processes construed as psychological affairs in the artist's mind, creative acts are "such that in performing . . . one or more of them a man is creating . . . a work of art."[21] Consequently, scratching a word out from a rough draft of a poem, giving up the original theme or tune that initially led one to begin the writing of a poem, putting in an image that fascinates one, and so on are certainly factors which may be characteristic of creativity, though they are not peculiar to the creation of artworks. The concept of inspiration or critical control or spontaneity, singly or together, designed to name and define the process of creativity, must defer to other, public manifestations for description and justification of the concept itself. Thus although inspiration may, for instance, solve serious knots in the writing of a poem, a description of this inspiration does not lead us to "something behind" the words of a poem, to the process of creativity. To get to something behind the words is to develop a sense of the intention that informs the poem. And to construe the intention is to figure out how to organize its complex of elements together in a coherent interpretation. This construal of intention does not entail the "intentional fallacy" since here the intention is seen as something structured in the work itself.

The idea of artistic creativity nevertheless derives its considerable support from the concept of inspiration, a concept that is as old as early Greek thought.[22] Some theorists consider inspiration to be the central element that distinguishes artistic creativity from any other kind of creativity. Thus Jack Glickman, who has recently made some important arguments against the idea of the creative process, has also argued that creating is generically different from making.[23] I will not deal here with Glickman's specific arguments but with the general distinction between creating and making, a distinction which has become central to a great deal of aesthetic theory since Kant. For Kant as well as for the German romantics, regardless of the differences among them, artistic creativity is the unique capacity possessed by the Genius. The Genius in creating art does not follow logical or conceptual rules but rather by some unconscious productive power (often characterized as inspiration or intuition) creates works that are uniquely new and original. Harold Osborne has clearly stated this case in a recent essay: "There are no principles and no rules by which non-aesthetic elements can be put together by logical and intellectual planning in such a way as to bring into being foreseen aesthetic characteristics. This adequately accounts for the difference between artistic creation and skilled craftsmanship and for the fact that fine art cannot be brought into being only by the conscious application of learned rules and know-how." [24]

How justifiable is the sharp distinction between creating and making or between art and craft? It is true that making and craft signify purpose as well as the value of learning rules, whereas art and creating seem beyond the necessity of rules or learning. Yet the ability that the Genius, capable of creating art, exhibits is not possible in the absence of both rules and the knowledge and mastery of a tradition. Indeed, the ability exhibited by the Genius is not fundamentally different from what is acquired through discipline and learning, unless these two are conceived as mechanically applicable guidelines or rules. Moreover, as Wittgenstein has taught us, the language we use in daily life is not a matter of the conscious application of rules. Rules are a matter of intuitive mastery, and they reveal themselves in informal but complex ways not reducible to clearly definable guidelines. And even the concept of exactitude is itself relative to the question and the discipline under consideration and does not have a straightforward application to all questions and disciplines requiring some notions of exactitude. Indeed, exemplary cases of making often tend to claim for themselves a creativity which immediately appropriates the concepts of inspiration and imagination that the theorists of creativity would like to reserve for art alone. Thus though creating and making allow for a difference, they also overlap at times, disclosing a complexity in the use of our concepts.

The concepts of originality and novelty used by critics are themselves meaningful within the institution of criticism and do not derive any real significance from a postulation of radical distinction between making and creating. This distinction is at the basis of spurious oppositions at times proposed by theorists between art and philosophy, art and history, art and science. If making and creating did not at some point overlap, it would be impossible for critics ever to say that some works of art, even if they are powerful, are flawed. Indeed, criticism would cease to be an activity of critical response, and would turn into an activity of praise or description. As praise, however, it would have no meaning or value because it would not know what it is not to praise, and as description it would be naive inasmuch as it would not know that to describe is to engage in an act of interpretation.

WHAT, THEN, IS THE STATUS of the testimony of creative artists? No doubt speculations about the nature of artistic creativity stretch at least as far back as Plato, and since the rise of romanticism there has accumulated a considerable body of testimony from artists themselves.[25] The fact, however, that there is a great deal of testimony does not necessarily establish that there is a special process of artistic creativity. It is plausible to say that the testimony will seem relevant to one who already believes that there is such a special creative process. Yet the testimony of creative artists is often unreliable[26] or contradictory: some emphasize inspiration, others critical control, and still others certain events or moods in personal life. Consequently, the theorist who seeks to base his theory of artistic creativity on the testimony of artists must formulate a proposition that allows for the entire variety of factors.[27] Alternatively, he may have recourse to the creative process specific to individual artists. The first version means no more than our early admission that creativity is a complex matter. But this admission does not entail that there is a special process of artistic creativity, that creating is radically different from making. The second version, that each artist has his own special process of creativity, while it appears to be more scrupulous than the first version, is open to at least two objections: first, artists of the past have left little testimony, though that fact does not prevent us from experiencing and interpreting their works; and second, the emotion presumed to be evoked by an artwork may be different from either the emotional make-up of its creator or the mood of the creator at the time of creating the work.[28]

It is, therefore, interesting that while creativity *seems* to be a process with a single significance, theorists tend to describe it at times in a host of divergent forms, each of which is offered as a competing theory of artistic creativity. Since there is no regular consciousness of one or another accompanying mental process and since there is no way of knowing that there does occur a particular mental process when artists are, so to speak, in the throes of creativity, one's postulation of its existence is simply hypothetical. When one has achieved a certain mastery in the creation of artworks, or in critical interpretations of them, one is at times tempted to seek an inner process that will stand as the basis of the various artistic products of one's mastery. It is here that our intelligence is bewitched by the language we use (in this case the "creative process") and that our head is bumping against the logical grammar of that language. Hence the postulation of various hypotheses about artistic creativity.

The most interesting sort of confusion occurs when attempts to prove one's concepts of art and criticism seek to derive them logically from a supposedly indubitable theory of artistic creativity. The temptation comes in some such form: How do words and sentences manage to become parts of a poem or to constitute a poem? The critic or theorist who is interested in the problem of creativity often rightly feels that the process of words and sentences becoming poems is so complex and difficult as to be inscrutable, a mystery. From this entirely plausible feeling he is then tempted, wrongly, to see it laid open before him, to have the knots untied by some theory. The point here is that this is precisely the confusing thing to do, that the problem that needs to be solved is the disentanglement of its various assumptions. For the diversity of modes which make possible the diversity and richness of works of art is closely connected with the diversity and richness of the modes of response itself. Thus my argument here that hypotheses of artistic creativity derive from the concepts of art and criticism that critics possess; concepts of criticism are not made possible by, and do not spring from, hypotheses of creativity.

SINCE THEORISTS often concern themselves with artistic creativity in order to define artistic imagination, it is important now to ask for a

49

clarification of the use of defining imagination. Is it to be used as a means of identifying works of art, or is it to be understood as a criterion of creativity such that we can understand the specific stages through which a given construct must have gone before becoming a work of art? The first question is inadequate to comprehend the complex and indeterminate modes in which critics use the concept of imagination in their practical criticism, and the second question we have already shown above to miscomprehend the logic of aesthetic theory. Here too Wittgenstein's probing on imagination can be helpful to us: "One ought to ask not what images are or what *happens* when one imagines something, but how the word 'imagination' is being used. But that does not mean that I want to talk only about words. For the question as to the nature of the imagination is as much about the word 'imagination' as my question is, and I am only saying that this question is not to be decided, neither for the person who does the imagining nor for anyone else, by pointing; nor yet by a description of any process."[29]

Our attempt, or the artist's attempt, to describe what exactly went on, even if we put aside the question of its accuracy or desirability, would not constitute an answer to the question what is artistic creativity or what is the nature of imagination. For we can arrive at a concept of creative imagination, not by a consideration of the process of artistic creativity, but by examining carefully what we say about works of art. And this consideration should in turn enable us to avoid (1) hypostatizing the faculty of imagination (as for instance in Coleridge); (2) comparing art with nonart in order to establish the intrinsic value of art; (3) making the distinction of kind between ordinary and poetic language, neither of which is precisely definable anyway; and finally (4) making the category mistake by confusing the concept of art with that of nonart. Yet, however insufficiently defined one's concept of art, in actual practice one is able to distinguish it from other concepts. To be able to make this distinction is not to make a value-judgment about the relation of this concept to the latter, for the concept of art has value within the context of other concepts. And that is what makes the attempts to articulate one or another type of poetics both difficult and valuable, for the context of concepts within which different concepts of art have their value is unstable and variable. This instability of cultural concepts directly or indirectly exerts a pressure upon concepts of art and forces them to undergo rearticulation and recharacterization.

III

MY ARGUMENT that hypotheses of creativity derive from the concepts of art and criticism does not mean that the concept of artistic creativity is itself devoid of value. Consequently, my position differs from that of Monroe Beardsley, who considers the concept of artistic creativity, if accepted as having any significance for criticism, to commit one to genetic criticism, a mode that he and Wimsatt have characterized as a critical fallacy. I discuss the question of intention in the next chapter. Yet I may be allowed to state here that regardless of whether an object conceived as a work of art is made by a human being, to see it as art is to attribute to it an intentionality.[30] To interpret a work of art is also to construe its intention. Thus human beings (and their actions) and works of art are best characterized in the Kantian sense as intentional entities, embodying "purposiveness without purpose."

There is of course another way of recognizing the value of artistic creativity without getting caught in the erroneous theory of the artistic process. And that is by attempting to come to terms with the diversity of modes of creativity that one notices through the history of art. Such a concern will tend to seek explanations of changes in the forms of artistic expression. One can explain, for instance, the changes in art history as transformations from one dominant modality in a given art at a particular time to another modality which replaces it. Here we verge on the rhetoric of artistic creativity as this creativity manifests itself through the dominance of different artistic modalities through art history, and thus on the rhetoric of criticism itself. The theorist who is concerned with constructing a theory of changes that have occurred in the modes of creativity must of course be conscious of the dialectical relationship between his own mode of figuration of the field of art history and the problem of figuration itself. In analytical terms, the criteria that a critic employs in order to articulate his apprehension of a field of art history must themselves be recognized as a problem, since they are not immutable yardsticks.

I HAVE ARGUED above that neither the theory of the creative process nor its various subconcepts such as inspiration and imagination can help us formulate a defensible theory of artistic creativity special for works of art. For the sharp distinction between creating and making presumed in order to separate art from the rest of the products of human endeavor is unjustified. Creating makes sense not only against the background of making, but also in conjunction with making. When creating is considered a unique process it leads, on the one hand, to the myth of the mental process, and, on the other, to the Crocean, extremist notion of the uniqueness of art, for both of which criticism becomes not only futile but also impossible. The variety of factors that contribute to the production of artworks and to the divergent forms of art and criticism show fairly adequately the futility of both the belief that artworks spring, as it were, from a single, unique process of creativity and the hope that satisfactory response to art must derive its standards of interpretation and judgment from that process. In neither case can the creative process serve as the determinate guide to proper comprehension of art, since the concept of creativity is closely intertwined with the concepts of criticism and no single determinate characterization of creativity can adequately elucidate those concepts.

Moreover, the theorizing that is designed to show how qualitatively unique aesthetic objects originate in a process of artistic creativity that is itself uniquely peculiar to those objects cannot succeed because it is not possible to have that kind of description of artistic creativity. For even if we assume that such creativity is independent of our thought about aesthetic objects, we can still analyze it only in terms of our thought about these objects. This implies that we cannot validly distinguish between those features of aesthetic objects which arise from our theory of artistic creativity and those features which arise from our concept of aesthetic objects. Even if we do make this distinction it will not help aesthetic theory, since the resulting description of artistic creativity presupposes a concept of aesthetic objects. This treatment of artistic creativity does not invalidate the central insight of romanticism, for which art and self are mutually implicated, but it will certainly invalidate the scientistic ambitions of genetic criticism.

CHAPTER THREE
Intention and Contemporary
Literary Theory

For more than three decades the question of the relevance and value of intention for literary criticism has been the subject of considerable critical debate, and the controversy surrounding this question is far from reaching a satisfactory resolution.[1] In Anglo-American discussions of it the controversy has tended to center on the arguments that William K. Wimsatt and Monroe Beardsley first proposed in their famous essay. The importance of the question of intention is aptly stated in Wimsatt and Beardsley's words: "There is hardly a problem of literary criticism in which the critic's approach will not be qualified by his view of 'intention.'"[2] They resolutely characterized intentionalist criticism as committing a "fallacy," and resolved the question in favor of the New Critical formalism. Since works of art, according to this formalism, are self-contained, organic entities, they create a privileged mode of discourse not available to other kinds of objects.

In this chapter I want to examine the New Critical rejection of intention and to articulate some crucial features that characterize the concept of intention in criticism. My thesis here is twofold. First, this concept is an "essentially contested"[3] concept and therefore cannot be *logically* resolved in favor of either the intentionalist or the antiintentionalist. It is nevertheless a rationally debatable concept allowing for argument and evidence that in principle can lead to clarification and enrichment of both positions. Second, because a decision on the concept of intention has a significant bearing on the concept of criticism

53

that one holds, a full characterization of the controversy on intention should help illuminate not just the issues at stake but the concept of criticism itself. If the concept of intention in criticism is an essentially contested concept, then the concept of criticism itself reveals its own nature as a highly complex, essentially contested and contestable one. My second thesis, as we shall see, has implications for all the central preoccupations of this book.

The Nature of Controversy on Intention

I SHALL FIRST CHARACTERIZE the critical context in which the question of intention became a serious issue.[4] Such a characterization is necessary because the antiintentionalist position derives some of its power from its attempt to redefine the concepts of art and criticism and to lend theoretical rigor to the principle of aesthetic autonomy. The latter part of this section will concern itself with a further scrutiny of the dispute on intention by focusing on the relevant views of E. D. Hirsch and Hans-Georg Gadamer.

Wimsatt and Beardsley do not deny that there does reside an element of intention in the structure of a poem; they rather deny the usefulness of any genetic analysis of the concept of intention. This point requires some clarification. A genetic approach to art is one which claims that there can be a causal explanation of (how) works of art (are created). An intentionalist approach therefore entails a genetic theory only insofar as it attempts to delineate and exhaust all, or necessary and sufficient, conditions that presumably create a poem. But it is not a genetic theory insofar as it locates the intention within the structure of the poem itself. Most genetic theorists, however, do not rest content with just one or another genetic theory for poems; they tend to assert further that their particular versions of causal accounts provide the criteria for appreciation and judgment of that particular quality in virtue of which we recognize a work as a poem. It is in order to reject this latter assertion that Wimsatt and Beardsley argue that intentionalist criticism commits a serious "fallacy."

Wimsatt and Beardsley do not simply deny that knowledge of a poet's intention is necessary to the proper critical appreciation and judgment of his poems. They extend their denial to the romantic claim for the relationship of the poet's personality to his poems. They join the first issue with the second in order to provide a theoretical foundation for T. S. Eliot's attempt[5] to disconnect the link that the romantics had claimed between the personality of the poet and his poems. They lend their position further theoretical support with this argument: poems are verbal structures made out of public language which is governed by the conventions of a language community.[6] This is their most powerful argument. If there is obscurity or ambiguity in a poem, they would argue, it is not because elements of private language have crept into the poem, but because the convention permits ambiguity, since it adds to the aesthetic richness of the poem. Where a presumed ambiguity in a poem does not seem to contribute to the aesthetic value of the poem, the responsible critic must select those meanings that are permitted by the total context of the poem. If the conventions of a language community permit it, the critic is free to choose a word to mean, provided he keeps to the context of the poem, something other than what the poet might tell us extraneously about it.[7]

However, it is often difficult for critics to keep separate questions about poems and questions about the process that presumably brings them about, because in literary criticism, owing to the fluidity of its concepts and terms, one tends to move, imperceptibly as it were, from one claim to another. Wimsatt and Beardsley therefore argue that these claims can be, and ought to be, kept separate. On logical considerations, their argument would seem to be plausible, for a great deal of criticism would seem to confuse inquiries beginning with "why" (the reason one finds the poem holding together its diverse elements and acquiring its aesthetic value), with inquiries beginning with "how" (the way the poem came about), reason with cause. When, for instance, a critic says that a poem is spontaneous or sincere, he can give two kinds of explanation for his proposition. Either he can confine himself to the words of the poem and, if he wants to give a theoretical explanation, explain what it is to talk about spontaneity or sincerity in poems; or he can talk about what the poet did when he wrote the poem so that the claim about spontaneity or sincerity can be validated. The alternative account, in order to be justified, has to be related to its creativity, the way the poem was created. Antigenetic theorists would argue that the causal account cannot explain the poem better in the sense of leading one to realize it aesthetically, since that account must rely on factors that are presumed to have contributed to the making of a poem, factors that are at best conjectural and do not in any case solve the question concerning the poem's value.[8]

It is in order to keep these two inquiries separate that Wimsatt and Beardsley are tempted to revamp the romantic poetics: "It would be convenient if the passwords of the intentional school, 'sincerity', 'fidelity', 'spontaneity', 'authenticity', 'genuineness', 'originality', could be equated with terms such as 'integrity', 'relevance', 'unity', 'function', 'maturity', 'subtlety', 'adequacy', and other more precise terms of evaluation—in short, if 'expression' always meant aesthetic achievement. But this is not so."[9] It is Beardsley's conviction that the "variability of their meaning makes them handy for critics who do not want to bother to be clear about what they are talking about, and therefore you can only decide in each particular case how a critic is using one of those terms."[10] If a critic uses the internal evidence of a poem in employing any of those terms, he is not committing the intentional fallacy; but if he is using the external evidence, then he is.

Now, it is true that as long as one keeps the personality of the poet and his poems separate, the criterion of whether a particular expression is spontaneous and sincere cannot be employed genetically. Instead, one employs the criterion in terms of the convention that has been developed to recognize whether a poem is spontaneous and sincere. With this application of the criterion neoclassical principles of criticism are in perfect accord, since considerations of biographical detail are not required. But as soon as neoclassical principles of imitation of reality, decorum, and so on are put into question, as soon as there develops a new dynamics about the primacy of the individual temperament by which the world is not merely viewed but also constituted, then the genetic method makes a competing claim, which is an "essentially contested concept" and cannot be logically refuted or reduced to some other concept.[11] However, as the history of modern criticism shows, the neoclassical and romantic criteria of criticism do not exhaust the ways in which a literary work may be realized. As Roman Ingarden, an antigenetic theorist of criticism, has argued, there are other ways of actualizing the intentional object, the literary work, which transcends both the intending act of the author and the actualizing act of the perceiver.[12]

But, then, on what grounds can we say that the genetic method makes a competing claim, that it is an essentially contested concept? For, one may argue, the empirical fact or premise that this concept has been contested does not authorize us to deduce a necessary proposition. It is my contention here that this concept exhibits certain peculiarities which enable its proponents to defend, refine, and recharacterize it.[13] For instance, both neoclassical and romantic concepts of criticism are embedded in history, and given the contingent nature of history these concepts are liable to be highly complex. To recognize contingency as an irreducible datum of history is to recognize that events and concepts that occur in history cannot be brought under a single scheme of rational explanation. One may ask, however, whether history, because of its contingent nature, might not also bring about eventual reconciliation among, say, conflicting concepts of criticism. This question can at best make us realize that conflicts do at times cease, giving us a sense of general conceptual stability in criticism. But that is illusory. The triumph of the New Criticism in the forties and fifties in America seemed to give a sense of stability, but that was no more than a temporary, though doubtless significant, suppression of other contending trends in criticism. Yet this triumph cannot account for the fact that on the Continent phenomenological criticism flourished and would soon seek to replace the New Critical formalism in America. The equation that Wimsatt and Beardsley desire is not possible, not because critics are intransigent and do not bother to use words in a logically tidy manner, but because concepts of criticism do not have a single significance which can be fixed once and for all by logical scrutiny. Consequently, the romantic theory of self-expression cannot be equated with formalism, nor can it be reduced to formalism, without conceptual distortion.

The attack on intentionalist criticism is part of a larger and more comprehensive modernist attack on romanticism initiated early in the century by T. E. Hulme and T. S. Eliot. For the modernists the antagonist is the romantic critic—Walter Pater, Sainte-Beuve, and Taine, for instance—whose method of appreciation and judgment of poetry is genetic.[14] Yet romantic thought itself, however complex and ambiguous, was partly the result of a reaction to the neoclassical modes of poetry and criticism. For the neoclassicist, both poet and critic had available to them objective criteria with respect to subject, character, and diction; and the emphasis was to be on typical experiences because individual experiences, not being typical enough, cannot have universal appeal. Thus Pope emphasized, at least in theory, "what oft was thought but ne'er so well-express't," Gray suppressed his personal feelings in his elegy, Dr. Johnson condemned the metaphysical poetry for its violent yoking of heterogeneous materials and for its consequent failure to exhibit respect for rules of content and form in poetry.[15]

The romantics, on the other hand, rejected the neoclassical concern with rules, and recognized the importance of any diction if it was organically suitable, for the analogy between form and content was for them skin and body, not clothes and body. There is here an emphasis on individual experiences and inner vision, which constitute the nature of the works that an artist produces. On this view artists no longer have a common set of problems that critics can understand in their study of poetry by employing either the Aristotelian concepts of probability and necessity or the Augustan concepts of appreciation. Given the romantic emphasis on the peculiar qualities of the poet's vision, sincerity, spontaneity, originality, and adequacy become the criteria of criticism. Romanticism thus brought about a fundamental shift in the definition of a work of art. As M. H. Abrams has observed, "Wordsworth . . . reverses the cardinal neoclassical ideal of setting only accessible goals, by converting what had been man's tragic error—the inordinacy of his 'pride' that persists in setting infinite aims for finite man—into his specific glory and his triumph. Wordsworth shares the recognition of his fellow romantics, German and English, of the greatness of man's infinite *Sehnsucht*, his saving insatiability."[16]

That the controversy on intention centers on the two opposed definitions of poetry can be shown simply by juxtaposing them. The eighteenth-century definition can be construed in terms of the structure of a poem, its relationship with the world it represented (the quality of its decorum, the fidelity to general social experience, the avoidance of emotional indulgence), and its effect on the audience. For the romantic definition, on the other hand, "A work of art is essentially the internal made external, resulting from a creative process operating under the impulse of feeling, and embodying the combined product of the poet's perceptions, thoughts, and feelings."[17] Without minimizing the differences between the two definitions, we can grant that the romantic definition is not narrowly literary. Indeed, "Wordsworth's criteria are as much social as literary, and . . . by their egalitarianism they subvert the foundations of a view of poetry inherited from the Renaissance."[18]

In general terms, then, romanticism has brought about the emergence of intentionalist criticism (however variable and complex its features) and, as a modern offshoot of it, psychoanalytic criticism. There are, of course, other contributory factors that complicated the scene of cultural criticism in nineteenth-century England and Europe. Among the most important of these factors was the desire to extend the scientific methods of explanation to literary works, for the contention of critics such as Sainte-Beuve and Taine was that because literary works are natural phenomena they should be amenable to naturalistic explanation. This conviction led them to carry out an intensive search for the causes of literary phenomena and to propose a number of genetic theories which were vigorously put into practice and defended by their proponents. "The essence of biography, especially the nineteenth-century biographies of artists and poets," Gadamer has said, "is to understand the works from the life." [19] Literary works, in other words, acquire a more intense and richer kind of meaning if we place them in the context of their writer's experiences.

It is clear, then, that the characterization of intentionalist criticism as a fallacy is part of a larger, modernist attack on romanticism and its critical principles. The attack, moreover, is systematically motivated, for the antiintentionalist position conceives the theoretical problems of creativity and criticism to be definitional and conceptual ones which can be properly articulated and settled by a rigorous logical scrutiny. Wimsatt and Beardsley thus argue, "It is not so much a historical statement as a definition to say that the intentional fallacy is a romantic one." From their initial premise that aesthetic objects are autonomous, Wimsatt and Beardsley want to establish a logical separation between historical and definitional problems and to argue that the former are irrelevant to proper criticism. It is here that the antiintentionalist position runs into serious difficulties, since it refuses to see that in criticism and cultural thought historical and definitional problems are closely intertwined. Furthermore, it refuses to see that critical concepts are essentially contested and contestable concepts which operate differently from the way in which conclusions deriving from formal logic operate, since all parties to a dispute accept this logic as a valid modus operandi. Wimsatt and Beardsley thus argue: "What is said about a poem is subject to the same scrutiny as any statement in linguistics or in the general science of psychology." [20]

The controversy on intention is part of a larger dispute on the more fundamental questions about the characterization of what is a work of art and what is proper criticism. Though the dispute is a conceptual one, it is inevitably complicated by the contingencies of history. Disputants are therefore forced to articulate and refine the logic of their respective positions, while exposing the weakness of the position that is rejected. Consider, for instance, the modernist attack on romantic criticism, an attack which focuses on the inadequacy of the romantic criteria: adequacy, sincerity, spontaneity, and originality of expression. Antiintentionalists reject the first and the last on the ground that one can argue for the adequacy of a poem only when we compare the poem and the poet's original experience, but what is at issue is its availability. And they ask further, At what stage is the experience original and the expression adequate to it? The antiintentionalist position has a convincing argument in the following words of T. S. Eliot:

> And what is the experience the poet is so bursting to communicate? By the time it has settled down into a poem it may be so different from the original experiences to be hardly recognisable. The "experience" in question may be the result of a fusion of feelings so numerous and ultimately so obscure in their origins, that even if there is communication of them, the poet may hardly be aware of what he is communicating; and what is there to be communicated was not in existence before the poem was completed.[21]

Antiintentionalists therefore gladly accept Croce's statement that a work of art is a voyage of discovery, for the artist does not know what he is going to express until he has expressed it.

As for sincerity and spontaneity, antiintentionalists contend that the first is relevant only when considering content, whereas the second is relevant when considering process, but that neither criterion is adequate for criticism. Thus, although the romantic criteria are usable, they are extremely inadequate since they are neither necessary nor sufficient for criticism, which needs a criterion of value. Moreover, the romantic criteria, even if they can be used, cannot give a clue to the poet's original experience: they are not dependable, nor can they be employed as criteria of value. A persuasive, antiintentionalist example is that some poets write, as Keats reportedly wrote "Grasshopper and the Cricket," without any articulate original experience. And if a poem is revised, how can we use the criterion of sincerity without arbitrarily distorting its meaning? Antiintentionalists therefore insist on the organic and self-subsistent nature of poems, for once the poem is written and published, it is public property since it can no longer be controlled by the poet. Hence the insistence by Eliot, the New Critics, and other antiintentionalists such as Ingarden that criticism ought to confine itself to the task of appreciation and evaluation of literary works. Contrary to the opponents of these theorists, this position is not reducible to a mechanical and sterile formalism. The insistence that criticism concern itself with the aesthetic dimension as an autonomous realm of human endeavor does not entail a denial of either meanings or the literary work's relation to the world. Postponing a further discussion of this position until the following chapter, I need only stress here the antiintentionalist insight into the complex modes by which meanings and values acquire their aesthetic significance in literature and the arts.

The antiintentionalist position can be summed up in a number of points, some of which overlap and some of which are independent but all of which are important. First, in the process of writing their poems poets often abandon their original intentions. Second, poets often include things that are not central to their original intentions. Third, if there is a change in intention in the course of writing a poem we can no longer consider the original intention as the standard for judging or interpreting the poem. Fourth, in the case of anonymous poetry, Homer, Shakespeare, and most of the poetry of the past there is no way of determining the poet's intentions. And finally there is the Socratic argument, cited by Wimsatt and Beardsley, about the unreliability of the poet's capacity to explain his intentions.[22]

All of the above five points are plausible. Their plausibility derives from the fact that writing poetry is a complex achievement, and that all the numerous factors that contribute to a poem are not likely to be present in the forefront of the poet's consciousness. Yet a sophisticated intentionalist need not find these points in any way detrimental to his position. He would readily agree that if pressed to describe his intentions or moved to promote a particular interpretation of his poem, the poet may well describe at best what was uppermost in his mind and perhaps superfluous to our understanding of the poem or at worst what may be completely irrelevant to the poem (his motives of getting money or fame, for instance). But this does not commit the intentionalist to the argument that the factors that do not get described in the poet's description are as a result counterintentional or unintentional. Because the factors that are presumed to be not in the forefront of the writer's consciousness can be construed as essentially intentional, it is possible for some critics to make the rather dramatic but conceivable claim that Milton was of Satan's party; they can plausibly make this claim because they are consciously or half-consciously committed to the concept of art as self-expression. Antiintentionalists, however, because of their prior decision as to what is to count as proper talk about Milton's poem and therefore what is to count as permissible evidence for talk about Satan, would find the argument about Milton's being a Satanist both unintelligible and extravagant. It is clear that their rejection of the intentionalist claim about Milton rests finally on their concept of poems as self-contained entities or as objective structures. The intentionalist can argue that anything that is characterizable as expression is necessarily self-expression. Underlying this argument is a conviction that all human actions and expressions differ from natural objects, that they differ because human beings engage in specific activities for which they can and often do give reasons and explanations.

It would now be important to test the power of the antiintentionalist position by examining a major attack launched against it by E. D. Hirsch. Hirsch's attack is carried out on two fronts: first at the level of literary theory, where he seeks to question the antiintentionalist banishment of the author and to reinstate the recovery of authorial meaning as the central task of literary interpretation; and second at the level of the phenomenological concept of intentionality, where, following Husserl, he criticizes Gadamer's Heideggerian concept of interpretation.[23] Hirsch's radical opposition to the antiintentionalist stand is signaled by his counterproposal to Wimsatt and Beardsley's contention that "poetry differs from practical messages which are successful if and only if we correctly infer the intention."[24] Poetic language, on this view, is an end in itself, whereas ordinary language is a means to an end and is therefore limited to the speaker's intention. Hirsch not only rejects this distinction, he also insists that all uses of language "are ethically governed by the intentions of the author."[25]

Meaning, according to Hirsch, remains constant, whereas responses to it are changing and can be accounted for by articulating changes in its significance for different critics at the same time and at different times. The function of criticism is therefore to grasp words in the original sense in which the author intended them. It is, then, not changes in meaning but changes in the significance of a work that make it necessary for each new age or critic to reinterpret the work. Yet insofar as critics defining a verbal work's significance claim at the same time to offer its meaning, Hirsch argues, they must accept the author as the determiner of the meaning of his work, because without that we have no compelling normative principle for validating one interpretation and rejecting others. "It may be asserted as a general rule that whenever a reader confronts two interpretations which impose different emphases on similar meaning components, at least one of the interpretations must be wrong. They cannot be reconciled." [26]

Hirsch's logico-experimental approach consists in subjecting one's interpretive hypotheses to the control of observation which is provided by the invariant verbal construct, a poem. But note that Hirsch, correctly, does not call this construct "unambiguous," [27] because otherwise the question of seeking for the most probable interpretation will not even arise. The verbal construct is ambiguous, though it allows for one most plausible interpretation, which it is the (ethical) function of criticism as objective scholarship to establish. Hirsch is, of course, more demanding than this, for he insists that no one interpretation will be satisfactory enough to put criticism of a poem to rest. This argument is thoroughly consistent with his Popperian conviction about the logic of inquiry in criticism. The reason Hirsch argues for a single, most probable interpretation of the meaning of a poem is that he holds a theory of intentionality which links the poem to its creator, to the mind that produced it. Yet he does not go by simple notions of examining what the poet said in his notes, essays, or memoirs, though he would not altogether reject them. In proposing an objectivist conception of meaning he seeks to oppose the confusion underlying the psychologistic conception of criticism, which identifies meaning with mental process.

Interestingly enough, then, Hirsch, like Wimsatt and Beardsley, seeks to avoid psychologism and the search for the author's private meanings, though, contrary to them, he also seeks to reinstate intention as central to interpretation. Hirsch's argument thus does not really confront the antiintentionalist position, since in order to deny that position he would have to recognize the importance of private meanings. The question, then, becomes whether Hirsch's reinterpretation of the concept of intention succeeds in countering the antiintentionalist position. The answer, it seems to me, has to be No, because Hirsch's authorial intention does not entail a biographical person but rather a "speaking subject," not really distinguishable from the New Critical persona. For Wimsatt and Beardsley intention is not an anomaly as long as it is construed as subsisting in the inter-relationship among the parts as they make up the totality of a poem. Those who insist on the connection of intention to consciousness, however, do not search for authorial meaning in the sense intended by Hirsch. Hirsch has indeed transformed what seemed to be a psychologist criterion into a scientistic one inasmuch as his theory must develop a logic of validation for which, while correctness is the goal of interpretation, "it can never be known to be achieved."[28] But for those who consider meaning an affair of consciousness, the emphasis is not on the standards or validity of interpretation, but rather on the experience and articulation of the nature and quality of a literary consciousness.

Consider, for instance, the Geneva critics, who do not concern themselves either with providing interpretations of discrete literary works or with the question of validity of interpretation. The Geneva critics are preoccupied, not with questions of structure or genre, but rather with literature as experience. The concept of literary autonomy directing critics to interpret and evaluate literary works as autotelic entities has no significance for the Geneva critics because it is the total consciousness of an author which is central to grasping the experience of the works he produces. These critics focus on the imaginary subject generated in an author's works, not the authorial self that may be presumed to subsist outside his works. The act of criticism engaged in this manner dissolves the boundaries critics generally assume between literature and criticism, and criticism becomes indistinguishable from literature. This is because if language at its most self-conscious conducts a meditation on its own nature, then criticism to the extent it penetrates to the inner workings of an author's consciousness recreates that consciousness. Criticism becomes a kind of metacommentary, and literature discloses itself as metaliterature. For Georges Poulet criticism is a form of literature, just as literature is a form of criticism. The Geneva critics thus hold that each writer has his own unique experiential patterns, which are at the basis of all his activities. The works that a writer produces do not refer to his consciousness but rather duplicate it, and criticism mediates the incarnations of the authorial *moi* in the writer's various works. In J. Hillis Miller's words, "The pervasive stylistic traits of a writer, his recurrent words and images, his special cadence and tone, are as personal to him as his face or his way of talking. His style is his own way of living in the world given a verbal form."[29] Consequently, though the question of art and personality came to be closely connected in romantic literature and criticism, a defense of that connection can no longer be made by seeking to establish an interpretation in terms of authorial meaning. As the Geneva critics do, a defense can be made by seeking to experience the personality or consciousness of a writer through a reading of all his verbal works. Moreover, given a variety of points of departure from which to apprehend the complex ligatures of a writer's consciousness, the Geneva critics would deny that there can be an unvarying and determinate form of consciousness.

The antiintentionalist could, of course, argue against the Geneva school of criticism that the Geneva method is applicable to the verbal productions of any nonliterary writer and therefore provides no usable criteria by which to distinguish between literary and nonliterary works. His attack on intention, he might add, was to provide some usable criteria precisely for such a distinction and thereby to invest criticism with legitimate status as a discipline. The Geneva critic, here construed as a committed intentionalist, would counter by saying that the value of criticism as a discipline resides in apprehending the consciousness of a writer, since the world of his literary works and his consciousness are mutually implicated. An answer to the question whether a given work of art is valuable or not would then depend, for a Geneva critic like Georges Poulet, on whether he would succeed in his effort of identification with a writer.[30] More strictly, the question of value-judgments is an illegitimate one for the Geneva critics both because it creates distance between the critic and literary works and because it conceives of literary works as autonomous objective entities charged with varying degrees of meanings and values. The writer's subjectivity is, of course, immanent within works, not to be replaced by the biographical person outside the works. The dispute between the intentionalist and the antiintentionalist is thus an essentially contested dispute, and it turns on what criticism is and how one should engage in it. Unless one of the parties to the dispute changes its position or experiences a loosening of the hold of its own position, the possibility of refinement is always open, though the arguments of one or another position may at times be simply a stubborn and unreasoning refusal to engage in genuine dispute.

Despite their radical opposition, both the Geneva school of criticism and the Wimsatt-Beardsley position seem to share a methodological assumption regarding critical neutrality. Thus while the Geneva school believes in the possibility of neutrality so that the mind succeeds in "its effort of detachment from itself" for "the apprehension of a subjectivity without objectivity," [31] Wimsatt and Beardsley believe in the organic nature of poems construed on the model of physical objects. Both positions are subject to a serious theoretical objection from Gadamer's theory of interpretation. Recall first, however, that Hirsch too proposed a logic of validation requiring neutrality for reaching the most probable interpretation.

Gadamer denies the very possibility of a historical reconstruction of the past, though he does not consider this denial to entail a denial of rational discourse. [32] For Gadamer linguisticality and historicity are the conditions of possibility of understanding, so that it is methodologically impossible to transcend the hermeneutical viewpoint. The interpreter, in other words, brings to the text a horizon of expectations that characterizes his own life-world. This horizon enables him to make a preliminary projection of the meaning of a text which is then revised, leading to new proposals and projections. The entire process is one of the gradual modification of the sense of the parts in terms of the whole that emerges in an interpretation. If, as Gadamer argues, a successful interpretation is necessarily the result of a fusion of horizons, there is no such thing as the correct interpretation. Gadamer's views on intention and interpretation are clearly expressed in the following statement:

> The real meaning of a text, as it speaks to the interpreter, does not depend on the contingencies of the author and whom he originally wrote for. It certainly is not identical with them, for it is always partly determined also by the historical situation of the interpreter and hence by the totality of the objective course of history. . . . Not occasionally only, but always, the meaning of a text goes beyond its author. That is why understanding is not merely a reproductive, but always a productive attitude as well. [33]

Gadamer's view is a highly sophisticated theory of interpretation and provides a serious insight into the nature of the human understanding. If it would expose the Geneva critics' theories for their somewhat simplistic conceptions of subjectivity and objectivity, it would expose the New Critics for their illegitimate assimilation of literary works to physical objects. His theory would thus disclose the inadequacy underlying the concepts of interpretation held by both theories. Yet Gadamer's theory cannot dissolve the central crux of the dispute on intention. A committed Geneva critic can profit from Gadamer's hermeneutics without abandoning his conviction about the indissoluble bond between art and consciousness; and he can adhere to his refusal to study literary works as discrete, autonomous aesthetic objects. With some willingness for self-criticism he can see both that Gadamer's hermeneutics provides a richer theoretical foundation for his critical practice and that Gadamer returns history to art and unites both with criticism. An advocate of the New Criticism, on the other hand, can accept Gadamer's notion of the fusion of horizons and study literary works as autonomous aesthetic works. Equipped with Eliot's view of the interdependence of the past and the present, the New Critical theorist can begin to purge theoretical excesses of the organic metaphor, and show greater theoretical self-consciousness about the nature of his own interpretive assumptions.[34] For both theories there is the possibility of recharacterization and refinement, allowing for rational discourse though never for a logic of validation that would put the dispute to rest (except, of course, by the end of history itself).

I have argued so far that the concept of intention is an essentially contested concept. One's decision on it depends on one's insight into the concepts of art and criticism. Consequently, while the New Critics can certainly consider intention as at best an element structured within a poem, a writer's intentions are nevertheless part of a broader category logically not reducible to that element within the poem. That category includes the genetic concept of personality; and this concept, if accepted as a valid principle of criticism, brings in all the things related to the writer's life, his other literary works, his diaries, essays, and so on; and this in short prepares the way, on the one hand, to psychoanalytic criticism, and on the other hand, to a criticism of consciousness. It is true, however, that once the search for antecedents begins there is no limit to it in principle. One can extend the search for causes, for instance, from the individual psyche to the artistic traditions, the national dream or myth, the racial memory, and finally the human psyche or the collective unconscious. That the search tends to move off into the "boundless," as Wimsatt complained,[35] does not mean that the insight that informs intentionalist criticism is thereby disproved as logically misconceived. For the perspective that romanticism opened up by establishing the connection between art and artist, aesthetic creativity and social existence, remains an important one. And the controversy between intentionalists and antiintentionalists is not empirical but conceptual.[36] To say that it is not empirical is to say that more evidence or new facts will not alter the conceptual decision that bears on the question of intention. If one accepts intention as a fallacy then it is logically incumbent on one to show the limits within which certain intentional considerations can validly operate in criticism and to reject those considerations that involve search for causal antecedents. This is one reason why Wimsatt and Beardsley wish to remove the question of intention from its historical, conceptual context, where the question became urgent, and to characterize it as a logical, definitional one.

The Concept of Intention

IT WILL BE PERTINENT now to focus on the concept of intention and characterize the features that identify it. No one will deny that the usefulness of the concept of intention is at first connected to the reasons an agent gives for his action. But the concept does not remain confined to the reasons which seemed to give an expression or action its meaning. This is why any expression or action could be removed from its original context, and yet be called intentional if someone could give compelling reasons for it. Thus it is that Kant, without attributing intention to any mind, conceives even nature itself as revealing a purposive organization; he thereby extends the domain of intention not just to the human mind or to works of art but also to inanimate nature.[37]

What does it mean, then, to say that any explanation of what human beings say or do or what works of art do is intentionalist? Conceived in this way, does not the notion of intention become too sweepingly general and devoid of any force it was initially conceived to possess? The answer to these questions is as simple as it is complex, since the concept of intention is not construed separately from the concept of interpretation. The two seemingly different concepts are closely interconnected, for knowing what a text means or intends involves our being able to explain it, justify it, elaborate it. And how we elaborate and explain and justify will depend on how we mean it, how we take it, and what it means *to us*. To be able to do this is to characterize intention in the sense of how someone may have meant us to take that text, regardless of our possession of any other intentional statement given by the writer of the text. Such a construal of intention recognizes that it is not separable from interpretation, that one constitutes intention and interpretation together. In Gadamer's terms, the relation between reader and text is one of dialogue which precludes both subjectivism and authorial meaning. The meaning of a text is the result of an interaction between the questions posed by the text to the reader in his historical situation and the expectations of the reader that pose questions to the text.[38]

A recognition of the interdependence of intention and interpretation has implications which are particularly fruitful for recharacterizing the concept of self. One would then see that the concept of self is enormously complex and is founded in moral discourse and requires considerations of other selves. For every expression of a self is also an invitation for as well as an implication of other selves. The concept of self therefore does not refer to or imply absolute autonomy completely set apart from the world of other human beings. If it were completely autonomous, we would not be able to characterize or know it as self. The self, as ordinarily understood with all its contradictions and tensions, is a social and moral concept and has its meaning and value in intersubjective human contexts.

It is in order to illuminate the otherwise elusive and difficult concept of self that Wittgenstein shows the link between the self and human expressions and actions. He argues that sensations are not simply felt by the person who has them, but can be known by those who do not have them. In thus linking (private) feeling and its public manifestations Wittgenstein counters solipsism and restores a certain objectivity to our discourse.[39] This objectivity need not involve us in the structuralist project of articulating rules of comprehension, since the rules underlying language are not logical or mechanical regularities. Our conventions make sense because they enable us, among other things, to communicate our experiences to others and to achieve mutual agreement or understanding. This agreement or understanding makes up what coherence our expressions acquire, what certainty we acquire in our response to art and nonart.

That there are tensions and contradictions within language, within the use of words, within our conventions means that there can be no universally agreed upon definitions of concepts that underlie our use of words. When we learn the use of the word *self*, this learning does not teach us to *describe* its use, for when we do attempt to describe that use, the concept covers a heterogeneity of phenomena called self. Consider, for instance, the romantic preoccupation with self in relation to the literature that precedes the romantic. Eighteenth-century literature cannot be conceived as devoid of a certain notion of self, though one may argue that for the neoclassicists self is not as problematic a notion as for the romantics. Despite this immediate difference the same word is used for its various manifestations. We are therefore tempted, Wittgenstein would argue, to seek a clear picture which turns out to be a false one, and he admonishes us not to expect that words such as *intention, self, thinking, meaning*, and so on "should have a unified employment; we should rather expect the opposite." [40] They do not have "unified employment" because we do not learn their use, nor do we use them efficaciously, by learning their "essential" meaning.

IN THE FIRST SECTION I argued that intentionalists and antiintentionalists hold different theories of the nature of works of art and that neither theory can be reduced to a version of the other. And in this section. I have argued that a construal of intention is logically implicit in any act of interpretation. One may now object that on my account both intentionalists and antiintentionalists are necessarily intentionalist in that a construal of intention is implied in any act of interpretation.

This objection is easily answered. Its concealed presupposition is that there is a distinction between intention and intentionality, that intention is what the speaker of a statement means and intentionality is what is inherent in the statement in its context for a listener or reader. Now, antiintentionalists make or imply this distinction in order to reject what they consider to be the absurd consequences that follow from a search for the authorial meaning of a poem. They therefore redefine the concept of intention in order to characterize what according to them is proper criticism. And this logical step is based on their concept of art. Thus antiintentionalists are intentionalist insofar as they must construe the meaning of a work of verbal art; their dispute centers on what constitutes the correct mode of such a construal and on what constitutes a satisfactory characterization of the nature of art. Yet there is no single correct mode of construing intention, though each competing mode offers itself as the correct one. The reason, however, that none can be established as the valid one is that the logic of inquiry in criticism differs from that in the sciences, and the concept of intention is therefore a contestable concept generating different and conflicting construals of it, none of which can be set up as the general and valid construal.

Our answer to the question whether poems belong in the intentional matrix as other human actions do or, by some special qualitative fiat, they fall outside this matrix, depends entirely on the insight one has acquired into the nature of poetry. Consequently, the romantic contention about poetry as "the spontaneous overflow of powerful feelings" (however qualified in the original Wordsworthian statement) on the one hand, and Eliot's contention, on the other, that "poetry is not a turning loose of emotion, but an escape from emotion"[41] constitutes a head-on conflict on the concept of poetry. Those who defend intentional criticism attempt to articulate the particular function that it fulfills and thus to defend it as the valid function of criticism. Those who reject intentional criticism attempt to articulate the concept of self-sufficiency of poems, and thus to defend the function of criticism underlying that concept.

Take, for instance, the argument that many poets do not begin writing with a clear intention in mind. But this does not entail that no poet ever writes a poem with a clear intention. Consequently, where a statement of intention is available it is entirely appropriate, though not conceptually compelling, for a critic to consult it for his critical interpretation.[42] Whether that statement will be compelling depends on a given critic's concept of what poems are. Thus the dispute about the relevance of intention is a peculiar one, and it reveals its nature at a peculiar depth where the conflict about the nature of poems is no longer empirical, but fundamental and conceptual. No amount of new facts that an opponent can discover will persuade an antiintentionalist that an external intentional statement is crucial to the understanding of a poem. For the antiintentionalist holds that a poem, being a public object, possesses no private significance, since the function of criticism is to articulate the poem's public meaning. The intentionalist critic, on the other hand, would not deny that poems have public meanings; he would rather insist that at least part of the meaning of a poem has a private dimension that cannot be apprehended by means of objective criteria.

71

A scrutiny of the controversy on intention thus reveals the peculiar and complex features of the concept of criticism. Wimsatt and Beardsley, for instance, did not deny that intention is an element in a literary work itself; they rather deny that a search for intention outside the work is a legitimate critical function. Rather than banishing the category of intention, they simply redefined it, in order to promote their concept of art. Similarly, rather than rejecting the notion of response from art criticism, they simply wanted to curb the play of mere subjective and impressionist response, in order to distinguish aesthetic experience from other kinds of experience. Committed to the concept of literary autonomy, they attempt to articulate and validate the logic of their position. And they succeed in giving considerable logical power and coherence to their position. Antiintentionalists, then, succeed in showing the limitations of the romantic criteria. Yet they cannot show that the romantics are entirely wrong, nor can they succeed in grounding their rejection of certain modes of criticism in some unassailable logical basis. They cannot do so, not only because no such logical basis is available, but because the concept of art is a disputed concept, one that cannot be resolved by future discovery or better logical equipment.

CHAPTER FOUR

The Concept of Poetic Autonomy

The concept of poetic autonomy is perhaps the most important doctrine of both modern aesthetics and modern literary theory. The concept itself is perhaps the most influential insight into art because to speak of modern aesthetics and poetic theory since Kant is to speak of the doctrine of autonomy. And to speak of the history of modern criticism is to speak of the emergence and sophistication of that doctrine. Moreover, its power inheres in the fact that almost all other competing concepts of criticism must not only take cognizance of this doctrine but also seek to derive their power from strong antithetical relation to it.

In this chapter I attempt to examine the concept of poetic autonomy. My intention is to discuss the logical implications of holding some of the central assumptions of this concept. I shall not argue that the concept of poetic autonomy is inherently misguided, nor that its central assumptions are erroneous. Instead, I shall seek to clarify these assumptions, and suggest when and why they harden into rigidly logical notions, subverting the very concept which they initially sought to characterize and defend. I shall first examine its central assumptions; then I shall discuss a modernist definition of aesthetic experience that seeks to support the concept of poetic autonomy; then we shall look, rather briefly, at a powerful defense of the concept of poetic autonomy made by Gadamer, a defense that has given a serious criticism of the Kantian autonomist tradition in a way that provides the concept of poetic autonomy with a philosophy of criticism; and finally I shall make some concluding remarks concerning the importance of this concept in the history of modern literary theory and criticism.[1]

Poetic Autonomy and Critical Practice:
A Critical Paradox?

THE ASSUMPTION of the inseparability of meaning from its formal trap-
pings in literary works has been the most important principle of both
philosophical aestheticians and literary theorists who subscribe to the
organic theory of poetry. For instance, the theory of poems by Croce
and A. C. Bradley (who are idealists in philosophy) and that by O. K.
Bouwsma (who is an analytical philosopher) are, once the idealist
theory is stripped of its metaphysics, essentially similar,[2] and they
take on an added significance in view of their radically different philosophical orientations. Moreover, they have a significant relationship
with the romantic theory of organic form, since for all of them form is
organically connected with content and is therefore not separable
from it. In the words of the most important English romantic exponent of this theory, Coleridge, "the organic form . . . is innate; it
shapes as it develops itself from within, and the fullness of its development is one and the same with the perfection of its outward form.
Such is the life, such the form."[3] Coleridge's notion has found general
acceptance among the New Critics who do not accept the affective
component of his theory.

The central thesis of this position is that a literary work is a unique
verbal structure embodying a unique complex of heterogeneous and
often contradictory meanings brought into unity by a paradoxical
logic of poetic creativity. Since its form is unique, its content too is
unique, and is not separable from the form. In Wimsatt's words,
"complexity of form is sophistication of content."[4] Each is dependent
on the other; neither is separable in priority or importance from the
other. Nothing can be removed from a literary work without either
distorting or altering the original whole. To substitute any other expression for the one already in a literary work would be to deny that
the work is perfect and that all its expressions are perfectly adapted
to a unique complex of meanings which is the work itself. Literary
works, then, do not allow for synonymous expression, nor do they
allow for translation or interpretation. This is a logical or conceptual
principle and not an empirical one, for interpretation of a poem cannot avoid paraphrase. Theorists who reject paraphrase hold that since
literary works are unique objects, to ascribe paraphrasability to them
is to be self-contradictory. If literary works are unique entities, and if

their unique ontological status is the result of a complex qualitative fusion of form and content such that no other kinds of objects achieve it, then this concept of literary works and the concept of paraphrase are logically incompatible. Paraphrasing literary works is therefore, in Cleanth Brooks's well-known phrase, a heresy.[5]

The concept of poetic autonomy may seem strange, and practicing critics may want to dismiss this theory, since literary works have not only been translated but also interpreted and reinterpreted. Yet the fact that several conceptual analysts, such as Bouwsma and Hampshire, have also held this view gives one pause for reflection.[6] What cannot be dismissed, moreover, is that recently there has occurred a resurgence of the modernist concept of poetic autonomy, a resurgence that has taken a radically negative form. This negative form is best captured in de Man's announcement of the inevitability of criticism's failure before literary works, or "the impossibility of reading" literature as an unavoidable condition of any significant criticism.[7]

Modern theorists of poetic autonomy hold a specific theory of language. Comprehension of nonliterary verbal expressions depend, according to this theory, on the necessity, or at least the possibility, of separation of its meaning from that expression, whereas comprehension of a literary expression does not depend on the necessity, or even the possibility, of such separation. Ordinary language, on this view, requires understanding, which in turn requires translation or paraphrase. Understanding can take place only if there are criteria that will enable readers or listeners to infer intentions and references.[8] Ordinary language, being a vehicle of truth-value, results from the "platonizing" and reductive nature of man's relation to reality; it functions by reducing the dynamic swirling chaos of reality into our narrow and fixed categories. Poetic discourse, on the other hand, has no difficulty with the contingent and chaotic nature of reality, since by means of the miracle at the heart of all poetic metaphors it cherishes "the world's body."[9] The distinction, in other words, is a difference of kind rather than of degree, since it holds that semantically equivalent expressions do not exist for the language of poems.

One critic has persuasively argued that the distinction between poetic and ordinary or scientific language is a spurious one; he cites a sentence from J. L. Austin's *Sense and Sensibilia*, which is an attack on the sense-data theories of A. J. Ayer, and suggests that formal strategies such as the witty analogy and the effect of exaggeration in Austin's sentence would make one "hesitate to contend that the mode of expression could be altered without altering the full meaning of the sentence." Austin's sense is as follows: "In these paragraphs we already seem to see the plain man here under the improbable aspect of Ayer himself, dribbling briskly into position in front of his own goal and squaring up to encompass his destruction." [10] The objection here is that there is no essential qualitative difference between poetic and nonpoetic language, especially if a nonpoetic sentence is as well written as Austin's is. It would follow then that the unity that poems possess cannot in principle be different, not in kind anyway, from the unity that we can assign to Austin's sentence.

But this is precisely what the New Critic would not accept. He would argue that such a collapsing of the distinction simply ignores the actual distinction underlying the reading of Austin's sentence and the reading of a literary work. And he would insist that the New Critical distinctions argue for a conception of truth-value for ordinary language which it considers inapplicable to the poetic. How would the New Critic defend this position? I think he would defend it precisely by distinguishing the nature of reduction involved in analyzing and understanding Austin's sentence from the kind of reduction involved in understanding a poem. For instance, the undeniable truth-component of Austin's sentence is that without Ayer's knowing it himself, his arguments are self-refuting. If somebody tells us, while recounting Austin's criticism of Ayer's sense-data theories, that the former made interestingly witty and sarcastic remarks in his discussion, we may want to ask our informer to tell us more about Austin's wit and sarcasm. But if our interest is seriously philosophical we will ask him to explain Austin's essential points. It would make no difference if we changed the sequence of questions or if we simply ignored Austin's witty analogies. A genuine philosophical concern here would require a scrutiny of how Ayer's arguments are so evidently self-refuting, for an emphasis on the literary power in Austin's writing is not centrally relevant to an inquiry into the philosophical status of his criticism of Ayer. If, on the other hand, we ask someone about *Paradise Lost* and are told that the poem is about man's fall from Paradise and his eventual redemption through the sacrifice of Christ, we are likely to say in dismay that the Bible says the same thing, that we could know about man's fall and redemption from any Christian. Surely one could question the value of Austin's book if someone proved that, long before Austin's attack on Ayer's theories, somebody had written a book that makes all the damaging and brilliant arguments that Austin makes later. Responsible reviewers would then at most note the literary distinction of Austin's style while saying, if they wish to avoid making the charge of plagiarism, that this book makes no contribution to the existing body of knowledge in the field and that all these arguments are essentially a repetition of what was said years ago by someone else. Thus, given our hypothetical evidence, Austin's criticism *could* involve plagiarism. In art, however, the question of plagiarism becomes enormously complicated. One can take the matter to its logical extreme and point to a poem which lifts fifty lines from a Donne poem and which has some lines interspersed in and around them—the issue here is clear. But take the case of *Hamlet*. We do not call it a work of plagiarism even though it is a virtually proven fact that there existed at least one manuscript play *Hamlet* by Thomas Kyd, from which Shakespeare presumably derived his story. Nor do we call Eliot's use of the lines of other poets an act of plagiarism. Rather we have a respectable critical term for Eliot's "lifting," *allusion*; and we have complex explanations of the literary value of such allusions.

The New Critical defense of the fusion of form and content would thus consist in arguing that it is no essential reduction to insist on getting at Austin's basic arguments, nor a violation of art to seek the intellectual propositions underlying, say, *Hamlet* as long as one does not try to "abstract" mere intellectual assertions implicit in the play. For the assertions could be understood, such a defense would insist, only within the context of a grasp of the whole. The New Criticism would thus refuse to extend the mode of understanding of ordinary or nonpoetic language to the mode of understanding of poetic language, and it would insist on a qualitative difference between the wit of Austin's sentence and the wit in *Hamlet*. This qualitative difference, to repeat, is construed by the New Criticism to be a difference of kind and not degree, since a reading of a literary work is an aesthetic experience and since, as aesthetic experience, it is an experience of value which is different from any nonaesthetic experience. In Brooks's words, "the essence of poetry is metaphor, and metaphor is finally analogical rather than logical. The presence or absence of strict logic, therefore, has no *direct* relation to the kind of coherency to which good poetry aspires, and without which it cannot be 'good.'" Consequently, the statement that many instances of ordinary language, too, are not paraphrasable is not the same as the statement that poetry is unparaphrasable because insofar as instances of nonpoetry are unparaphrasable, we are faced with two kinds of nonparaphrasability. Even the propositional element, insofar as it does exist in a literary work, exists in ways and by means that transform that element so thoroughly that it is no longer recognizable as centrally propositional as it is in Austin's sentence. Thus we have Richards's assertion in what is perhaps the earliest espousal of the New Critical dogma about the fusion of form and content in poems: "It is never what a poem says that matters, but what it 'is.'" [11]

The distinction between poetic and ordinary or scientific language is thus a theoretical contribution made by the New Criticism. It is intended to make a positive advance beyond philosophical idealism since this idealism fails, as does Coleridge, to account for the function of language in poetic creation. [12] The New Critics, in search of clearly articulated differentia for poems, have a significant affinity with T. E. Hulme. Though many of his theories are a tissue of contradictions, Hulme still provided the New Criticism with a compelling initial characterization of the nature of poetic language. Ordinary or scientific language is for Hulme a means of communication, whereas poetic language possesses nuances of meanings which are multiple and irreducible, and is therefore an end in itself. Poetry, said Hulme,

> always endeavors to arrest you, and to make you continuously see a physical thing, to prevent you from gliding through an abstract process. It chooses fresh epithets and fresh metaphors, not so much because they are new, and we are tired of the old, but because the old cease to convey a physical thing and become abstract counters. . . . Visual meanings can only be transferred by the new bowl of metaphor; prose is an old pot that lets them leak out. Images in verse are not mere decoration, but the very essence of an intuitive language. Verse is a pedestrian taking you over the ground, prose—a train which delivers you at a destination. [13]

The New Critics adopt Hulme's argument by claiming that the poet achieves a discourse "which can break through the inherent incapacities of all nonpoetic uses of language." The language of ordinary discourse, they claim, is "inherently poor," whereas the language of a poem constitutes a "new world" and a "new word" in its intramural referentiality and is therefore inherently superior to ordinary language. [14] Closely bound up with, or rather following from, this conception of ordinary discourse is a New Critical notion that science, history, philosophy, and all other nonaesthetic discourses are constituted in their very nature by the freezing and schematizing violence that ordinary language as propositional discourse must perform on the data of empirical reality in order for these disciplines to claim their legitimization.[15]

There is an important complicating factor in the New Critical notion of poetic language which deserves consideration here. This factor is the relationship that the New Critical notion has with Richards's well-known distinction between fact and value, which logical positivists made. The latter sought to define sharply the nature and scope of knowledge and to separate the activities that give knowledge from the ones that do not. Facts, according to the early logical positivists, are verifiable and are therefore carriers of truth-value, whereas "values," being expressions of likes and dislikes, are not amenable to rational inquiry.[16] The New Critical theorists inherit this distinction from Richards, though they attempt to turn this distinction to their advantage. For Richards poetic language is emotive and nonreferential and therefore has no cognitive value, whereas scientific language is referential and conveys knowledge. For the New Critics, on the other hand, ordinary or nonpoetic language, though a vehicle of truth-value, is a vehicle of truths that are necessarily referential since they result from the "platonizing" and reductive nature of our relation to reality. The New Critics then attack science and all other propositional discourses (which on their view do not include literature and the arts) as being necessarily reductive. Thus we have logical positivists on the one hand and the New Critical theorists on the other, each group privileging its cherished interest at the expense of the other.

One might suspect that the distinction between fact and value and the opposition between positivism and New Criticism are the result of a conceptual confusion or rather a pseudoproblem. For recent developments in the philosophy of science have exposed some serious shortcomings in the positivist conception of scientific inquiry and exploded the arbitrary separation of fact and value which was the cornerstone of logical positivism. These developments suggest that observation is not and cannot be independent of theory and that there is no such thing as knowledge which is indubitably true and verifiable.[17] It is possible that the New Critics are caught in an anxiety which perhaps the positivists created in them, since the positivists relegated poetry to the realm of mere emotions and emotive stimulation. This anxiety, conjoined with a sense of the loss of belief in religion for the culture voiced earlier by Arnold and later by Richards, contributes to the complex interplay of aggression and defense in the New Critical apologies for poetry.

Nevertheless, Richards and Brooks, from different viewpoints, propose important arguments on the nature of poetry. For Richards poems do not make statements because their value resides in the affective realm of our experience of them. For Brooks, on the other hand, poetic language is constituted and given what dramatic force it has by the interanimations among the parts of the entire context of a poem. Brooks, of course, opposes the psychologism of Richards, whereas Richards would reject Brooks's organicistic and objectivist conception of poetry.[18] They share, however, a fundamental agreement about the value of poetry, though they disagree on how this value should be conceived. Their agreement here is also an agreement on the value of the language of poetry, for they agree that the scientist's use of language is guided by a desire to communicate a single and unambiguous meaning, whereas the poet's use necessarily carries a rich and complex aura of suggestive associations and meanings.

Though Richards and Brooks seem right to me in opposing abstraction of propositions from poems, their distinction between poetic and ordinary language becomes extreme as soon as they reject, Richards through his emotivism and Brooks through his organicism, all propositions from poetry. The total emergent context of, say, *The Waste Land* makes possible certain statements which significant criticism seeks to articulate. That does not mean that the task of criticism will be easy or that a reading will give the final, determinate meanings of the poem, for the complexity of literary works reveals itself in the difficulties it poses to criticism. Moreover, since language is the constitutive medium of literature, literary language is bound to possess an opacity that calls attention to itself: in other words, it suspends, or at least complicates, our pragmatic and referential relation to language. The opacity of literary language is a constant reminder that the understanding of a poem is a complex phenomenon not reducible to a set of propositions that could capture the poem's meaning or experience. But it is an illegitimate extension of this insight to say that, because of the poem's complexity, there is no statement involved in our experience of it. This extension is illegitimate because it turns a sound insight into the poem's qualitative nature into a strict and abso-lutist position. It transforms a difference of degree into one of kind. Once this difference is conceived as a difference of kind, the New Critics then go on to posit oppositions such as poetry versus science, poetic versus ordinary discourse, poetry versus history, and poetry versus philosophy.

As I shall argue more fully in the next section, the process of liter-ary understanding is highly complex and does not allow for a single and unitary theoretical articulation. However complex, various, and conflicting the construals of its nature, this process constitutes the ex-perience of literature. The experience of reading literature makes pos-sible things that the experience of reading history, philosophy, and science does not, although the primary constitutive acts of these do-mains are perhaps not distinguishable from the primary constitutive act of either artistic creativity or literary understanding.[19] And the putative oppositions that the New Criticism sets up between litera-ture and other domains are not genuine contrasting oppositions at all. A consciousness of the need for distinction has thus taken an extreme theorizing form in the New Criticism, and it has ended up positing oppositions. There is another source of this difficulty for the New Critical theory, and that is the New Critic's sense of his status as an apologist for poetry. He is defending, on the one hand, poetry's unique ontological status against Plato's relegation of it to an inferior status, and, on the other hand, its special cognitive efficacy against the positivist relegation of poetry to the noncognitive realm of emo-tion and exclamations.

Yet the New Critical endeavor to grasp poetic language and to dif-ferentiate it from other modes of language is no doubt significant. For even though patterns of language in poetry are not radically distin-guishable from those in ordinary language, our experience of poems does not really allow us to construe the use of language in poems as one specifically designed for making plain statements. This percep-tion of the poet's expertise in controlling his medium led the New Critics to posit a notion of complexity, conceived variously as irony, paradox, ambiguity, and tension, as the most important aesthetic value. Hence they argue that the greater the poet's power to exploit the potentialities of language as carrier of polyvalencies the better the quality of his art. William Empson and the New Critics therefore at-tempt to show how this principle of complexity works in poems.

It is possible, then, to argue for a distinction between poetic and ordinary statement, because the first is surrounded by an aura of associative meanings and ambiguities, whereas the second is not. But from this preliminary distinction we cannot extrapolate a further and more radical opposition between ordinary and poetic language. While ordinary statement may partake more of plain statement than of the poetic, the difference between the two is simply one of degree rather than of kind. The objection, however, that theorists have not succeeded in formulating a theory of poetic speech does not mean that there is no difference between poetic and ordinary language.[20]

The unavailability of a clearly definable set of criteria with which to distinguish between poetic and ordinary language does not expose the impossibility of the distinction. It only exposes the inadequacy of those modes of theorizing which must propose clear and indubitable distinctions for literary criticism. The pursuit of such distinctions, when one is aware of its futility, turns into an opposite form of theoretical violence, and announces the impossibility of reading literature. Both forms of theorizing forget that significant proposals of criteria for poetic language tend to be more complex than at first appears because the criteria a sophisticated proposal offers are bound up with an entire conceptual framework. It is within this framework that the criterion of poetic language possesses its value and force. Consider, for instance, the fact that in order to validate his notion of poetic language Brooks had to ask for support from the entire dramatic context of a poem. Thus what may initially seem to be an isolated thesis about poetic language finally has its depth, its significance, in what Brooks has all along conceived it to be: an organic theory of poetry for which he must invoke the categories of parts and whole. Apart from the conceptual context within which one can provide an operational criterion for poetic language, such a language is no more than a technique among other techniques of poetry. By itself this or any other technique cannot successfully attempt the difficult task of talking about either literary theory or literary experience.

THE NEW CRITICISM'S most important doctrine is that what a poem says is more complex than what the "abstractionists" tend to think it does. Inasmuch as a poem is a complex organic entity constituted by interanimating relations among its parts, what content it possesses is informed and made qualitatively rich and complex by its form. If the content of a poem is thus unique by virtue of its organic relationship with its form, then every poem by definition is a concrete universal and no two poems can have constituents that are identical. Thus Wimsatt, while discussing the nature of the concrete in poems, says: "The fact is that all concrete illustration has about it something of the irrelevant. An apple falling from a tree illustrates gravity, but apple and tree are irrelevant to the pure theory of gravity. It may be that what happens in a poem is that the apple and the tree are somehow made more than usually relevant" (*Verbal Icon*, p. 76). This conception of poems asks us to determine, as precisely as we can, the nature of this relevance in our criticism of poetry. Once everything in a poem is made relevant, a simple duality of universals and particulars indispensable to characterize non-art, has to be given up. To accept the category of concrete universals for works of art is to deny the distinction between form and content, for to accept the distinction would be to accept the notion of means and end. Thus, in Wimsatt's words, "in literature a part is never a means to another part which is the end, or to a whole which is the end—unless in the organistic sense that all parts and the whole are reciprocally ends and means, the heart, the head and the hand. The end-means relation in literature (so far as the end is outside the means) is a relation between us the readers and the poem, by means of which the poem may be aiming at us. Inside the poem there are no ends and means, only whole and parts" (p. 243). On this view, a literary work is a complex of associations, values, and meanings which cannot be transported into its paraphrase or critical description.

The New Critical concept of poetic autonomy thus rests on a concept of the uniqueness of poems, on poems as peculiar verbal structures, as concrete universals. A strict adherence to this concept would lead to some very drastic consequences such as the denial of aesthetic and literary theory. Ethical actions, as Stuart Hampshire has said, are repeatable, and without their repeatability ethical norms will have no value in life; but in the case of poems there are no aesthetic norms, except that a poem is its own justification. Hampshire has therefore questioned the legitimacy of aesthetics, since works of art as unique entities do not allow for general theoretical inquiry, except presumably for the inquiry that argues for the uniqueness of works of art.[21] Yet adherents to the uniqueness thesis want to maintain that a work of art is both unique and communicative. They are therefore logically compelled to say that its communication is also unique, that its content in-formed by its form is irreducible.

If every poem is unique then the idea of cultivating sensibility by sustained commerce with poetry will have little point to it because the critic will be unequipped for responding to each unique work. The uniqueness thesis, when pushed to its logical extreme, would render impossible the activity of criticism since critics at best can experience rapturous wonder and be silent in the presence of aesthetic objects. The concept of uniqueness is not offered as a functional notion which can be construed as an empirical question resolvable by observation of facts, because no such observation could really prove that works of art are unique entities. The concept of uniqueness of works of art is a concept about the peculiar "mode of existence" of works of art, an ontological concept.[22] It logically entails the epistemological category of uniqueness. Once a theorist adopts this category, as for instance Croce does, it is logically inescapable for its proponent that uniqueness resides everywhere in the world. For Croce, whenever we intuit a particular as a particular, we express; and since every expression is an expression of feeling and since he equates expressions with beauty or art, every intuition of a particular is a work of art.[23]

ONE MIGHT OBJECT, however, that Croce is a philosophical theorist, whereas Brooks is a practical critic with theoretical leanings only in a polemical historical-cultural context. But the objection loses its force when one realizes that both positions imply a logic that establishes a philosophical closeness between them. Otherwise there would be no justification in examining the New Critical theory except in order to situate it in its historical context. Yet the differences between the New Critical theory and Croce in his early extremist position are genuine, and they are best represented in Wimsatt's theoretical contributions.

As distinguished from Croce's often tortuous dialectic, Wimsatt maintains a sort of homespun dialectical attitude in his theory of criticism. Noting that a central tradition in Western critical thought is that of poems as concrete universals, he argues that it offers two opposed theories of this paradoxical notion, one emphasizing individuality and the other emphasizing universality. If the first generates a mode of criticism more unstable, elusive, and private than responsible criticism need be, the other generates a mode of criticism excessively rule-bound, mechanized, and finally inhuman. "Neither of the extremes give a good account of art and each leads out of art" (*Verbal*

Icon, p. 74). Thus the theoretical problem for critical theory is to elucidate how a work of literature can be both more individual and more universal than works of other kinds (p. 75). This may be defined as the central concern of the New Critical theory, a concern which is intended to elucidate the special significance of literature for man and culture as a whole. It is perhaps best expressed in Wimsatt's definition of literature, which is also a definition of the value of literature: "A literary work of art is a complex of details . . . a component so complicated of human values that its interpretation is dictated by the understanding of it, and so complicated as to seem in the highest degree individual—a concrete universal" (p. 77).

This conception is basically a celebration of poems which Wimsatt carries out by making a sober and difficult adjustment among multiple and complex discriminations, and these discriminations form what is perhaps the most important feature of his critical endeavor. Consider, for instance, his following words: "One of the faults which Plato found with poetry was that in imitating the actions and feelings of men, poetry discovered the lack of unity in their lives, the strife and inconsistency. Recent schools of criticism . . . have likewise noted the importance to poetry of the elements of variety and strife in human living and have seen the poem as a report made under tension or an ironically suspended judgment rather than a commitment to solutions" (p. 99). These observations show Wimsatt's remarkable capacity for making subtle and intelligent connections between two ideas which, taken on their own terms, are mutually opposed. It is in this sense, then, that Wimsatt perceives continuity in the history of criticism and conceives its problems to be common and converging upon one another. In the same paragraph Wimsatt continues his gifted rewriting of some important critical theories:

> And this view would seem to put the poem clearly in the realm of the amoral or premoral. But again, recent critical theory has noted with approval the Coleridgean doctrine of a resolution or *reconciliation* of opposites, a doctrine which may not read so well with the ironic. To the present writer it would seem that though poetry is inclusive it is also exclusive in the sense that a poem has a presiding idea, attitude, and coherence and thus at least a tendency to an assertion. [*Verbal Icon*, pp. 99–100]

Thus what seemed to be courting with the amoral or premoral is simply overcome by the New Critical adoption of Coleridge's doctrine mentioned in the passage quoted. But notice that Wimsatt recognizes a certain tension between the New Critical concept of irony and the Coleridgean one of reconciliation. He therefore attempts to overcome this tension by going to the very source of the New Critical interest in irony and reconciliation: I. A. Richards. Richards had argued, in *Principles of Literary Criticism*, for a poetry of inclusion as the poetry that makes for the maximum possible synaesthetic harmony among the important and conflicting impulses and had therefore recommended it as the most valuable source for organizing experience. And he had suggested that the poetry of exclusion is the poetry that does not possess the richness and ambiguity that the other does and is therefore not amenable to the most satisfactory organization of experience.[24] Richards's distinction between these two kinds of poetry is correlated with another important distinction he made between the language of poetry and the language of science. Wimsatt, in the passage quoted above, has concentrated a rich history of thought on the problem of cognition in poetry and at the same time attempted his own resolution. Richards denies propositional content to poetry, whereas Wimsatt grants it, for he considers poetry "objectively . . . as a body of cognitive and analyzable meaning" (*Verbal Icon*, p. 86). He does not, however, consider the cognitive value of poetry as a scientific body of knowledge. He rather defines its cognitive value by placing it in "a system of values in which poetic is distinguished from moral and both are understood in relation to the master ideas of evil as negation or not-being" (p. 100). Wimsatt has thus placed the problem of cognition in poetry in his oblique manner within the context of Christian ontology, and he has consequently denied the value of psychological considerations for talking about our experience of literature.

Wimsatt's theory, however, faces serious difficulties which are present most directly in what is otherwise his remarkable scrutiny of the theories of the Chicago Aristotelians (pp. 41–65). He is right in saying that the "dogmatic side of the Chicago theory is necessary if they are to have any theory at all" (p. 47). Wimsatt's own attempt is far from any simpleminded, rigid dogmatism. He does not construe poems as things except analogically, and he significantly modifies the organic metaphor for poems. Wimsatt also rejects the general New Critical contention that the language of poetry is radically different from ordinary language.[25] And there is an element of truth when he rejects Richard McKeon's view "of the systems as parallel, discrete, and aloof from one another," and substitutes for it his own view of them as "successive, partial, and overlapping in an attempt upon common problems" (p. 48). For he argues that no critical method can justify its own central claims without at the same time not only taking cognizance of the claims of other theories and methods but even using them. Nevertheless, what Wimsatt finds good in rival theories is often guided by the assumption about the nature of poetry that he has already made. It is owing to this assumption that he is led not only to modify a number of theories of criticism but to reject some of them. The assumption Wimsatt has made here is the central New Critical proposition about the fusion of form and content in poems, a fusion which lies at the heart of his characterization of poems as concrete universals. He conceives poems to be so thoroughly integrated entities that it is conceptually wrong to make a distinction between form and content.

Wimsatt fails to recognize that the Aristotelian theory, while retaining elements of the organic theory of poetry which it first introduced in critical theory, is still a theory whose enabling categories are means and end, which make possible the distinction between form and content. The methodological consequence of my objection here is that the kind of explanation one can give of poetry within the framework of the Aristotelian theory will necessarily be different from the kind of explanation possible within the framework of the New Critical theory. For instance, the talk about plot and characterization in a novel or play is generally likely to be an Aristotelian mode of criticism, whereas the talk about symbolic configurations of meanings in the same work is likely to be a New Critical mode of criticism. Moreover, Wimsatt's argument that the analogy between poems and things is necessary because that is "the only way criticism of a poem can be conducted" is questionable (*Verbal Icon*, p. 50). The sense in which there can be objective criteria that will enable the members of a society to achieve consensus about a physical object does not apply to cultural objects. Postponing further discussion of this point until Chapter 6, I should say that Wimsatt's theory courts here the difficulties that inevitably plague all theorizing that has not reflected on criticism as a distinctively hermeneutical endeavor.

Wimsatt's theory cannot explain why critics offer at times radically opposed interpretations of the same structure of words presented as a poem. This problem involves a consideration of the nature of literary experience which Wimsatt has not really examined. He has indeed taken for granted the complexity of literary experience that Brooks emphasized in his altered and spatialized version of the notions about it, which Richards and Empson had first developed. If Wimsatt had examined the difficult question of literary experience, he could have still sustained his claim that critical systems are partial and at times overlapping, though he would also have been forced to recognize the moments at which they become divergent and lead critics to constitute the poems they study differently. For Wimsatt, however, while poems invite indefinitely variable interpretations, they cannot be constituted in ways that are incompatible or mutually opposed except by an erroneous or extremist theory of poems. It is in the nature of poems as concrete universals, as unique objects, that their interpretations, though differently reached, converge and evolve toward a growing and translucent totality. Thus Wimsatt's discriminations have not prevented him from espousing a rather idealistic version of a critical formalism that sets poems apart from history and society.

IF THE UNIQUENESS THESIS necessarily entails everything as a work of art, including "the news-jottings of the journalist"[26] (if intuited as particulars), there is all the more reason to accord the status of artworks to literary interpretations. Indeed, they too will be unique and exclusive as, for instance, both Paul de Man and Harold Bloom, from their different viewpoints, have argued.[27] Such a conception construes each literary interpretation to possess its own unique internal structure. The question of dispute or genuine confrontation among different critical interpretations of a poem will have little significance, since all of them claim to be both original and irreducible. The question of validity or faithfulness of a critical interpretation will be irrelevant, since either notion requires a standard that necessarily resides outside the specific act of criticism which it desires to judge. As we know, however, the logic of the autonomist conceptual framework has denied legitimacy to any critical standard. Misinterpretation becomes the mode, and logic reveals its nature as rhetoric. The idea of critical judgment is revealed as the delusion of a criticism that takes pride in its capacity to judge good from bad, art from propaganda. The situation is indeed ironic. The theory that started out by distinguishing art from non-art, literary language from ordinary language, could not escape its internal logical dynamics, and ended by losing the very capacity to make discriminations necessary for its survival.

A glance at the actual practice of criticism, however, reveals a different situation. Critics generally attempt to sharpen readers' critical sensibilities and to revaluate, as Eliot suggests in "Tradition and the Individual Talent,"[28] the old in the light of the new and the new in the light of the old. They often recognize the new as valuable not because of its novelty but essentially because though it is related in some subtle way to the past and though it is not derivable from the past, it nevertheless shapes as well as is shaped by the sensibility of its own historical context. Critics compare patterns of artistic development in one or several authors' works. They read, for instance, Chaucer's early poems and find him growing in terms of aesthetic control, almost stage by stage, from his first poem to *Troilus and Criseyde*; they may argue that there is a developing pattern, from the first poem to *Troilus*, of the artist struggling to discover his identity, to the creation of a complex whole of rich aesthetic perspectives. *Troilus* thus is unique, in a manner of speaking, because its excellence has its defining features in a structured whole of aesthetic values which do exist in a more or less limited sense in Chaucer's early poems.

Stretched beyond a point, then, the notion of the unique mode of aesthetic discourse is theoretically vacuous, for in terms of an extreme autonomist position a unique poem must elicit speechless admiration. Take, for instance, Croce, who said that the critic's task is to separate the nonpoetry from poetry and that poetry alone does not need interpretation.[29] Yet in actual practice critics use the word *unique* in an honorific sense in order to compare and contrast literary works. This use of *unique* is not the same as the concept of uniqueness as articulated in their different ways by Kant, the idealist aestheticians, and the New Critics. And my brief elucidation of the concept as it is actually put into practice is no more than a theoretical extrapolation from traditional criticism, T. S. Eliot, and common sense. The uniqueness thesis as proposed by the autonomists entails, in its extreme logical form, a radically confused concept of interpretation.

If we believe that all of the associations or meanings in a poem are its essential features, then it logically follows that both translation and criticism are impossible. Not only will every literary interpretation be unique, but no steps in the direction of intelligibility can be taken. Take, for instance, the problem of translating a literary work. If one is an autonomist in the extreme logical sense, one will insist on the impossibility of translating literature. The translator, however, does not attempt simply to give a rough approximation of the literary work. He also seeks to make his translation as compelling and elegant as the original. He cannot do this by a literal faithfulness to the original. For words in each language possess their own historically sedimented cultural associations and meanings which cannot be rendered literally in another language without often grossly distorting them. Consequently, the translator has to take recourse to the content of the work, since it is more easily accessible than the formal complexities which present the greatest difficulty. The translator, in other words, cannot do without subordinating form to content. If he does not, he cannot carry on the act of translation. This logical necessity does not of course exempt him from making an attempt to build an appropriate formal complexity in his translation. Otherwise his translation could be a grossly prolix retelling of the work.

The situation of the literary critic is fundamentally similar to that of the translator. Critics do not make the entire complex of meanings and formal values the defining characteristics of a literary work. Indeed, critical practice requires one to abstract some characteristics as the defining ones, which are then distinguished from those that are construed as contingent. If a critic succeeds in giving an intelligent and sensitive interpretation of a poem in terms of the essential features, then his interpretation is faithful. Thus the institution of criticism, regardless of its flaws, does not regard literature in the way the autonomist theory in its extreme logical sense does. We need not deny, however, that the critic, like the translator, is in some respects like the creator of a literary work. For he must have a capacity for grasping the complex nuances of language, structure, and action in a literary work. The critic nevertheless differs from the literary artist in that, in some recognizable sense, he is expected to remain faithful to the literary work. But if one accepts the extremist concept of the uniqueness of literary works, the concept of faithfulness has no meaning. For the first concept already prescribes the inaccessibility of poems to either translation or criticism.

The extremist theorist of poetic autonomy, however, ends by allowing two opposed categories or insights to overlap in his mind, since while theorizing he defends the uniqueness of literary works and while practicing criticism (even if he seeks to "prove" the theory) he inevitably engages in a process of abstraction. Caught in the movement of this contradiction, the autonomist at times claims not only that literary works are unique verbal configurations but that every interpretation is unique. The autonomist who seeks to differentiate literary works from interpretations is also caught in the contradiction, since, given his concept of poetic autonomy, he must insist on the inevitable failure of criticism. Criticism is then construed in the mode of either heresy or crisis. The specter of failure that haunts these two versions of poetic autonomy can be put to rest by disentangling the contradictory insights which have forced the autonomists to their extreme metaphysical theorizing.

Poetic Autonomy and the Aesthetic of Detachment

SOME OF THE MOST IMPORTANT DISCUSSIONS of poetic autonomy take the form of a characterization of aesthetic experience. Indeed, many theorists consider a clear and theoretically defensible notion of aesthetic experience to be crucial for aesthetics and literary theory, for it is rightly supposed that the definition one gives of the nature of aesthetic experience will affect one's definition of both the nature of aesthetic objects and the nature of criticism itself.[30]

Because of the considerable role that the concept of aesthetic experience has had in traditional aesthetic and critical theory, I shall focus on the problem of defining it. Almost all major definitions of aesthetic experience agree on a number of premises, the most important of which is that the aesthetic experience is an experience of disinterested attention. This premise is already packed with a specific kind of significance, since it radically separates aesthetic experience from all other kinds of experience. In what follows I shall attempt to articulate the complexity underlying the *form* of the concept of aesthetic experience and by implication of the concept of criticism.

THE CONCEPT of the autonomy of aesthetic experience is central to an entire formidable tradition of aesthetic and critical theory of long standing. For instance, the eighteenth-century discussions by Hutcheson, Addison, Hume, and Burke prepared some grounds for it, though their theory is, in different ways, an empiricist theory of taste.[31] Kant provided a full conceptual definition and validation for this theory, and, though indebted to the British discussions of the theory of taste, he construed the concept of aesthetic experience as an experience of disinterested attention. In effect, he rejected the empiricist foundations of the British theory of taste and prepared the way for a new concept of aesthetic experience. Kant's theory exercised considerable influence on the late eighteenth- and nineteenth-century philosophical thought about art. Moreover, the idealists, too, we recall, considered the concept of the autonomy of aesthetic experience central to their aesthetic thought. In our own time philosophical aestheticians such as Jerome Stolnitz, Virgil Aldrich, and Eliseo Vivas have proposed theories that defend the concept of aesthetic experience as an experience of disinterested attention.[32] And, finally, a great deal of modern Anglo-American philosophical discussion of aesthetic theory attempts a conceptual clarification aimed at defending the autonomy of both aesthetic objects and aesthetic experience.[33]

Aldrich, a modern analytical philosopher, has proposed what is perhaps the most sophisticated recent account of aesthetic experience as an experience of disinterested attention. As Aldrich argues, an object, when considered as an aesthetic object, is lifted from the context of lived reality, the context in which the reader or spectator performs the activities of normal living. But during aesthetic apprehension the agent adopts an attitude which cannot be described by the language used in describing ordinary lived reality. After watching the performance of a play we do not ask questions we are liable to ask in an empirical context, nor do we expect a legal inquiry into, say, the situation of Othello and Desdemona. The action of *Othello* belongs to the world of what Aldrich designates as "categorial aspection."[34] Aldrich explains categorial aspection as a radical change in our perception at the moment of aesthetic apprehension. It is an experience during which, though we know the players who perform the roles of Desdemona and Othello to be real human beings, the action we see on the stage has undergone, in our perception, a categorial aspection. Because of this radical shift in our mode of perception the categories and attitudes of ordinary reality have no validity during an aesthetic experience of the play.

In this section I want to examine another version of this theory, one proposed by Vivas. There are three reasons for focusing on Vivas's theory: Vivas has provided a most succinct definition of aesthetic experience, his definition is supplemented by several of his theoretical essays, and his theory has found support in some modern discussions of critical theory.[35]

Vivas wants to propose a definition that "should throw light on the problems of aesthetics,"[36] for the critic of poetry "needs a definition of the aesthetic experience" which will function implicitly, in his analysis and interpretation of poetry, "to discriminate what he conceives of as poetry from other sorts of documents."[37] In order to propose such a definition, Vivas first discards two different theories of emotion, the one claiming that the aesthetic object arouses emotion in the spectator and the other claiming that the content of art is emotion. Second, he gives a definition of aesthetic experience which (1) propounds the "autonomy" of art, (2) correlates the aesthetic object and experience which (3) leads to the aesthetic judgment, and finally, (4) disposes of subjectivism. In effect, Vivas concludes that his "definition enables us to relate the perceiver to the object in a detailed, specific and verifiable manner."[38]

Vivas has given a full and extended defense of his definition, a defense which covers his reflections on aesthetic theory from 1939 to 1962 and brings these reflections into a cohesive unity around his definition of aesthetic experience.[39] In view of his having provided a very comprehensive definition of aesthetic experience, it is only fair to mention a few of his related views, views which are indeed implicit in his definition. Literature, Vivas argues, does not offer us philosophic or propositional "truth" about the world, primarily because the literary object is unique in status and thereby precludes such knowledge. This is true essentially when the literary work is functioning as art, a moment when the reader is engaged in a "rapt, intransitive attention." It is only during this moment that a work of art functions as a uniquely valuable and self-contained object, completely cut off from the referential world outside its own structure. At the moment of "rapt, intransitive attention" the cognitive, moral, and religious functions are denied any direct participation.[40]

The definition Vivas proposes is this: "An aesthetic experience is an experience of rapt attention which involves the intransitive apprehension of an object's immanent meanings and values in their full presentational immediacy."[41] Vivas, of course, does not intend to give us a set of defining aesthetic traits in terms of which we respond to a work of art, for there may be several ways in which we respond to a work of art and presumably Vivas would not want us to commit the fallacy of exclusion or reduction. In this sense his definition is quite harmless. But it makes some specific claims which do not allow for these several ways to operate in our experience of art. Of these claims the most important is that the aesthetic experience is an experience of rapt, intransitive attention, a claim which announces the "autonomy" of art. It is because of the autonomous nature of art that *Hamlet* presents a unique aesthetic situation. We do not question Hamlet's inadvertent murder of Polonius, nor does Hamlet himself initially feel any remorse for his act, and yet it would seem that his delay and moral agony are related in some way to his rather ambiguous concern over whether it would be ethically justifiable for him to murder his uncle. The aesthetic tension in the play is so conceived that what seems to be flagrantly violating the world of ordinary moral and cognitive values proves itself to be a part of the growing organic complex of the play. The hiatus at that stage between the two worlds of ordinary human discourse and of art would seem to us to be complete. In the total complex of meanings in the play, however, is the discontinuity between the two worlds complete? It would seem to me that Shakespeare has distorted an aspect of our perception by making the reader as well as Hamlet undisturbed over Polonius's murder, and in effect, has intensified the other aspect of the *same* perception by concentrating on Hamlet's ethical dilemma.

What is important is to recognize a certain ambiguity inherent in the very nature (and therefore in the concept itself) of aesthetic experience. Since the world of *Hamlet* or *Herzog* cannot be extended beyond that particular world in the literary work, aestheticians like Vivas tend to emphasize the discontinuity between these two worlds and claim that the art experience is *sui generis*. But we do continue to use the categories of ordinary discourse not only in our self-conscious critical analysis but in our response to art. We can say, for example, that Lear's failure to recognize Cordelia's love and his other daughters' treachery is the "cause" of the disintegration of his psyche; and that Lear is "after" and "during" his suffering morally chastened. Serious imaginative literature presents the profound issues of life and these issues, as they are dramatized and reconstituted in a work of art, facilitate and control our response to the work. The moral and cognitive dimensions become operative in our critical response to it.

Vivas, then, makes a distinction between feeling and emotion and seeks to exclude emotion from a valid definition of aesthetic experience. He says, "The feeling is a by-product of the experience and is a concomitant not only of aesthetic experience but any other activity which is successful." As for emotions, Vivas says that "the same object is capable of arousing different emotional reactions in different spectators or even in the same spectator."[42] Insofar as different emotional reactions are not related to the aesthetic dimension of the work in our experience, it is entirely proper for us to ignore them. In Vivas's words, "whether the value of the artistic experience depends wholly or in part on the presence or absence of emotion, the definition of it does not depend on emotion." Construing emotion as a problem of psychology, Vivas asserts that "psychology does not know anything about a *sui generis* aesthetic experience." But Vivas does not deny that emotion is relevant to a consideration of aesthetic experience; he simply denies its relevance as emotion: "emotion is part of the [aesthetic] object, but not as emotion."[43]

In order to criticize Vivas's argument, and implicitly the whole tradition that his modern version supports, I shall first state some counterexamples and then clarify my objections to it. Let us briefly consider an experience of *King Lear*. The kind of feeling we have at the meeting of Cordelia and Lear in the fifth act is surely not a by-product; for the feeling to be just a by-product it will have to be possible out of the context of the play. The feeling we experience at the meeting of Cordelia and Lear is indeed in no way identical to any extraaesthetic experience; and in some sense that meeting lends a new density to our experience of the play. That the feeling is comparable to extra- or nonaesthetic experience underlies the nature of communication and communication implies, among other things, perception of similarity and dissimilarity. In other words, although the feeling we experience at the meeting of Cordelia and Lear may be different from the feeling we experience from any extraaesthetic context, these two share some elements in our response. For it cannot be denied that both of them derive from and relate to the context of life. Moreover, we are emotionally moved in some slight way by Wordsworth's "The Solitary Reaper," his "Immortality Ode" affects our sentiment-structure, and *Lear* and *Ulysses* deeply influence our very perception of life. Thus there is a range of emotional involvement which extends from the minimal to the very deep. Vivas's animadversions against theorists who lay exclusive stress on emotion or feeling are, to be sure, valuable; excessive stress on emotion in art tends to lead to the vagaries of impressionism or the flabbiness of expressionism in art and in criticism. But to say, as Vivas does, that "the emotion is an accidental consequence of aesthetic apprehension"[44] and to reject emotions as mere by-products or concomitants of many other activities is to ignore the complex nature of art and to simplify the relation of art and experience.

Dr. Johnson, I might add, has an interesting discussion of this problem in his "Preface to Shakespeare":[45] the spectator recognizes that he is moved at seeing Lear or Hamlet suffer, but he also knows that he is in a theater and that the character on stage is an actor who is not really suffering. The theorist is then faced with the enigmatic problem of how the spectator could be moved in these circumstances at all. Most theorists of criticism see the problem suggested by Dr. Johnson, but they would be willing to ignore some aspects of the actual art experience since they are in search of a coherent theory of art. In effect, some theorists[46] conclude that we apprehend, for instance, Raskolnikov's suffering but are not ourselves in any way affected by it—at least our being moved by his suffering is not aesthetically relevant. There are theorists,[47] on the other hand, who suggest we share the total emotional meaning of a work of art. In order to avoid simplifications of our actual transactions with art, we should see that there are degrees of both detachment and identification and that in paradoxial ways they may coexist and that the best works of art often show these extremes as coexisting in some relationship in aesthetic experience. Another way of explaining this would be to say that there are different degrees of involvement. Insofar as the situation in a literary work resembles ours, the involvement will be very deep; insofar as it does not, involvement will tend to be minimal. In any case, since both dimensions of involvement and detachment operate in aesthetic experience, we face here a problem in characterizing the nature of aesthetic experience that most definitions of it fail to comprehend fully.

Once we admit that the aesthetic experience has both these supposed extremes operating in a complex mode, we shall see that our apprehension is no longer either merely intransitive or merely transitive. They both operate in their unique, contrastive capacities and create a discourse which critics from ancient times on have tried to identify with imitation of reality, pleasure, aesthetic emotion, significant forms, or ambiguity and irony. There is of course some configuration of reality, of man's moral and psychological condition, but by itself art is not life or reality or any of its situations. There is some configuration of history in art, but by itself art is not history. And there is some configuration of nature in art, but by itself art is not nature. Together, all these elements and many more constitute the differentiae of art. Our experience of literature becomes narrow and limited, because as theorists and critics we often tend to emphasize exclusively certain aspects of literature. It is important to recognize that, although as critics we can select just a part of the total descriptive range of meanings of art and aesthetic experience, the nature of art is much more complex than our inadequate critical apparatus generally enables us to realize.

The word *emotion* is a rich and ambiguous one and its meanings cannot be fixed permanently. If emotions are taken as vague feelings that may or may not occur depending on various external factors, they may well be ignored in a consideration of aesthetic experience, since their occurrence or nonoccurrence is not predictable. But the idea of emotion conceals a far more complex set of meanings insofar as in reading, say, Dostoevsky we experience a profound disturbance in our total structure of response to life. We are led to ask fundamental questions about the nature of man and his existence. What I am saying in effect is that in order to understand the nature of aesthetic experience in a manner that will not simply mark itself off from other kinds of experience, we need to take into account factors that cannot be brought under a single set of criteria. My stronger thesis here is that no definition that we propose will in the last analysis do justice to the complexity of our experience of literature, for literature—our experience of it—reveals patterns of complexity that do not yield to our demand for definitions that are coherent, economic, and elegant. Our experience of literature, if all these factors are taken into account, is such that the more we understand it the less it is amenable to a definition or a set of rules by means of which we can claim to explain all our encounters with literature.

The upshot of my argument here is that our talk about, and ascription of, emotion in aesthetic experience makes sense in particular contexts. There is an indeterminate but vast spectrum in the variety and richness of our experience of literature which allows for varying degrees of emotion. As long as we confine our talk about emotion in aesthetic experience to specific contexts, to discussions of specific literary texts, it is easier to gain clarity about it. But as soon as we extend our talk to the more general context of defining the aesthetic experience, it borders on vagueness, generality, confusion, or vacuity. Vivas saw, rightly, the difficulty of talking about emotion in a generalized fashion but proceeded, wrongly, to exclude emotion from the concept of aesthetic experience. If Vivas had seen the arbitrariness of his exclusion he would probably have come to question both his definition and eventually any attempt at defining once and for all the aesthetic experience.[48]

Consistent with his exclusion of emotion from his definition, Vivas tries to transfer the psychological basis of aesthetic experience from the reader to the object, perhaps in order to escape the charge of the crude psychology of response-mechanism as well as to assure autonomy to the aesthetic object. More important, however, Vivas is reacting to the psychologism of I. A. Richards, who had suggested in *Principles of Literary Criticism* that poetic experiences are valuable because they reconcile a large number of conflicting impulses, thus creating a "synaesthetic" state in the mind of the reader or spectator.[49] In contrast to Richards, Vivas recognizes the need for "the generic traits of aesthetic objects," which would be the defining characteristics of art-experience. Vivas here is back to a sound commonplace of non-Kantian, traditional aesthetics. But of course he has already given his definition of aesthetic experience and "any list of truly generic traits would do."[50] In saying this Vivas is incorporating the findings of the psychologists and arguing that generic traits are the ones that psychologists have found to be central in our attention to aesthetic objects. But Vivas's statement nevertheless leaves us with serious unresolved difficulties. Does he mean to say that there are or can be many lists of truly generic traits? At least he does not seem to imply that there are different lists of truly generic traits. This would seem to involve the assumption that, with any list of truly generic traits, it is possible to have the *same* aesthetic experience, although one may experience it more or less fully. In other words, despite the difference in interpretations of a literary work, Vivas is postulating the possibility of the same experience. Vivas's answer thus simplifies the question of the conflict among different interpretations of a literary work and its relation to the nature of the aesthetic object.

Since meanings, according to Vivas, are immanent in the aesthetic object and entrap the reader, in a manner of speaking, in the aesthetic object, "it is of interest to know exactly what point by point correspondence is there between the aesthetic object and the experience."[51] It is important to recognize, however, that the valuational framework that we possess plays an important part not merely in our experience of art but in the way we characterize the very nature of aesthetic objects. For, as I said earlier, our perception is necessarily selective, and we see in terms of the categories that we possess for perception. (This nature of our perception Kant calls "categorial.") This is what makes the insights of Dr. Johnson, A. C. Bradley, and L. C. Knights so different, and that too is what makes the insights of Sartre, Jane Austen, Proust, and Conrad into the condition of man so different. The categorial perception satisfies the human need for a coherent and consistent explanation of a work of art even as it implies some ultimate limitation of all critical frameworks; this qualification, however, does not propose the impossibility of enrichment of one's categorial framework. In fact, we base our ordinary notion of aesthetic experience on a rule-of-thumb formulation that there are degrees of the aesthetic experience, for instance, of *King Lear* or *Ulysses*, and that the more sustained our contact with that work and the more sophisticated our critical framework, the better our appreciation of the full embodiment of meanings in the work. It is with these implications in mind that one may believe Bradley to have given us better insight than Coleridge did into Hamlet as a character, and Eliot better than both Dr. Johnson and Coleridge into Donne. This is what makes comparative evaluation of critical works, besides works of art themselves, meaningful.

It is clear that Vivas is an autonomist in aesthetics who rejects both cognition and morality from his concept of aesthetic experience, which for him is an experience of "rapt, intransitive attention" during which "the self disappears along with the emotion." In saying this Vivas claims to be making a phenomenological, not an epistemological, statement. Our analysis has shown that though a phenomenological statement may look different from a conceptual statement about what we mean by literary works, the strength of the former is closely intertwined with how we answer the latter. When Vivas admits that he cannot experience *The Brothers Karamazov* as art because of its complex moral and cognitive dimensions, his admission discloses the inadequacy of his definition. For the category of the aesthetic should not be conceived as radically different from or opposed to the moral and cognitive categories. When they are conceived as radically different or opposed, they invite confused theorizing that tends to oppose knowledge to aesthetic experience and reason to imagination. And it eliminates history and lived social reality from the experience of art. It is an appropriate and historically recurrent irony that, though concepts such as Vivas's definition of aesthetic experience should claim to be both a "normative definition" and a universalist criterion, they fail precisely when literary works such as *The Brothers Karamazov* reveal the inadequacy of our theoretical articulations of the concepts of art and art-experience.[52]

Gadamer and Poetic Autonomy

DESPITE MY CRITICISM of the various modes of defense of the concept of poetic autonomy, I have suggested that the concept itself, regardless of the difficulties implicit in its many defenses, is certainly powerful. The difficulties that attend these defenses spring mainly from an inadequate grasp of the concept of interpretation and from a related inadequacy in grasping the concept of change that is central to the history of literary interpretations. In *Truth and Method* Gadamer has provided a defense of the concept of poetic autonomy which is free from these inadequacies. Gadamer's most important philosophical contribution is, of course, in seeking to explore the phenomenon of understanding, and he attempts that by developing Heidegger's ontology of understanding into a dialectical hermeneutics. The central question Gadamer seeks to answer concerns the nature of understanding. In asking how understanding is possible Gadamer seems to be asking a Kantian question, but he complicates it by construing the question as an ontological one, one that would account for the whole of man's historical experience. Gadamer's importance for aesthetics and critical theory, however, resides in his radical questioning of the tradition of aesthetics stemming from Kant. Positively characterized, his questioning seeks to offer another account of the concept of poetic autonomy.

Gadamer signals his opposition to the Kantian and idealist traditions of aesthetics by arguing that "the idea of taste was originally more a moral than an aesthetic idea."[53] He therefore criticizes Kant for his purification of ethics "from all aesthetics and feeling" (*Truth and Method*, p. 34). The concept of taste is for Gadamer inseparable from its variability because "taste is a testimony to the changeableness of all human things and the relativity of all human values" (p. 53). As Gadamer argues, by ascribing subjective universality to aesthetic judgments Kant denied any knowledge of the aesthetic object. Consequently the "radical subjectivisation" implicit in Kant's aesthetic theory discredited "any kind of theoretical knowledge apart from that of natural sciences" and "compelled the human sciences to rely on the methodology of the natural sciences in self-analysis" (p. 39). The result of Kant's theory is the denial of a philosophy of art, since Kant argues that art cannot give knowledge or truth. Gadamer's defense of poetic autonomy, though directed toward a questioning of Kant's aesthetic theory, intends the questioning to help him propose that "aesthetics is possible only as a philosophy of art" (p. 53).

Gadamer's critique of the Kantian aesthetic tradition focuses, among other things, on the concept of aesthetic distance central to the tradition. This concept, Gadamer argues, is the result of an abstraction of aesthetic consciousness, one that conceives of aesthetic experience as empty of its own historical nature and as enjoying the immediacy of sensuous form. The most crucial consequence of this abstraction is the denial of the possibility of criteria for apprehending works of art. Thus if there are no criteria for aesthetic apprehension and if the aesthetic experience is the enjoyment of pure sensuous form, there can be no philosophy of criticism. Its inevitable consequence is the vogue for "art for art's sake." It follows that such an aesthetic must reserve knowledge and truth for the natural sciences. This aesthetic, moreover, ascribes a transcendental ontological status to artworks and removes artworks from society and history. Through the abstraction of aesthetic consciousness "the work of art loses its place and the world to which it belongs insofar as it belongs to aesthetic consciousness." And this loss is "paralleled by the artist losing his place in the world" (p. 78).

At this stage Gadamer questions the eighteenth-century cult of genius and the nineteenth-century sacralization of art. Both forms of theorizing separated aesthetic objects from ordinary objects because they argued that the latter derive their criteria of perfection from the purpose for which they are intended and to which they are answerable. But what, Gadamer asks, is the criterion of perfection for a work of art? Since it does not derive "the measure of its perfection from such a purpose," it logically follows, as Gadamer argues it did for Paul Valéry, that the work of art is not completable at all. Indeed, the work results from "a chance and random breaking-off of a formative process" (pp. 84–85) and therefore cannot contain anything binding. Consequently, not only is no criterion for correct reception and understanding available to the critic, but what he does is entirely left to him. "One way of understanding is then no less legitimate than another. There is no criterion of an appropriate reception. [It is] not only that the artist himself does not possess one. . . . Rather, every encounter with the work has the rank and the justification of a new production. This is an untenable hermeneutic nihilism." Thus the artist who was initially characterized as the genius in creating unique aesthetic entities gives way to the critic who now becomes the genius in understanding. "But genius in understanding," argues Gadamer, "is, in fact, of no more help than genius in creation" (p. 85).

Similarly, the idealist aesthetic of experience, too, by positing the absolute discontinuity of art-experience from man's historical life-world, impoverishes the experience of art. Gadamer therefore rejects the idealist tradition which makes everything begin with reflection. Though Gadamer construes the aesthetic experience as a mode of self-understanding, he insists, in contrast to the idealists, on the temporal and dynamic nature of this experience. "Inasmuch as we encounter the work of art in the world and a world in the individual work of art, aesthetic experience does not remain a strange universe into which we are magically transported, for a time." But Gadamer does not deny the necessity of adopting an aesthetic attitude; rather, he relates that necessity to the "historical reality of man" (p. 86). A work of art is not an object that stands apart from the subject who experiences it. "Instead, the work of art has its true being in the fact that it becomes an experience changing the person experiencing it" (p. 92). Consequently, the experience of a work of art is not simply a replay of the subjectivity of the person experiencing the work, but is a fusion of the horizons of the work and the person. Central to this notion of aesthetic experience is what the work of art says to us. What it says to us (the *Sache*) is the subject of the experience of art, not reducible to the content of the work of art.

Gadamer thus seeks to reappropriate the concepts of truth and knowledge for art. He does not deny the power of aesthetic experience to overwhelm the aesthetic agent. His explanation of the mode of being of the work of art is important here. Instead of adopting an attitude of aesthetic distance, one loses oneself as a spectator. But this kind of immersion cannot occur without one's moral, historical world. "It is the truth of his own world, the religious and moral world in which he lives, which presents itself to him and in which he recognizes himself" (p. 113). In aesthetic experience there occurs a recognition of oneself, since to be absorbed into an experience of a work of art is to be absorbed into what is, into the way things are. This experience of what is, that is, of reality, rather than a removal from it, is the essential feature of aesthetic experience. In terms of Gadamer's remarkable discussion of the structure of play (pp. 91–99), primacy is given to what is being played, not to the players. The players engage in a free-play of play that is at the same time bound by the rules of the game that underlie the fusion of horizons. Gadamer, then, does not abstract aesthetic experience from the rest of man's moral, cognitive experiences. Instead, he takes the concept of experience itself to be "a determining feature of the foundations of art." He therefore recognizes an essential ambiguity in the concept of aesthetic experience. As he explains it, the concept of *Erlebniskunst* "meant originally that art comes from experience and is an expression of experience" (p. 63).

In contrast, moreover, to the extremist theorists of poetic autonomy, Gadamer recognizes the inevitability of translation. "The situation of the translator and that of the interpreter are fundamentally the same." Both translator and interpreter bring to the text their own horizons of expectations, and both must recognize "the value of the alien, even the antagonistic character of the text and its expressions" (p. 349). Gadamer does not suggest that the gulf between the alien text and the interpreter or translator can be removed. Those who insist on its removal base the notion of faithfulness to a text on a scientistic objectivist conception of meaning. For Gadamer, however, the notion of faithfulness derives its authority from an interpreter's recognition both of what is already known and of oneself (pp. 310–25). He thus rejects the Kantian distinction that insists that science provides truth, whereas art does not. Gadamer indeed turns the Kantian distinction around and proposes that science deals with theoretical knowledge, while art deals with practical knowledge. Consequently, though he rejects the Kantian and idealist traditions that defend the concept of poetic autonomy, his rejection does not imply a rejection of the concept itself. His real goal is to provide a new characterization of the concept that would also help him reappropriate aesthetics within the human sciences.

Gadamer's version of poetic autonomy thus seeks to restore the essential integrity of the concept of art with the rest of the concepts of the human sciences. Some theorists will no doubt challenge Gadamer's or any other version of the concept of poetic autonomy and argue that in the context of actual living art ought to be subordinated to other human endeavors. One could construe this objection in radical political terms and say that, despite the theoretical sophistication of his concept of interpretation, Gadamer fails to realize that art belongs in the complex matrix of power-relations that obtains at any given historical time. This objection, then, charges the concept of poetic autonomy with an inability to realize that the reception of an artwork at any time depends on the ways in which power-relations form and control the institutions of society. Yet the objection is convincing only to someone who has already committed himself to one or another radical political perspective. But there is no guarantee that beyond the abstract logic of the objection long known to the West the objector will be able to propose sophisticated interpretations of literary works, that he will not simply superimpose the political category on art but also insist on the unquestionable primacy of the first over the second. The radical theorist of politics and ideology thus assumes a superiority for his perspective that is not necessarily justified. Nevertheless, the conflict between the critic of ideology and Gadamer could, if probed, reach a point when it would become fundamental and unresolvable. The concept of poetic autonomy, in other words, is not in itself unassailable, but rather requires for each new age more sophisticated defense and definition. One who holds a radical political commitment can never be brought to defend the concept of poetic autonomy, just as one who conceives poetic autonomy to be central to literary criticism can never give primary commitment to the political doctrine. But this argument leads to considerations that I want to reserve for a later discussion on the nature of inquiry in criticism.

Poetic Autonomy

THERE IS NO DOUBT that the concept of poetic autonomy has at times led its proponents to make confused and contradictory arguments. Yet the concept itself would not be a compelling modern dogma, to borrow Wayne Booth's useful phrase,[54] if there were not present in contemporary culture some elements that other accounts of criticism could not properly deal with. These elements generally had to do with the enormous success of science in our time and with a concurrent sense of the lessening of the value of art for a culture in which practical considerations were fast becoming the basis for the rise and stability of institutions of knowledge. The New Critical version of poetic autonomy, stemming from Kant and Coleridge, defends art by showing that the order we experience in literature is not of a scientific or logical nature but of an *alogical* nature. For such a conception of literature a recognition of the interdependence between complexity and value in literary works was minimum equipment. The New Critics therefore attempted to save literature and the concept of literature from the encroachment of mechanical categories of science and from the habitual modes of thinking about things. And they considered their concept of poetic autonomy to be necessary for us to remain human. Thus their defense of poetry is in the long tradition of the defense of poetry which both set literature in opposition to science, thought, and action, and conceived literature as providing man with the highest moral or psychological wisdom. Behind this confidence in the autonomy of literature, the last refuge of certainty in a world progressively rendered precarious by the conditions of living, was Kant's philosophy, a philosophy whose reassuring feature was the autonomy of man's moral vision. With this vision the Kantian man did not have to flinch before the Humean vision of the contingent nature of the external world. The New Critics, too, with their conception of poetic autonomy, argue for literature's capacity for loving the accidental, contingent, mad swirl of reality and at the same time for achieving a coherence denied to this reality. Poems therefore become unique objects.

The New Critical version of poetic autonomy is essentially Christian in that, though a poem is conceived to embody the "world's body" within itself, it is also conceived at the same time to escape the condition of the world, which is that of ambiguity or contradiction. For though the poem comprehends the real, it remains ideal. Such a conception of irony or tension is metaphoric, not in the sense that all concepts, since they are verbal, are metaphoric, but in the sense that poems are constructs which contain within themselves both terms of the metaphor. If the world of experience and concrete particulars is one term of this metaphor, the transcendence of it by the unique mode of poetic creativity is the other. This is why what Wimsatt calls the tensional poetics of the New Criticism is Christian.[55] Given this nature of its presuppositions, this poetic has to resort to paradoxical assertions: poetry does not give knowledge as science does, yet it gives the highest kind of knowledge; it deals with the real but is itself ideal; it is historical, yet it is universal. The ambiguous and contradictory nature of human experience that it claims poetry to embody is thus annulled in the vision of the totality. This poetic therefore attempts the enclosure of what appears to be an ironic characterization of poetry within the Christian humanistic vision of the possibility of man's deliverance from the world—with its brazen and swirling chaos of particulars—to the world of transcendental objects, that is, to poems.

There is an important truth in the position of Kant, the idealists, the New Critics, Vivas, Aldrich, Ingarden, Wellek, and many other aestheticians and literary theorists who argue for the autonomy of aesthetic experience. It certainly accounts for some of the crucial features of literary experience. We recognize, with Aldrich, that Othello's murder of Desdemona is an enactment of murder, that our intense interest in and involvement with Othello and Desdemona occur under a "categorial aspection." Proponents of the autonomy thesis are right insofar as we can say that while Lear goes to his death, and Raskolnikov is sent to Siberia, readers experience deep aesthetic pleasure. Yet they also experience the emotional impact of *Lear* and *Crime and Punishment*. Thus the power and complexity of serious literature derives, not simply from some rarefied rhetorical manipulations of language, but from compelling dramatizations of the moral, cognitive, and affective issues of life. It is the interanimations in serious literature of the aesthetic and the moral-cognitive dimensions that leave us profoundly moved. Despite a certain undeniable plausibility, then, of the definitions of aesthetic experience as an experience of disinterested contemplation or intransitive attention, they cannot explain the experience of involvement that is closely bound up with the experience of detachment in literary response. If they were true, readers' involvement would have to be impossible and their experience of literature would have little relation to lived social reality. Moreover, we would not know what the experience of literature is, since, cut off from the categories of lived social reality (and language constitutive of that reality), there would be no criteria with which to identify literary experience. The category of uniqueness has once again intruded generating the uneasy feeling in the autonomist's mind that interpretation is unrelated to experience, that literature forever remains inaccessible to criticism.

CHAPTER FIVE

The Concept of Affective Response in Contemporary Literary Theory

One of the most visible features of a group of contemporary literary theories is a rather constant and repetitive attack on the New Critical and traditional theories of criticism. The goal of these theories is to offer supposedly newer and more radical methods of experiencing literature. These new theories separate themselves from the notions of aesthetic experience and aesthetic objects and substitute for those notions the idea of literary response, which is then construed in several different ways. One influential version conceives of the central task of criticism as that of description of what happens in the mind of the reader as he reads words on a page. By characterizing itself as a theory of affective response it has signaled opposition to the well-known strictures of Wimsatt and Beardsley against affective criticism. And it has sought to substitute for the spatial conception of form held by the New Criticism, a radical notion of form such that the form of a literary work cannot be distinguished from the form of one's response. This mode of criticism has become well known as reader-response criticism.[1] There is another group of theorists who study the transaction between reader and text in order to account for the impact of the reader's psychological makeup on his response to literary works.[2] The second form of theorizing has become well known as psychoanalytical critical theory.

In this chapter I shall examine both these kinds of critical theory. My purpose is to characterize the difficulties involved in the very *form* of each version, especially as these difficulties arise from the kinds of questions involved in talking about literary response. I shall not deny the significance of a close analysis of one's reading experience, nor shall I deny the significance of psychoanalysis for criticism. Rather, I shall question the ways in which this significance has been construed. My analysis will indicate how the relation between psychoanalysis and criticism may be nontrivially and nonreductively construed. Finally, I shall try to show how the concept of affective response may valuably illuminate the concept of criticism.

Psychoanalysis and Criticism

THE REASONS for considering psychoanalytic critical theory are several. First, because of a desire to reenergize criticism, many critics now look for conceptual models in disciplines such as psychoanalysis, anthropology, and linguistics. Second, several critics claim that psychoanalysis can provide a more dynamic and rigorous account of literary response than can the traditional forms of criticism. And finally, since interdisciplinary studies are becoming an important mode of cultural scholarship, it is necessary to examine how other disciplines may illuminate problems of criticism and critical theory and how they might obfuscate or trivialize those problems. For the sake of consistency in discussion I shall focus on some aspects of Anglo-American psychoanalytic criticism, taken from Norman Holland's work, and then turn to French psychoanalytic critical thought, mainly that of Jacques Lacan.[3]

An important element of Freud's psychoanalytic thought is that the libido is the prime mover of the human psyche; this principle he claimed to have arrived at through extensive empirical investigation.[4] Psychoanalytic critics generally accept this as a presupposition on which both to develop their theories of criticism and to found the practice of criticism. To state this presupposition in the form often considered useful for criticism: fantasy is a driving force behind all human activities; it is a constant feature of the human organism and is capable, under all circumstances, of manifesting itself through various defense mechanisms; and these defense mechanisms are the formal properties that facilitate the displacement of fantasy (*Dynamics of Literary Response*, pp. 31–62). This is, of course, no more than a generalization imported by some critics from psychoanalysis, and as we shall see, it obscures and even trivializes some vital aspects of psychoanalysis.

Though he conceives psychoanalysis to be an art of interpretation, Freud realizes that the therapeutic problem is highly complex. He acknowledges that the patient "cannot remember the whole of what is present in him," though access to this repressed material is essential to the therapeutic treatment. Indeed, the important part of the treatment consists in making the patient conscious of the unconscious repetition of the repressed, because the patient tends to take the repetition "as a contemporary experience instead of . . . *remembering* it as something belonging to the past."[5] The repetition-compulsion causes a severe neurosis, making it impossible for the patient to distinguish the past from the present. If the patient's compulsion to repeat is transformed into "a motive for remembering" he can learn to live in the present. The psychoanalyst can help the patient accomplish this release from the past by a proper handling of transference. For Freud, however, transference is more than a mere naming of the resistance the patient's behavior discloses, since it awakens the memories and facilitates a disentanglement of the present from the past. Therapeutic practice acknowledges that the patient not only resists treatment but indeed intensifies his resistance during the treatment. Consequently, the psychoanalyst cannot simply inform the patient of his resistance, because that might only exacerbate the conflict within the patient and further complicate an already delicate and sensitive situation. These elements are among the significant dimensions of psychoanalytic practice and require, not an imposition of systematic categories, but a careful handling of the specific features of a given case. As Freud cautions, the possibility of failure, on the part of both psychoanalyst and patient, is a real one, and a sustained "working through" is necessary, though not accomplished simply by a mere application of the technique by the analyst.[6]

The psychoanalytic critic of literature, however, must modify this notion of psychoanalysis. He would conceive of literary works as sublimated fantasies, form and meaning being strategies of psychic defense which literary writers inexorably employ, and language being an instrument of displacement which transforms a writer's fantasies into a complex form and meaning available to readers as a literary work. The function of criticism, then, becomes twofold and follows logically from the psychoanalytic critic's conception of literary works.

On the one hand, the critic must uncover a literary writer's latent fantasies in the manifest content and form of his works, and, on the other hand, he must examine his own response in order to discover psychic defense strategies which manage that response to a literary work and its psychic substrate. As Holland puts it: "What is needed is simple: more study of the ways people feel as they read various works employing various types of fantasy and defense—works which are primarily drive-gratifying; works which mingle anxiety-arousal with wish-fulfillment; works in which the fantasy is strongly managed; works in which the fantasy is weakly managed. The results may lead not only to a firm explanation of our affective response to literature, but also to a deeper understanding of our emotions in life."[7]

Construed in this way, psychoanalytic criticism claims to explore the "dynamics of literary response" in two ways: it articulates the presumed links between a writer's psychic defenses (as stimuli), which prompt his literary creativity, and his actual literary products (as sublimated behavior); and it articulates the links between the reader's psychic defenses (as stimuli), which prompt his literary response, and his actual literary response (as sublimated behavior). Both writer and reader thus exhibit latent fantasies which have been displaced by strategies of form and meaning; psychoanalytic criticism seeks to trace such displacements and to expose the primal scene, the infantile fantasies, lying at the heart of both literary creativity and literary response. By involving writer and reader in criticism Holland intends to "confront (and overcome) our old *bête-noire*: the problem of subjective and objective" (*Dynamics of Literary Response*, p. 108). This strategy involves more than an empirical examination of specific reader-responses to specific literary works, for Holland hopes to provide a theoretical scheme conceived in terms of a general causal principle that links poems to their writers and readers. If everything is thus embedded in the Freudian secret—the archetypal sources of the self's activities—Holland can thus make the "empyrean speculation that the poet's secret, the novelist's, the film-maker's, perhaps the mere literary critic's lies in his being able to take pleasure not only from the drives but also from the very defenses inherent in what he does" (pp. 132–33).

How does Holland put his theory into practice? A full and detailed application occurs in his discussion of Arnold's famous poem, "Dover Beach" (pp. 115–31). Holland first gives what he considers to be a

New Critical objective response to the "text by itself"; second, he gives some general considerations relevant to a psychoanalytic criticism of the poem; and finally, he explains his own response to the poem. When these three are brought together in a coherently articulated relationship, he would consider literary response to the poem to be psychoanalytically founded (pp. 116–17). The second and third stages, as they articulate the reader's response to the poem, discover the objective and determinate structure of the fantasy underlying the text. Taking an important line ("ignorant armies clash by night") as crucial to a reading of the poem, Holland argues that a critic who confines himself to the "text by itself" would give merely "ordinary explication" which "offers little basis for the armies while psychoanalytic criticism offers considerable" (p. 121). The New Criticism, construed as "ordinary explication," thus suffers from an interpretive debility beyond its preliminary observations about the poem, whereas psychoanalytic criticism enables Holland to grasp the hidden fantasies which the strategies of the poem displace into a manageable form. Holland, for instance, selects these details: "grating roar / of pebbles which the waves draw back, and fling," "melancholy, long, withdrawing roar," "naked shingles of the world," "confused alarms of struggle and flight," "ignorant armies clash by night." These phrases and images make up for Holland the psychic substrate of the poem:

> There is a well-nigh universal sexual symbolism in the heard-but-not-seen, naked fight by night. This is one way Arnold's poem turns our experience of disillusionment or despair into satisfaction, namely, through the covert gratification we get from this primal scene fantasy. Arnold is talking about hearing a sexual "clash by night," just as children fantasy sex as fight. . . . The image ["darkling plain"] here operates defensively. As elsewhere in the poem, the image deflects our attention from a pair of lovers in a sexual situation and sublimates into a distant, literary and moral experience, a darkling plain from Thucydides. [*Dynamics of Literary Response*, p. 121]

To say, however, that "children fantasy sex as fight" is to propose a theory but not to establish that "clash by night" is covertly about a sexual clash. The psychoanalytic critic might reply that the equivalence "operates defensively," so that there are no one-to-one relationships but rather layers of hidden causal relationships. Yet Holland does establish such one-to-one relationships, and at the same time he offers them as causally determined connections. Consider, for instance, Holland's assimilation of Arnold's allusion to the historical battle (originally described by Thucydides) to the universal sexual fantasies that, from the psychoanalytic perspective, govern all activities. "The final image ['ignorant armies clash by night'] brings a still stronger feeling of rhythmic withdrawal, a child's excited but frightened vague awareness. That other, separate adult life has a naked, night time, rhythmic sound. It does not lie there like a land of dreams—rather, it is violent, passionate, brutal; the bright girdle is withdrawn and bodies clash by night" (p. 122).

This is the result of an uncritical adoption of some of the elements of Freudian theory.[8] Holland draws out certain sexual associations of a word, phrase, or image and puts them together as a repetition of the primal fantasy. The selection of details and associations is controlled by the desire to reduce everything significant in the poem to a defensive displacement of the primal fantasy. In psychoanalysis full articulation of associations is theoretically necessary until the patient grasps the compulsive repetition of his past that prevents him from living in the present. Freud therefore insists on patience and on letting "things take their course" in order to spare "the illusion of having failed"[9] because success in psychoanalysis is not a matter of the analyst's application of a technique but rather a matter of his intuitive mastery of knowing what to say, when, and how, under specific, often unforeseeable, circumstances. It should be admitted, however, that Freud himself conducted some highly questionable analyses. For instance, his analysis of Dora, even if we grant him his basic theory of the case, shows him forcing "interpretations upon Dora even before she is ready for them or can accept them."[10] Moreover, not all the associations that a patient is likely to bring up are connected with his dreams. Consequently, while specific causal connections between the life of a patient and his infantile experiences can be made, those connections do not justify the authority of a general causal law about the psychic life of man.[11] This is intended as a fundamental objection to psychoanalysis as a science, not to it in its humanistic aspirations to investigate the complexities that constitute the human self.

These complexities inhere partly in the fact that the information which the patient gives is necessarily fragmentary and incoherent, and the analyst must participate in ways that both facilitate dialogue and build suggestions that can create the conditions for a story that the patient himself cannot tell. It is in learning to comprehend the phenomena of distorted communication in one's own life that the psychoanalytic situation reveals itself as a process of self-understanding. Psychoanalysis, in other words, is a hermeneutic discipline; it is, as Habermas would put it, context-dependent rather than context-free.[12] As Freud himself recognized, neither the patient's explicit consent nor his explicit resistance provides grounds for the psychoanalyst to believe that the requisite changes are beginning to take place within the patient, or that the repetition compulsion has been brought under control and halted. This is why the psychoanalytic situation calls for what one might call a "depth" hermeneutics, a kind of second reading that subtly but unobtrusively examines the phenomena of distorted communication in the patient's psychic life.

My discussion so far reveals certain difficulties in the project of psychoanalytic criticism. How do we know that a particular fantasy underlies the work of a writer and the response of a reader, except by an arbitrary a priori adoption of a general law about the human psyche? If such an adoption is involved, how could we claim it as knowledge? Can it help us better interpret literary works? Moreover, it is possible to argue that knowledge of a particular fantasy does not commit one to explain the poem in terms of that fantasy. This is not to deny that a knowledge of the psychological makeup of an author can help one to interpret his literary works in interesting ways. There would still be the question of how such knowledge might be profitably used, the force and the limits of the criteria that operate explicitly or implicitly in application to the interpretation of literary works.[13] In the case of a particular literary work, certain psychological factors might impressively converge (as for instance in the case of Sylvia Plath's poems), making it plausible or interesting to claim that they provide grounds for explaining the work, particularly its content. Yet all criticism, even that which seeks to give the historical, authorial meaning of a text, involves interpretation and is therefore an activity of reason-giving, not of causal ascription.

Moreover, there are many internal changes that have been taking place in the discipline of psychoanalysis. Some of its concepts have become more sophisticated, some have been thrown out, some have been substantially modified, and some new ones have been proposed. Psychoanalytic critics therefore must redefine their own strategies and concepts. For example, Holland has now modified his position in order to focus more fully on the recent psychoanalytic investigations into the concept of identity.[14] Holland thus argues that each person is made up of an "unchanging inner form or core of identity" which facilitates his transactions between himself and others. This unchanging core constitutes a primary identity, "an invariant which provides all the later transformations of his self."[15] He apprehends the world in such a way that his apprehension "replicates his identity."[16] Consequently, all "interpretation is a function of one's identity."[17] There are four specific modalities that underlie the principle of identity re-creation: defenses, expectations, fantasies, and transformations. One shapes an experience in order to (1) avoid anxiety, (2) gratify one's unconscious wishes, (3) absorb a particular event as part of a series of events, and (4) shape that event in that series. As a result of this transaction one experiences a meaningful totality in reading a literary work.[18] Thus there is no doubt about a shift in Holland's views. If formerly he held that autonomous texts embody psychological processes, he now holds that they don't. The shift, however, is not a serious one. The recent view still gives a place of centrality to the earlier concept of defense and adaptation. The difference resides in the introduction of the concept of identity, which he says must be considered "from the point of view of defense and adaptation." "We work out through the text our own characteristic patterns of desire and adaptation." The fantasy-content located in the text is created "by the reader . . . to express his own drives."[19]

The reason Holland insists on the personal element in reading is that he finds impersonal much of the criticism being written today. He therefore asks: "Why not acknowledge and welcome the personal in a reading? In a theory of reading why not take into account as much of the personal as our twentieth-century psychology allows?"[20] For Holland's contention that a person's capacity for acceptance of a literary work is contingent upon his capacity "exactly to re-create" by means of the work "in a verbal form of his own particular pattern of defense mechanisms."[21] His example of George Bernard Shaw will illustrate the point. "Shaw was a lifelong teetotaller, a non-smoker, and a vegetarian—a man much concerned with his mouth, but less with taking in, more with keeping things out of it . . . a response to an absent mother and an empty mouth." As Holland reads him, Shaw "responded to hunger and perhaps a fear about things coming into his mouth by a decision to make things go out of his mouth."[22] Thus in terms of this theme of variations around the central core of one's identity, Holland seeks to trace an individual style through the entire life of a person.

Finally, given his initial assumptions, the psychoanalytic critic would conceive of psychoanalytic criticism as the valid understructure of all interpretations of a literary work. When confronted with incompatible interpretations he would want to reveal the presumed psychoanalytic structure and spread it over them like a tarpaulin, for these interpretations are by definition sublimated manifestations of the infantile sexual fantasy.[23] Thus what may appear from our ordinary critical perspectives to be a hopeless conflict among different interpretations of a literary work is dissolved. Its concepts of literature and criticism (and finally of any human expression or action) may be formulated in one sentence: each way a reader understands a poem is a particular manifestation of the universal psychic defense mechanism in all readers; each poem is a subliminated version of the infantile sexual fantasy at the heart of all human creativity.[24] Or, in terms of the concept of identity: "each reader seeks out the particular themes that concern him. Each will have different ways of making the text into an experience with a coherence and significance that satisfies."[25] It is a coherence that is the result of his own pattern of defense mechanism.

I have argued, however, that psychological facts are complex and cannot be singled out like experiments in physics. Literary response partakes of this complexity, and it therefore does not follow a deductive or inductive physicalist model. This simple fact plagues psychologists and psychoanalytic critics alike in all their inquiries because they tend to construe facts of human behavior or literary response or human psychic life as if they were simple, manipulable entities. Thus psychoanalytical models of defense mechanism and the primal scene are like so many pulleys and levers in a mechanical experiment. Moreover, psychological experiments are to a large extent context-dependent; their conclusions are not self-evidently valid generalizations about other actions and events. And finally there are limitations set by the mind of the experimenter or psychoanalyst; this is a difficulty that cuts at the very foundation of psychological inquiry, its presumed scientific objectivity. Freud, at his most lucid moments, was aware that his particular mode of apprehension enabled him to construe and interpret his data and that recalcitrant data revealed the problematic nature of his apprehension. As Lionel Trilling has said, "it was left to Freud to discover how, in a scientific age, we still feel and think in figurative formations, and to create, what psychoanalysis is, a science of tropes, metaphor and its variants, synecdoche and metonymy." [26]

The difficulties that confront psychoanalysis and psychoanalytic criticism are, however, not generally recognized, because the convenience of a methodological model derived from the physical sciences is hard to give up. Giving it up would involve an acceptance of flexible, analogical, tentative, and indeterminate formulations of questions and answers, and the acceptance of informal, intuitive procedures of reasoning which do not yield easily transportable methods. Critical interpretations of poems may seem to be part of an empirical inquiry, but actually involve a complex mode of quasi-inductive and quasi-deductive reasoning informed by an insight critics have acquired into literature.

IF ANGLO-AMERICAN VERSIONS of psychoanalysis and psychoanalytic criticism seem simple, schematic, and often rigid, French psychoanalytic thought, especially that of Lacan, if not free from a kind of schematism, is highly obscure, difficult, and complex. Instead of insisting on the cheerful and self-confident ego of the American version of Freud's thought, Lacan insists on the need for interpretation of the master's theories. And he attempts his interpretation by means of the structuralist linguistic theory, which asserts that the universal laws of man or society are to be found in the structure of language. Lacan's important thesis here is that there is a structural homology between language and the unconscious, that the unconscious is structured like a language. Consequently, psychoanalysis becomes a kind of textual analysis of the unconscious. Lacan's theories, when employed for reading literature, seek to open interdisciplinary questions concerning psychoanalysis, literature, and reading.

Rather than being oriented toward cure, Lacan's psychoanalytic thought is oriented toward theory and toward a unification of knowledge of man. Lacan therefore rejects the American ego psychology, whose basic premises are that the ego possesses a healthy part and that this healthy part can adapt itself to reality. At stake in this conception of the ego, health, and reality are certain assumptions concerning objectivity, reality, and the possibility of our knowing them. Contrary to this version of psychoanalysis, Lacan argues that the ego is part of man's problem because it is incapable of distinguishing between the desire of the subject and the desires of others. Thus the ego is forever entrapped in a process of alienation and identity-confusion that occur in the "mirror phase" of one's development. Shorn of its presumed autonomy, the ego is the locus and instrument of neurosis. To rely, then, on the ego for a healthy adaptation to reality is, for Lacan, to abandon the goal of psychoanalysis.

Lacan's most important contribution to psychoanalysis seems to me to be his theory of the "mirror phase" (*Écrits*, pp. 1–7). The child from the age of six to eighteen months sees its body as a totality, rather than as fragmented, and totally identifies its body with its mirror image. These unmediated identifications constitute the child's *alienation* because the child during this stage is always subordinated to its image, to the other child, to its mother. This phase Lacan characterizes as the "imaginary" order (*imaginaire*) which he constrasts with the "symbolic" order (*symbolique*). If the first is narcissistic and alienating and brings about the Oedipal crisis, the second orients the child toward the social. Lacan does not construe this transition to imply some kind of affirmation, but rather, consistent with his insistence on Freud's darker insights into the human psyche, construes the symbolic to be inexorably infected by the imaginary. Though the chronologically later phase makes possible symbolic and therefore more complex identifications, the imaginary identifications made during the mirror phase constitute the child's concept of identity. The subject therefore becomes constituted as the alienated self, a self that Lacan calls the ego (*moi*). The ego is inescapably neurotic because all its attempts to constitute the self are always infected by the inevitability of misrecognition (*méconnaissance*) characteristic of the mirror phase. The self, then, is forever like an other, one that was in the beginning for the child its mother. Psychoanalytic practice, implicit in Lacan's theory, can never help one eliminate these initial misrecognitions which determine one's alienated identity. It can only help one comprehend this *méconnaissance* at the heart of one's being. Further, Lacan argues that beyond the symbolic phase and its inhabiting by the imaginary constructions lies the "real" (*réel*). But the "real" cannot be captured in language, though it is always defined in relation to the linguistic system as something that forever eludes our knowledge and understanding.[27]

Yet the object of psychoanalysis for Lacan is intersubjective communication. When the patient learns to address the analyst as an Other, when he learns to express his subjectivity to an Other as a subjectivity, he has acquired his own true subjectivity. The subject, the patient, is then no longer a set of objectifications, a function in either the information theory or the collectivist project of a scientific theory. The relation between analyst and patient is constructive in that the centrality is given not to the dream, but to the conversation about the dream. Consequently, the psychoanalytic situation is primarily linguistic in character. The self is neither autonomous nor a repository of boundless possibilities. When the self, the true subjectivity of the patient, speaks, its speech acquires its significance because it recognizes and addresses the subjectivity of the other. Its speech therefore is necessarily the discourse of the other (*Écrits*, pp. 30–113). "The Other" is for Lacan an inclusive term and concept, and cannot be restricted to the other person; it also means the order of the language and the subconscious in the subject. Thus for Lacan the unconscious is structured as a language and it is the discourse of the other. The compelling interest here of Lacan's theory of the mirror phase, a psychoanalytic reworking of Hegel's concept of desire, is in his illumination of fundamental inner relations among language, desire, and the unconscious, relations that make it impossible to clearly separate them from one another (pp. 292–324).

Lacan's theories, however radical in his reinterpretation of Freud and however contemporary in his assimilation of Marxism, anthropology, and linguistics, are highly formalistic in character. Their formal nature, evident everywhere in his writings, shows most consistently in his psychoanalytic reading of Edgar Allan Poe's story "The Purloined Letter." [28] The story's power for Lacan resides in the letter, which illustrates the power of the signifier. Though the content of the letter remains unknown, the letter exercises great influence on the actions of all the characters. It possesses a meaning, unrelated to its socalled "real" content, by the differential oppositions to other units of meaning. Thus Lacan's reading of the story is highly formalistic in that rather than seeking to disclose the latent meanings, it discloses the disposition or form of the relations among the manifest units of signification. This form is the latent in the manifest structural relations within the story. The letter is a symbolic entity which represents an excess of signifiers over signified. It is in this plurality of signifiers that the activities of human beings reveal themselves as a ceaseless process of communication among signifiers. Lacan calls this process one of displacement and condensation, a process better known in structuralist thought as metaphor and metonymy. Metaphor allows for a suppression and concealment of one signifier beneath another, while metonymy allows for a replacement of one signifier by another. The operations of these two figures are, according to Lacan, formally identical with the operations of the unconscious. These operations, Freud had argued, are primarily displacement and condensation. For both Freud and Lacan psychic symptoms form a signifying system which can be read. For Lacan, moreover, "man cannot aim at being whole (the 'total personality' is another of the deviant premises of modern psychotherapy), while ever the play of displacement and condensation to which he is doomed in the exercise of his functions marks his relation as a subject to the signifier" (*Écrits*, p. 287). Consequently, man's real history consists not of the so-called chronological or objectifiable events but of his subconscious, and psychoanalysis facilitates the process which enables the patient to inscribe himself into the discourse of the Other.

Now, Lacan's thought may prompt some interesting and at times compelling formalizations of some elements in textual analysis, for literary narratives often become fascinating when their explicit meanings seem to conceal strange and in a sense unintended meanings or structural properties. Yet one cannot properly claim that Lacan's theory provides a theory of criticism nor that psychoanalysis can be a theory of criticism. His readings of certain texts do nevertheless suggest that psychoanalysis can ask questions of literary texts that criticism otherwise does not, and it may help criticism to discover possibilities that it may not have entertained. Thus Lacan's theories, like Freud's, may seem to lend complex instruments for interpreting literary works, but the result may often turn out to be repetitive and predictable, and the complexity deriving from psychoanalysis may often be no more than the complexity of a conceptual network superimposed on a text. Criticism, in other words, requires hermeneutic tact, and the contribution of psychoanalysis here is at best ambiguous. While it may reenergize criticism, it may also predetermine and trivialize the act of criticism. The fascination that some critics have felt for Freud and Lacan derives, I believe, from their hope that these thinkers provide solutions to some ultimate mysteries about human nature and its relationship with man's cultural and aesthetic endeavors. As Wittgenstein said of Freud, this seductiveness is the seductiveness of a mythology,[29] and for all its modernity this mythology is a dangerous one if adopted for criticism in an uncritical manner.

Nevertheless, Lacan's endeavor needs to be taken seriously. His insistence on the need for interpretation of Freud's texts and his emphasis on the significance of the master's darker insights into the human psyche are of great value. It cannot be denied that Lacan has sought to forestall trivialization that inevitably occurs in the works of those psychologists and physicians who hold simple-minded conceptions of authority, health, and cure. He has indeed posed a challenge to psychoanalysis aimed at restoring the rigor and the consciousness of the obstacles that Freud at his best always showed in thinking through the problem of the psychic life of man.

The preceding discussion does not seek to deny that psychological explorations can be valuable in literary interpretation, that some important literary works (for instance *The Prelude*) make it difficult to separate the concept of art from the concept of self. Consider for a moment the problem of reading "Dover Beach."[30] The poem evokes the speaker's sense of doubt and disorientation, a sense that is rendered poignant by a passionate personal element. In contrast to the powerful evocation of the harsh fate of mankind that almost dominates one's experience of the poem, and perhaps because of that, the speaker's words become a melancholy lyric of love. For if history and culture cannot provide man with faith, if there are no objective grounds for hope, love—sexual love—is perhaps the sole possibility of hope for human beings. Hence the speaker's plea: "Ah love, let us be true / To one another!" But there is no guarantee that the lovers will be faithful to one another. In the general chaos of history, the personal can afford us no certainty. Thus it is possible for a reader to experience the speaker's emotional vulnerability.

It is interesting that Arnold uses adjectives such as *fair, tranquil, moon-blanched, calm, sweet* to describe the beauty of the landscape, which is only heightened by his experience of the sea. But the landscape—or rather the seascape—is invested with emotional power by the ideas that stir the poet's mind. Compared to the scene's visual beauty and to the poet's immediate experience of it, the ideas are radically different. They don't simply introduce a negative perspective on the scene; they pervade and dominate; they constitute the reality of the speaker's sense of vulnerability. The sensuous surface that seemed to give pleasure is now entangled with the emotions aroused by the ideas. The ideas reveal the whole of man's historical experience to be futile or doomed to failure. It is in this context that love provides an anxious and vulnerable hope.

Consider now a rather more complicated case of the relation between the self and art. In Kafka's story, "The Metamorphosis," the protagonist, Gregor Samsa, suddenly leaves his usual form of life, a form that has been too oppressive for him. Kafka contrives with consummate skill the strange circumstances of Gregor's transformation—the circumstances that are a compound of waking and sleeping, of consciousness that is not quite conscious. Beginning with this change in Gregor's form of being, Kafka gradually strips Gregor of his assurance of love from his parents and sister. Indeed, having been their protector until now, Gregor had unwittingly created his self-alienation. His change provides him with an insight into the alienation which now separates him from his former illusory conception of his relationship with them. In a deliberately crude but powerful scene Kafka represents the love for which Gregor has nearly sacrificed his life for the family: when his mother and sister remove his furniture, Gregor, in a last desperate attempt to save some remnant of his human life, covers with his body the picture of the nude on the wall. The cheap picture already by itself captured the spiritual emptiness of his life. Gregor's act now repeats and encapsulates his condition. When Gregor finally dies, he does so not because of his insight into his alienation, but because his insight cannot liberate him from the complex and contradictory feelings he has toward his family.

Kafka's manipulation of the theme of parent and child, and his gradual exposure of the brutality of that relationship, suggest that the connection between Gregor and Kafka may be more profoundly personal than at first appears. When, on being asked if the story was autobiographical, Kafka called it an "indiscretion," he left no doubt about its painfully personal nature. For he asked, "Is it perhaps delicate and discreet to talk about the bed bugs in one's own family?" Yet the indiscretion is not just a matter of psychic defense-mechanism which conceals from the consciousness the unmentionable. On the contrary, the story is a systematic exhuming of the real relationship between Gregor and his family. Moreover, Kafka added to his remarks that "Samsa is not merely Kafka."[31] This is because Kafka's sense of his entrapment in his family was no more implacable than his self-destructive commitment to art. Consequently, "The Metamorphosis" is an intensely autobiographical story, not in the crude sense of being the author's personal record, but in the sense of bearing his personal testimony of suffering and entrapment in life. When Gregor becomes changed into a beetle, he has unconsciously taken a step toward the destruction of his situation in both family and society. Though he loathes his new condition, he also becomes aware of his family's hidden response to him. His change may be said, then, to be the result of the lack of love in his life. And he dies in full awareness of the impossibility of love in his life, an awareness that is dramatically reinforced since it comes only after his physical change.

If these two illustrations make sense, then we should see that literary experience is not a matter of re-creation of one's identity. It is not a matter of sheer self-enlightenment either, though we may be complacent enough to believe that it is. It may contribute toward a greater self-understanding, since it may at times threaten one's ordinary sense of stability and health. Literary experience is not a replay of one's mere subjectivity, though subjectivity does certainly come into play. If psychoanalytic criticism seems to involve a simplistic transposition of psychoanalytic concepts to criticism, it is because it often takes them too literally. Rigidly Freudian criticism tends to find literary correlates for every feature of the psychoanalytic situation, and rigid applications of recent psychoanalytic concepts commit the same mistake of finding literal correlates for criticism. Psychoanalytic thought, however, is a loose assemblage of interesting and often powerful speculative concepts. If used in a flexible manner they may bring about a deeper self-understanding and in turn energize and deepen our capacity for experiencing literature. But they may also predetermine and trivialize our literary transactions in a way that even psychoanalysts find embarrassing.[32]

An experiential reading of a literary work, whether or not it opposes a New Critical reading, cannot allow just any personal emotion or private association of the reader without trivializing the problem of literary response. The difficulty of theorizing intelligently about emotional response to literature and its relation to the nature of the self may suggest that literary experience possesses a complexity that cannot be captured in any neat, elegant, and economic formula. Since criticism is an interpretive activity, psychoanalysis, perhaps the most formidable interpretive discipline of this century, has an important bearing on criticism. Psychoanalysis is part of the romantic quest for self-knowledge and is informed by a moral effort to inquire into the nature of the self. Since one is not aware of the hidden forces within one's own self, psychoanalysis may certainly help one to articulate and understand them. That the experience of literature too can help one to confront and experience those forces and the forces within culture as well seems unquestionable. What is questionable, nevertheless, is a systematic transposition of the categories of psychoanalysis to criticism. When such transposition occurs, self-exploration, presumed to be made possible by literature, is prevented, since the results are already given in the systematic categories the critic has adopted from psychoanalysis. Both psychoanalysis and criticism deriving from it thus start from some ad hoc insights into complex, ambiguous, and often contradictory features of human experience, but they tend to make a transition from such important insights not just to a pattern of perceiving things but to both factual discovery and a general theoretical structure.

The Affective Critical Theory of Stanley Fish

IF PSYCHOANALYTIC CRITICAL THEORY seems elaborate and systematic, Stanley Fish has proposed a theory that is audacious in its self-conscious rejection of systematic categories. Indeed, the only category that has any value for Fish is that of the reader. In focusing on Fish's theory I shall try to explain three things: its entanglements with New Critical theories that Fish thinks he has either refuted or shown to be confused, the difficulties that he is not able to overcome or resolve, and finally, the radical skepticism implicit in his position that his recent discussion of the concept of interpretation cannot overcome.

FISH not only has dealt with most of the issues of critical theory, he has also claimed to have dissolved them, for he thinks that most of them do not spring from a correct conception of what is involved in the act of reading a piece of language. In direct contradiction of Wimsatt and Beardsley, he boldly says: "I am courting the 'affective fallacy.' Indeed, I am embracing it and going beyond it. . . . That is, making the work disappear into the reader's experience of it is precisely what should happen in our criticism, because it is what happens when we read." [33] Fish's theory claims to be both radical and natural: radical because traditional objectivist criticism and its theories create, according to Fish, a gap between description and interpretation and thereby fail to account for the complexity involved in the act of reading; and natural because Fish's "experiential analysis" attempts to bring to our "analytical attentions the 'events' one does not notice in normal time, but which do occur." [34] Fish thus embraces not only the affective fallacy but also the intentional fallacy, since his method is intended to enable the readers to have "the experience the author wished to provide." [35]

Fish has thus provided what he considered to be the only valid account of the process of reading. His claim for the indubitable universal validity of his theory rests on the conviction that it provides an account of the "sequence of the reading experience" (*Self-Consuming Artifacts*, p. 408). Such a conception, he avers further, does not distinguish the language of literature from the language of anything else. By denying the presumed distinction between literary and ordinary language Fish claims to offer "a theory that restores human content to language . . . [and] legitimate status to literature by reuniting it with a norm that is no longer trivialized." [36] Proponents of the distinction, Fish contends, extol literary language by trivializing ordinary language, for which there is no justification. Once this distinction is shown to be groundless, Fish can argue further that all traditional theories concerned with proposing the distinction between literature and nonliterature are wrong: "My method allows for no such aesthetic and no such fixing of value. In fact it is oriented *away* from evaluation and toward description. It is difficult to say on the basis of its results that one work is better than another or even that a single work is good or bad. And more basically, it doesn't permit the evaluation of literature as literature, as apart from advertising or preaching or propaganda or 'entertainment'" (*Self-Consuming Artifacts*, p. 408).

More specifically, Fish's theory rejects the formalist criticism that focuses on the "lines of plot and argument, the beginnings, middles and ends, the clusters of imagery," and therefore conceives of literary works as spatially observable structures. Fish's rejection, however, does not entail a denial of these features but rather a denial of any "necessary relationship between the visible form of a work and the form of the reader's experience." [37] The value of the formal features therefore resides, not in the visibly observable structure of a literary work, but in a structure of response that the reader experiences. Reading is thus a temporal experience which the spatial mode of criticism distorts. Fish's method therefore aspires to be radically empirical, since it prescribes "*an analysis of the developing responses of the reader in relation to the words as they succeed one another in time*" (*Self-Consuming Artifacts*, pp. 387–88).

Now, the temporal nature of the process of reading is an insight which has emerged in modern explorations in phenomenology, hermeneutics, and psycholinguistics.[38] Its value is undeniable for criticism. What is nevertheless open to scrutiny is how this insight helps critics and theorists to redefine or reconceptualize concepts of criticism. Fish, for instance, shifts critical attention away from the New Critical notion of poems as self-contained, organic entities to the process of reading itself. This process, moreover, does not allow any difference in the reading of literature and nonliterature. In consequence, the concepts of criticism become meaningless for Fish because, besides being predicated on a naive epistemology, they have little relation to the real act of reading. If, according to Fish, the concept of literature has little value, it follows that the concepts of success and failure that critics and artists use in order to distinguish, say, Shakespeare's *Much Ado about Nothing* from *The Winter's Tale* are misguided. It also follows that the possibility of confrontation among different interpretations of a poem, the significance of different conceptual frameworks as their proponents attempt to offer them as the valid ones as opposed to other frameworks, historical changes that contribute to changes in critical and cultural sensibility, and the very concept of dialogue among critics—these are simply dissolved or at best pressed into a descriptive analysis of the reader's developing responses. More simply, since there is no difference between literature and nonliterature, and since all experiences of language, if honestly faced, share the same fundamental pattern of responses in the minds of all readers, all we can have is a concept of effects.

More positively, vital criticism is one that concentrates fully on the experience of reading. "In the analysis of a reading experience, when does one come to the point? The answer is, 'never', . . . Coming to the point is the goal of a criticism that believes in content, in extractable meaning, in the utterance as a repository. Coming to the point fulfils a need that most literature deliberately frustrates (if we open ourselves to it), the need to simplify and close. Coming to the point should be resisted, and in its small way this method will help you to resist" (*Self-Consuming Artifacts*, p. 410). To the extent that Fish here underlines the complexities of the process of literary understanding, his observation is of course salutary, for too often criticism has tended to seek paraphrasable meaning and to offer it as the experience of literature. Remember, however, that Fish insists, not on the complexities of literary understanding, but rather on the process of understanding any linguistic utterance whatever. Even so, if he had wanted to underline the difficulty of conclusively distinguishing between literary and nonliterary works, his observation would once again be salutary, for it is becoming more and more difficult to offer criteria that can validly define literature.

Yet Fish does make various discriminations. He admits, for instance, that his "selection of texts . . . is itself an analysis of hierarchy" in his taste, for "literature is what disturbs our sense of self-sufficiency, personal and linguistic." He has here introduced a criterion of value that ascribes to literature a special significance. He is aware of the self-contradiction involved in his theory at this point, for he attempts to neutralize it by characterizing "this hierarchy to be the mere reflection of a personal psychological need [rather] than of a universally true aesthetic" (p. 409). Fish has to say this because his inaugural assumption prescribes that, whether or not the reader is aware, he does undergo all the fluctuations and uncertainties in responding to a piece of language. Consequently, he has substituted for "a universally true aesthetic" a far larger claim: a universally valid method of how readers do experience language.

Given the nature of his method, whatever discriminations he wants to make become problematical. For instance, the writers of "self-consuming artifacts" employ, according to Fish, ambiguous and confusing language in order to communicate, to make possible, an experience that is radically different from the notion of experience or reading based on discursive reasoning. For the author's wish is to push the readers to "a point where they are beyond the aid that discursive or rational forms can offer" (p. 3). This is scarcely any different from the antipropositional, qualitative, and irreducible structure of experience that Cleanth Brooks ascribes to poetry.[39] To say this about literature is to introduce a criterion of value. The New Critics and their defenders cannot make their apology for poetry unless they self-consciously follow the implications of their criterion of value. Unlike them, however, Fish has denied any such criterion in his initial assumptions. Yet the introduction of the criterion of "self-consuming artifacts" in terms of their writers' deliberate use of ambiguous and confusing language stakes a claim for the distinctive nature of the literature he values most. This criterion cannot allow that ordinary language too is used by speakers in order, as it were, to confuse the listeners for a peculiar sort of enlightenment. It follows that Fish must admit, through this criterion, a distinction between ordinary and literary language, that he must recognize the (pragmatic) communicative efficacy of ordinary language.

Yet Fish's perception that this distinction is an arbitrary and unjustifiable one is certainly valuable: "the very act of distinguishing between ordinary and literary language leads to an inadequate account of both." [40] For though literary language carries nuances of meanings which are more complex than those ordinary language can convey, they are not such that they can allow us a distinction of kind between the two. The New Critics, once they have seen the multivalent nature of poetic language, are tempted erroneously to see this nature reside in an intrinsic qualitative value that they claim poetic language to possess in distinction from ordinary language. In denying the distinction altogether, Fish makes the opposite mistake of conflating the two modes of language, which are interdependent and yet contextually different. From a denial, however, of a distinction of kind between ordinary and literary language, one need not deny the discriminations that Fish himself wants to make. He imports his discriminations, for instance, in terms of the "informed reader" who "is sufficiently experienced as a reader to have internalized the properties of literary discourses." But how can Fish introduce the notion either of internalizing "the properties of literary discourses" or of "literary competence" (*Self-Consuming Artifacts*, p. 406) without self-contradiction? Both imply a distinction between literary and nonliterary discourse as well as between literary competence and competence required for other discourses.

Fish's argument that the writers of "self-consuming artifacts" say what they do not mean also needs to be probed further, for it has implications that reveal its entanglements with the New Critical theory that he avowedly rejects. To say that writers say what they do not mean is to say that writers *mean* to say what they do not mean. Yet to assert this is to say no more than that they are often or generally ambiguous in what they say, or more appropriately, that their language is ambiguous. This in turn can mean no more than that not all the meanings that can be construed out of his work can possibly be in the forefront of a writer's mind. However, recognition of potential ambiguity inherent in most literary works finally points to the complex modes of response involved in reading them, and no critic or critical theorist would say that literary works have their meanings explicitly inscribed into them. Yet to say that writers go out of their way in order to say what they do not mean and thus through that circuitous and devious route let the reader experience what they do mean is to construct a theory that is ultimately no more than a theory of ambiguity of language. It cannot explain the historical nature of artistic creativity that makes *Paradise Lost* different from *The Waste Land* and that makes *The Waste Land* and *Ulysses* so similar in their cultural ambience. Nor can it account for either the conventions of reading that make possible the operations that readers perform in reading literary works or the differences in the conventions of reading that make Milton, Eliot, and Joyce so different. Fish's argument that ordinary language is not different from the literary is simply another version of the argument that complexity and unity are not specific to literary works but rather discoverable anywhere else. It is now easy for us to see that Fish simply conflates ordinary and literary language and that his conflation stems from an erroneous concept of literary response, since it cannot help him make, at least in his theory, discriminations in order to deal with the theoretical problems involved in talking about literary competence—for instance, the operations of reading that make literary competence possible and that distinguish the reading of literature from linguistic competence.[41]

Fish's theory is thus entangled with the New Critical theory, without logically allowing for a relation to it. His opposition, however, to the New Critical theory and practice comes from his significant affinity with I. A. Richards and William Empson on the question of literary response. Like Richards and Empson, Fish too emphasizes the logical and grammatical disorder as a means of achieving experiential or psychological complexity. Richards had argued in *Principles of Literary Criticism* that whenever we attend to something there is a margin beyond which our attention does not go, and that there occur things in our experience which are difficult to notice but of which we should be more fully conscious. Richards's idea occurs within a network of his general theory of value, a theory which construes value in terms of the arousal and satisfaction of impulses.[42] Consequently, the theory defeats his most important insight since it leads him away from talking about literary experience to talking about universal structure in terms of the organization of impulses.[43]

Empson, with his greater concern with the act of criticism, states more adequately the point Richards had first suggested: meaning "is grasped in the preconsciousness of the reader by a native effort of the mind."[44] He has here seized on an essentially right conception of the complexities of response that one often experiences in reading a poem:

> The conservative attitude to ambiguity is curious and no doubt wise; it allows a structure of associated meanings to be shown in a note, but not to be admitted; the reader is encouraged to swallow the thing by a decent reserve; it is thought best not to let him know that *he is thinking in such a complicated medium*. So it is assumed . . . that Shakespeare can only have meant one thing, but that the reader must hold in mind a variety of things he may have meant, and weigh them, in appreciating the poetry, according to their probabilities. . . . Very likely the editors do not seriously believe their assumption; indeed I have myself usually said "either . . . or" when meaning "both . . . and."[45]

This too is Fish's theory of reading, one that insists that the reader is always and necessarily thinking in such complicated terms. Thus he says, "What happens to one reader will happen, within a range of non-essential variation, to another."[46] Fish nevertheless is critical of both Richards and Empson because they do not propose "a sequential reading of the poem" or analyze "the developing responses of the reader as they succeed one another in time" (*Self-Consuming Artifacts*, p. 417). We should note, however, that Empson also holds a theory of taste or common sense with which he considers his theory of reading to be consistent. This theory enables him to reject specific interpretations as implausible or downright wrong.[47] For Fish, on the other hand, the interpretations he does not accept are not so much wrong or implausible as inadequate. These interpretations, too, are part of what happens in the reader's mind. He therefore says, "In an experiential analysis, the sharp distinction between sense and non-sense, with the attendant value-judgments and the talk about truth content, is blurred, because the place where sense is made or not made is the reader's mind rather than the printed page or the space between the covers of a book" (*Self-Consuming Artifacts*, p. 397). This is a clear rejection of the New Critical concept of poems as organic entities. That the New Criticism does at times construe the organic analogy on the model of physical objects is undeniable. Fish, however, goes to the other extreme of conceiving poems in a pre-Wittgensteinian[48] fashion and thus embraces an epistemology that is at once naive and radically confused. This is a point I shall develop a little later.

Consider, first, some consequences of Fish's theory of the experience of reading. If this theory is right, why should one study more than one poem, novel, or play, except to "prove" the theory again and again? Even the question of proving it does not really arise, since he has already assumed the truth of it. Even if Fish were to soften a little and allow different genres certain perlocutionary force, as he does by introducing his notion of the informed reader, one would have to be content with just one tragedy, one comedy, one satire, one epic, and so on. The intrinsic elements of the experience of any one of them would still not in any serious respects differ, if he were to be faithful to his theory, from one work to another. The whole vocabulary of criticism, whether New Critical, neoclassical, phenomenological, or Aristotelian, would be rendered useless. The notion of growth in the lifetime of a literary productivity, formal and other difficulties a literary writer faces and attempts to solve during his creative endeavors, would have no meaning, since all that a writer can do is to employ language in a manner that would evoke the patterns of responses that Fish has articulated for us. If critics were to adopt Fish's strategy, a strategy of stimulus-response to smaller units of words slowly and painfully emerging into what he calls the developing responses of the reader, the reader's experience of any narrative would be reduced to the simple categories of fulfillment and thwarting of his expectations. The real complexities of the narrative would be dissolved, and the characters in a dramatic poem or novel reduced to the fluctuations in the mind of the reader.

Fish's error, I think, is the error that he inherited from the Ricardian theory of reading. Richards had argued that thought or reference in poems is just a dispensable means and not central to the experience of reading poems.[49] Though he rejects Richards's rejection of meaning, Fish redefines the notion of meaning so that he would seem to be in agreement with the Ricardian and New Critical rejection of meaning as abstractable proposition from a poem. Fish, however, goes further in an attempt to show a radical fusion of form and meaning in the reader's experience and argues that meaning is the effects one experiences in reading a poem. He is certainly right in saying that meaning is the experience we have of a literary work, but goes to the extreme when he insists that he has thereby dissolved the concept of meaning altogether or reduced it to the concept of effects. For even complex experiences imply statements that can in principle be true or false, and critical disagreements arise at least partly because one critic thinks that some critics have failed to properly experience specific works and therefore misinterpreted them. From an experience of reading a literary work there emerge certain general symbolic patterns of meanings, conceived not as abstract formulas but rather as experiential meanings, which make the experience of romantic literature different from that of neoclassical literature, and both different from the experience of contemporary literature. It is the complexity of differences and similarities underlying these different experiences that makes any explicit vocabulary of evaluation arbitrary and rigid. It also makes the problem of evaluation harder to articulate when one does not erroneously consider it as simply dissolved or useless.

Fish's theory of reading entails radical skepticism, though it is not apparent in many of his trenchant formulations. For instance, he claims to show that poems dissolve or disappear into the developing responses of their readers. He does this in order to oppose the New Critical theory that he believes makes things out of poems and confers on them an objective ontological status which they do not possess. "The objectivity of the text is an illusion, and moreover, a dangerous illusion, because it is so physically convincing. The illusion is one of complete self-sufficiency" (*Self-Consuming Artifacts*, p. 400). His criticism *seems* to be valid since it attempts to discriminate between poems and physical objects. On close examination, however, it turns out that no such discrimination is possible, for if readers are constantly executing interpretive strategies on the world including poems, then what counts is the incessant cognitive process taking place in their minds.

Thus the utterance "There is a chair" derives its interest, argues Fish, from "the *sub rosa* message it puts out by *virtue of* its easy comprehensibility." "Because it gives information directly and simply," he continues,

> it asserts (silently, but effectively) the "givability," directly and simply, of information, and it is thus an extention of the ordering operation we perform on experience whenever it is filtered through our tem-

poral-spatial consciousness. In short, it *makes* sense, in exctly the way we make (i.e., manufacture) sense of whatever, if anything, exists outside us; and by making easy sense it tells us that sense can be easily made and that we are capable of easily making it. A whole document consisting of such utterances—a chemistry text or a telephone book—will be telling us that all the time; and *that*, rather than any reportable "content" will be its *meaning*. Such language can be called "ordinary" only because it confirms and reflects our ordinary understanding of the world and our position in it; but for precisely that reason it is *extra*ordinary (unless we accept a naive epistemology which grants us unmediated access to reality) and to leave it unanalyzed is to risk missing much of what happens—to us and through us—when we read and (or so we think) understand. [*Self-Consuming Artifacts*, p. 390]

On this view, we make sense of things through an ordering operation we perform on experience, though we cannot be sure whether anything exists outside us. Our skepticism with regard to the existence of things is no obstacle to the ease with which we understand experience. The utterance "there is a chair," then, not only makes easy sense, but also "tells us that sense can be easily made and that we are capable of easily making it." The meaning of the utterance is the epistemology of sense-making constantly performed by our consciousness, and ordinary objects such as a chair and a telephone directory constantly illustrate the epistemology fundamental to human experience. Now, it is not clear why Fish should want to distinguish this position from a naive epistemology, except that no one wants to embrace the latter position. By arguing that minds and objects are joined in an unproblematic cognitive process, Fish hopes to overcome skepticism. Yet the naive epistemology he embraces does not eliminate skepticism but rather cohabits with it. For to argue that a telephone directory asserts the "'givability' of information" and therefore illustrates our procedures of sense-making is to mystify communication by construing it in terms of some peculiar cognitive process of understanding. Indeed, the concept of communication is construed in a manner that entails a denial of any possibility of dialogue or conflict with others. If Fish were to adhere to his theory of reading, he could not legitimately claim to construe the propositional content of any theory. Nor could he legitimately challenge or propose another theory. But he does both. He therefore cannot consistently hold his theory.

In his recent essays Fish has attempted to overcome skepticism in his position and to refine his concept of interpretation. The refinement occurs in an explicit characterization of "interpretive communities." An interpreter, on this view, does not just read texts, but rather constitutes them. Consequently, one's agreement with another reader depends on sharing interpretive strategies that constitute a text. As Fish argues, "these strategies exist prior to the act of reading and therefore determine the shape of what is read rather than, as is usually assumed, the other way around." Now, it is true that the differences in conceptual categories make possible the differences in the text readers constitute through their readings. Nevertheless, the idea that interpretive stategies "exist prior to the act of reading" is not without some difficulties. For Fish the strategies are absolute determinants of one's reading: "I say what my interpretive principles allowed me or directed me to see, and then I turned around and attributed what I had 'seen' to a text and an intention." Verbal texts, it is true, have only experiential identity, and our experiential construals of texts entail a construal of intention. But Fish means something more radical than this. For him every response is a matter of executing interpretive strategies, and it is always a replay of one's expectations. He therefore argues that if he reads *Lycidas* and *The Waste Land* differently—he of course states he does not—it is because his "predisposition to execute different interpretive strategies will *produce* different formal structures." The logic of the argument here is that "it has always been possible to put into action interpretive strategies designed to make all texts one, or to put it more accurately to be forever making the same text."[50]

The consequences of this position are interesting. Perhaps the most important consequence is that he will have to abandon his criticism of Richards, Empson, the New Critics, and others. The only criticism he could retain against some of them is for their insistence on objectivity, on search for determinate meanings. At the level of practical criticism, Fish could either accept others' interpretive strategies and therefore their responses or, holding different responses, he could simply ignore them. In his practical criticism, however, Fish even now insists that one or another critic's response is limited or reductive because he has failed to achieve an experiential reading of a text.[51] But to fault someone is to say that an interpretive strategy is either inadequate or confused. Neither alternative is available to Fish,

since for him interpretation depends on one's predisposition to execute one or another strategy. This concept of interpretation does not
just rule out the possibility of a mistake; the concept of mistake has
simply no place in it. The logic of this position leads to a hermeneutic
nihilism, so that it is not just that everyone is constantly interpreting
but rather that, given the self-authenticating nature of each interpretative strategy, everyone is right.

The conceptual confusion underlying Fish's theory, then, springs
from a radically simplistic and theoretically impoverished concept of
criticism, and this concept is a direct consequence of an unexamined
and confused concept of interpretation that Fish holds. Take, for instance, the statements he makes about the concept of interpretation:
"A sentence is never not in a context. We are never not in a situation.
A set of interpretive assumptions is always in force." [52] The interpretive assumptions are here given such an absolute a priori force that
the concept of interpretation is emptied of its complexity. The consequence of Fish's theory here is not simply the unavailability of the
concept of mistake, but also a dismissal of the very idea of serious
effort involved in reading. If interpretive assumptions are insuperably
and everywhere operating in the way Fish describes, how could one
be said to recognize obstacles that one experiences in the process of
an intelligent and sensitive reading of a literary work? How could one
ever claim to read differently from the way one used to read before?
How could one ever claim to experience that one's assumptions have
become modified, enriched, or that one has come to experience a fundamental loosening of the assumptions one formerly held? On Fish's
view one is a prisoner of one's interpretive strategy, which one can
escape only by getting caught in another. No wonder he makes texts
disappear, for theoretically he has already denied the concept of the
text itself. "If intention, form, and the shape of the reader's experience are simply different ways of referring to (different perspectives
on) the same interpretive act, what is that act an interpretation *of*? I
cannot answer that question, but neither, I would claim, can anyone
else." [53] Fish thus conceives both his claims to be infallible; he has already defined the concept of interpretation, one which resolutely ex-
cludes any dialogue or conflict. If there is a dialogue it must be for
him a form of agreement, and if there is a conflict it cannot be genuine
because it must be the result of different strategies.

It is not surprising that, despite his goal of promoting humanism and despite his intention to characterize interpretation as a fundamentally human act, Fish only succeeds in privileging arbitrariness in interpretation, and even the arbitrariness thus privileged is curiously limited, since it insists only on the endless movement of contradictory responses at rather simplistic semantic and syntactic levels. If he had intended simply to reject the concept of the text construed as identical with the concept of physical objects, it would make some sense. For the act of reading involves a complex interaction between reader and text such that one's own strategies do not just articulate the possibilities implicit in their logical nature. The text exerts pressure, though not in terms of its presumed determinate meanings, but in relation to the expectation of meanings we bring to it. Consequently—and here I am following Gadamer—if the experience of a reading contains a negative component, it is because of man's finite, historical rootedness. Given the finitude of man's being, some of our expectations undergo modification and are revealed as false prejudices.[54] Fish, however, cannot accept this possibility as an important condition of the concept of interpretation because he has already assumed every expression and every response to be caught in a specific set of assumptions.

Fish's position thus entails a simple and unexamined version of skepticism, and it defeats the very purpose of formulating and defending a critical theory. Fish, however, professes to offer his theory in the spirit of genuine humanism. Now, no one need deny that the insistence of recent reader-response criticism to bridge the gulf between criticism conceived as a detached contemplative act and criticism conceived as an intense, participatory act of reading is of considerable value. Its seeming democratic liberalism, that all readers of literature bring their own assumptions to bear on their reading and are inherently correct in their responses, promotes critical thoughtlessness and complacency that are dangerous to the vitality of critical discourse. This is of course a deep logical implication of the concept of reader-response conceived in the manner Fish does. For if all of us are prisoners of our assumptions and all of us inevitably experience the implications of those assumptions in reading, then neither the concept of education nor the concept of cultivation of sensibility has any meaning. And reading becomes indistinguishable from hallucination. The act of reading, however, need not be conceived in such self-defeating terms. Considered at some level of semiotic or literary competence, the act of reading already suggests that all sophisticated interpretations, whether they claim to be contemplative or participatory, are in principle experiential readings. Otherwise, an insistence on the experiential nature of one's own reading, a programmatic feature of a great deal of reader-response criticism, has the questionable implication that some of the most exemplary instances of criticism—by Erich Auerbach, R. P. Blackmur, Theodor Adorno, Walter Benjamin, and Lionel Trilling, to mention only a few—are, because of their reflective detachment, poor in comparison with the experiential readings of reader-response critics. Nevertheless, the concept of criticism is an institutional concept, and allows for a variety of interpretive strategies, some of which are in conflict with others. Reader-response criticism is therefore bound to make a competing claim. Yet it is not simply the internal difficulties of Fish's theory that disqualify it as a genuinely competing concept. Its misconstrual of the concept of interpretation radically limits and defines the concept of criticism he holds. Consequently, his practical criticism, to the extent that it is controlled by his concept of interpretation, becomes vitiated. There is, I believe, no other explanation for the sameness of surprises repetitively experienced by Fish in his readings of literature. If Fish's theory is seriously confused, it is because his concept of interpretation misconstrues the relationship between a priori insights and verbal texts or the world. This confusion, I have argued, operates at various levels throughout his theoretical endeavor.

Affective Response and Criticism

It is clear that psychoanalytic critics tend to construe literary criticism as a subfield of psychoanalysis, just as some linguists want to construe it as a subfield of linguistics. It is also clear that both Holland and Fish claim that criticism, when it is functioning properly, is, first of all, a description of psychological response—of ambivalences, uncertainties, expectations—and not simply various descriptions and interpretations for which psychological response is one among numerous other things. Now if criticism did just this, if it focused primarily on response, on all that the reader goes through in responding to literary works, it would indeed seem to be just a part of psychology or psychoanalysis. Remember, however, that neither Holland nor Fish is saying that the reader is capable of responding to literature in such and such manner; each is rather explaining how the reader *does* do this, and each is claiming to illuminate what the reader *is* doing. This may indeed be the source of redundancy in Holland's critical interpretations, a redundancy that springs from his commitment to trace responses to their motivating fantasies and defenses, of repetitive moves in Fish's method that cannot allow his reader to learn from experience.

Both conceptions founder on their empiricist dogmas, since given these they cannot validly claim to have provided a satisfactory explanation of the nature of literary response. For even if we ignore other accounts of the nature of literary response, there are at least two rival, presumably empirical, accounts. But both cannot be empirically valid for them individually and for all who read literature; they must involve other considerations. These considerations, however, whether in the form of the concept of identity or in that of the concept of "interpretive communities," do not really affect the underlying logic of either theory. Consequently, the dogma that "this is what happens in the reader's mind when he reads a poem or a page" is a confused one. This dogma must be radically recast in order to understand that the concept of criticism is a complex concept and reveals its features in the practice of criticism through the peculiar interaction between the empirical and the conceptual.

We need to recognize, I should add here, that the experience of literature involves complicated patterns of involvement and detachment. If the experience of involvement were to be the only criterion of literary response, we would not be able to distinguish art from sermons, propaganda, or the simple joy and pain of daily life. For one who construes the concept of reading in an atomistic fashion, this dissolution of distinctions is no problem. Yet that is only an arbitrary stand. What is dissolved is not the problem, but one's knowledge that in actual practice we do make discriminations, that without our capacity for making distinctions, even if they are not unquestionable, we cannot claim to possess the concept of interpretation or the concept of culture, both of which are interdependent. Nevertheless, reader-response criticism has led to a resurgence of interest in grasping and characterizing the complexity of literary experience. Its contribution here, though it is theoretically often misguided, is important because no theory of criticism that refuses a peculiar efficacy of literary experience can throw significant light on literature.

PART TWO

Logic, Rhetoric, and Value in Critical Theory

*Compare a concept with a style of painting. For is
even our style of painting arbitrary? (The Egyptian,
for instance.) Is it a mere question of pleasing
and ugly?*

Wittgenstein

*Concepts lead us to make investigations, are the
expression of our interest, and direct our interest.*

Wittgenstein

CHAPTER SIX

Criticism, Critical Theory, and Rationality

The preceding chapters have examined a number of aesthetic and literary theories. Some of the results of that analysis can now be stated here. Kant and the philosophical idealists attempted to give a comprehensive philosophical defense of the autonomy of art and aesthetic experience. Yet their aesthetic theories are not simply closely intertwined with their philosophical systems, but hampered because of specific philosophical compulsions to subordinate art to their central theoretical preoccupations. Croce and Bosanquet, of course, sought to establish the significance of art on its own terms, and Hegel's aesthetics, however integral to his philosophical system, sought to examine both the relation of art to the history of culture and the place of art in the life of modern man. Kant's formalism, too, however austere its logical structure, sought to characterize the complexity and singularity of the nature of aesthetic judgments. Nevertheless, to the extent that their aesthetic theories remain implicated in the logical necessity of their specific philosophical systems, they fail to provide a philosophy of criticism.

A number of critics and artists, early in this century, attempted to make a sustained defense of the autonomist position. Eliot and the New Critics defended and rearticulated the autonomist position partly in reaction to the dominance of romanticism and impressionism in early and late nineteenth-century art and criticism, and partly in reaction to the erosion of religious belief and the increase in prestige of science and logical positivism. Thus, while their formulations do have certain metaphysical implications, for the most part they work within a recognizable literary context. This is most clearly put in the concluding statement of Eliot's well-known essay, "Tradition and the Individual Talent": "This essay proposes to halt at the frontier of metaphysics or mysticism, and confine itself to such practical conclusions as can be applied by the responsible person interested in poetry."[1] Eliot and the New Critics thus advocate a return to objectivity, a kind of "revival of neoclassical principles," though in "a different context and with an altered meaning."[2]

The doctrine of heresy of paraphrase is certainly the best critical recharacterization of the idealist intuition into the nature of art. Brooks does not mean to deny the importance of meaning to our experience of poems, but rather claims for poems a complexity that an excessive concern with paraphrasable meaning cannot comprehend. Yet the New Critical theories derive what power they have from the practice of criticism. But that fact does not make their theories immune to serious logical criticism. Nor need our knowledge that the New Critical theories were devised in a polemical cultural context and were the consequences of a pragmatic insistence on the need to read poems with special attentiveness exempt them from a serious theoretical scrutiny. The New Critics, for instance, distinguish between ordinary and poetic language, but they propose the distinction as a logical or conceptual opposition. And they set up further oppositions between literature and science, literature and history, literature and all other modes of human discourse. The argument I have made is that the endeavor to make discriminations between art and science, art and history, art and philosophy is certainly legitimate, and that without grasping the differences among the different realms of human endeavor one cannot claim significance for the concept of poetic autonomy. The New Critics, however, are in the grip of a compulsion (induced perhaps by the condition of art in modern culture) and are driven to offer their distinctions in terms of polemical oppositions between art and the other realms of human endeavor. Consequently, though the New Critics wish to propose sophisticated qualifications to their theories, their various distinctions conceived as oppositions vitiate many of their theories. The oppositions that they propose are false oppositions derived from their desire to establish the intrinsic superiority of art to non-art, of aesthetic experience to ordinary experience.

We saw the difficulties that arise when some theorists attempt to establish their concepts of art and criticism by seeking to derive them logically from a supposedly indubitable theory of artistic creativity. We also saw that the attempt to fix the logic of criticism by designating certain critical modes as logically fallacious is itself the result of a partisan view of criticism. And we analyzed several theories that purported to explain and define the nature of aesthetic experience or literary response. Detachment, we observed, is an important condition of aesthetic experience. Yet our analysis showed the experience of literature to be a complicated pattern of detachment and involvement; neither emphasis by itself gives a satisfactory account of the complexity that underlies that experience. Emphasis on detachment can lead to a rigid conception of objectivity in criticism; emphasis on involvement can lead to the vagaries of impressionistic and subjective response in criticism. Both emphases misdescribe the concept of aesthetic response.

Moreover, we saw that theories of affective response that depend exclusively on psychology simplify the real complexities of literary experience. Theories of affective response that insist on the temporal nature of reading do of course reorient criticism toward a greater awareness of the nature of literary response. But by construing literary texts as entirely mind-dependent they fail to see that literary experience involves, as Gadamer said, a complex interaction in which both the subjectivity of the reader and the objectivity of the text are transcended. Underlying all of this is an argument that the concept of criticism is an essentially contested concept that allows for a variety of conflicting construals.

The last assumption needs to be fully articulated and defended by an account of the logic of inquiry in criticism and critical theory. In what follows I attempt to give such an account by examining several theoretical positions on the logic of inquiry in criticism. While it is true that to argue whether criticism is a science is hardly a useful enterprise, it is, nevertheless, important to inquire whether and to what extent criticism is amenable to systematic discipline and progress. Moreover, if the first question is construed as essentially the same as the second, then there is nothing really useless or irrelevant about asking that question. It will be important, then, to see how successful endeavors to propose a science of criticism have been and what difficulties they have to overcome. I shall, then, attempt a consideration of both the nature of objectivity in literary interpretation and the nature of disputes in criticism. These issues will require a further discussion of the nature of critical understanding and its relation to tradition. The section following these discussions will briefly summarize them in a characterization of the concept of criticism. Finally, all of these considerations will lead us to discuss the most important question of articulating the logic of inquiry in criticism.

Criticism as Science: Richards and Frye

THE WORK of I. A. Richards early in this century gave a full and systematic expression to the efforts to put criticism on scientific grounds. For Richards, the psychological naturalist, the most important question of criticism in the age of science is, What is the place of art in the total scheme of human endeavors?[3] He answers it with two propositions which are fundamental to his own critical efforts: first, art has instrumental value for human beings or it is a means to intrinsic value, but it is not intrinsic value in itself; and second, though art is a means, it is an indispensable means, because what art can do nothing else can do. Richards's burden, then, as a theorist of criticism who must make criticism amenable to systematic and rational inquiry, is fourfold: to establish this value of art; given his initial assumption, to provide a general theory of value as well as of moral value; to prove his theory of value as a valid theory; and finally, since he is founding a science of criticism by attempting to articulate principles of criticism, to prove that his theory of value has application to criticism, that it can help us appreciate and judge literary works.

In order to prove his theory Richards began by mounting an attack on the state of critical theories, especially the idealist aesthetics of Croce, Bosanquet, and A. C. Bradley.[4] The idealist doctrine that he attempts directly to refute is Bradley's theory of art. Bradley's theory consists of four central theses: poetic experience has intrinsic value, the value of poetic experience must be judged from within, consideration of extrapoetic ends reduces the value of a poem as a poem, and finally, the world of poetry is autonomous and self-contained. Richards's refutation consists, briefly, in his counterproposals that art-experience is not different in kind from other experiences, that art has direct bearing on our emotional and psychic attitudes, and that the considerations rejected by the idealists as extraaesthetic are indeed part of aesthetic criteria. He would readily admit that considerations of end might ruin some poems, but he would insist that that is not true of all poems. Richards, however, is not in favor of propaganda or didacticism in art, for he shrewdly argues that whatever morality wants to achieve is achieved by art.[5]

If we accept, Richards argues, that the experience of life is the stuff out of which poetry is made, we will recognize that impulses and desires are satisfied by a work of art. He therefore contends that idealists made the mistake of putting the different aspects of man into different compartments and therefore failed to understand the substantive unity of the self. For, as he argues further, our reactions to things are reactions of a total personality. Thus to judge a poem is for Richards to place it in the context of total human endeavors, and to judge the value of a poem is also to judge its moral value. Hence Richards's insistence that what is needed is a general theory of value which would be applicable to both art and morality. "If a well-grounded theory of value is a necessity for criticism, it is no less true that an understanding of what happens in the arts is needed for the theory. The two problems 'What is good?' and 'What are the arts?' reflect light upon one another."[6]

Richards proposes such a theory of value to function as a cultural lever, to raise the cultural level of people in general, to make their sensibilities richer and more refined. He also hopes that such a theory would abolish the element of arbitrariness from discussions of literature and provide critics with means to conduct their inquiries rationally. Without putting it explicitly, Richards conceives such a theory to be a quantitative one, for he *seems* to admit that though qualitative differences can never be compared, they can be reduced to quantitative measures in order to facilitate a proper inquiry into them. Such a theory, moreover, must be psychological, since a general theory of value that claims to be applicable to literary criticism entails things concerned with our own experiences, tonal values, emotional attitudes, feelings.

Richards's theory of value is a psychological one and is derived from his theory of mind. The mind, according to Richards, is driven to seek satisfaction of impulses. He tries to develop this notion into a calculus of satisfaction, a calculus for which the greater the number of important and conflicting impulses harmonized, the deeper the satisfaction experienced by the mind. In effect the condition of value lies in a wealth of important and conflicting impulses balanced and harmonized, consistent with the frustration of the fewer impulses. Thus for Richards, "anything is valuable which will satisfy an appetancy without involving the frustration of some equal or *more important* appetancy." He defines the word *important* in a consistently psychological sense: "The importance of an impulse . . . can be defined for our purposes as the extent of the disturbance of other impulses in the individual's activities which the thwarting of the impulses involves."[7] Convinced that "that organization which is least wasteful of human possibilities . . . is best," Richards wants to avoid the extremes of interest and fulfillment that tend to be either too broad because they stem from disorder or too narrow because they stem from order. Poetry, Richards suggests, makes possible both the avoidance of such extremes and the realization of a complex organization of impulses.[8]

For Richards what is intrinsically valuable is synaesthetic experience, not the objects which induce it; the objects merely possess an instrumental value which is dependent on the intrinsic. Unless an object has become an object in experience it has no value, not even instrumental value, for only when it is realized by a human mind capable of experiencing it can it possess even that value. Richards argues, moreover, that synaesthetic experiences are in principle made possible by all kinds of objects and that the distinction between art and non-art ordinarily made in order to define the value of art over non-art is ill conceived.

Like all empirical investigators, Richards focuses on certain elements of the experience of reading poetry. Since he has already conceived this experience to be synaesthetic through a reordering of numerous impulses in the mind, it is necessarily an experience of feelings. Insofar as it is emotional it is necessarily constituted by neural sensations. It is therefore extremely difficult, Richards would seem to suggest, to articulate and explain such an experience in critical analysis. Thus he says: "A feeling even more than an idea or an image tends to vanish as we turn our introspective attention upon it. We have to catch it by the tip of its tail as it decamps. Furthermore, even when we are partially successful in catching it, we do not know how to analyse it. Analysis is a matter of separating out its attributes and no one knows yet what attributes a feeling may have, what their system of interconnection is, or which are important, which trivial."[9] Richards has therefore ended by equating the experience of reading poetry with those quickly vanishing feelings or sensations. If the mind achieves a balancing of impulses because of the experience of reading a poem, then it is an experience of value and the poem is good. If not, then either the poem is not good, or just as likely, the reader does not know how to read the poem and is consequently incapable of experiencing synaesthetics through poetry.

Because of his psychological theory of value, however, Richards is forced to draw wrong conclusions. In order to prove his theory, he has to misrepresent the fact that when one is talking about poetry one does not talk about impulses but rather about what arouses impulses. Besides, his theory of value as the organization of impulses can account only for one kind of experience of art, the art that we may characterize, following Nietzsche, as the Apollonian, the art that leads to the experience of balance, harmony, tranquility. It cannot account for the Dionysiac art, and at least some of our great literature leaves us profoundly disturbed and unsettled. It is ironic that Richards, who has made a very important contribution to a recognition of the emotional significance of literature and who opposed the idealist doctrine of aesthetic experience as an experience of detached contemplation, should arrive at the idealist conclusion about the detachment of aesthetic experience. Yet the modes in which this insight is achieved by the idealists and by Richards differ.[10] What was for the idealists a condition of the possibility of aesthetic experience has become for Richards the consequence, though with the causal apparatus of scientific inquiry Richards's conclusion is inevitable.

Convinced that the experience of poetry is an experience of arousal and organization of impulses, Richards also rejects the entire Aristotelian tradition of poetic theory, according to which a component of truth is necessarily present in poetic experience. It is Richards's contention that the organization we experience in reading poetry is alogical, not logical or illogical, and that statements in poetry are part of a structure of emotional attitudes and therefore acceptable even if they are false. On this view, when we accept falsity or empirical impossibility when reading poetry, we are not concerned with probability or necessity but with what goes on in our experience, and such an attitude does not have anything to do with verification. Richards thus does not just say, as Plato does, that poetry does not give knowledge; he asks whether poetry can give us knowledge. And this question involves a radical anti-Aristotelian step, since Richards maintains (with the logical positivists) that it is impossible that poetry should ever give us knowledge. He argues that poetry makes pseudostatements, not cognitively verifiable statements, that the language of poetry is emotive, not referential. He has thus joined his rejection of idealist aesthetics with a rejection of the Aristotelian tradition of poetic theory. According to the tradition that follows Aristotle, poetry gives an insight into the nature of truth, into the nature of man's experience in general. For Richards, on the other hand, such a claim could be made only if the poet did the scientist's work. But the poet, on his view, is concerned only with expressing and arousing attitudes rather than describing them, whereas it is the scientist's function to describe. Richards would therefore accept the Crocean proposition that poetry is the product of expression. Moreover, science cannot provide a foundation of values, for which we must turn to religion and ethics; when these fail us, we must turn to poetry, which makes men morally better.[11] Richards has thus construed the value of aesthetic experience within the framework of moral experiences. In other words, Richards, the naturalist, has subsumed aesthetic experience under the concept of moral experiences, and criticism under ethics, a subsumption which is not without some serious difficulties.

Richards's critics have pointed out the shortcomings of his theory as an ethical theory. First, granted that his theory is essentially liberal, it nevertheless suffers from being an egoistic theory, an account which would reduce obligations and duties to satisfaction of impulses. Second, the attitude of an ethical agent is one of involvement, whereas even if the aesthetic agent is not altogether detached, detachment frequently remains a crucial condition of the aesthetic experience. And finally, nobody would be criticized for acting in terms of a respectable moral code, but if someone should send a Shakespearean sonnet for publication under his own name, it would be taken for an act of plagiarism. Thus there is a sense in which aesthetic acts are unique and unrepeatable. There would be no point, however, in the concept of morality if good actions could not be repeated. It would then seem to me that the problem of relation between art and morality is not a pseudoproblem generated by professional critics and theorists; as Plato and Aristotle realized, whether or not we accept their specific answers, it is a genuine problem. A satisfactory answer ought to involve considerations that will not deny the complexity and singularity of art-experience even if the theory of value is to be conceived in generic terms. Richards has not succeeded in reducing art to morality, nor has he succeeded in resolving either concept in terms of scientific inquiry. Yet his importance for criticism and critical theory lies in his reorientation of both to examine closely the experience of reading poetry. And without collapsing the distinction between scientific and literary inquiry we can accept his conviction that that experience is one of value.

ANOTHER MAJOR ATTEMPT to construct a science of criticism has been made by Northrop Frye, primarily in his epoch-making *Anatomy of Criticism*. This time we have a theorist and critic who is not a scientist and who wants to defend the autonomy of criticism and to put it on a basis of neutral, objective inquiry. It is paradoxical in relation not only to Richards, a nonautonomist in criticism, but to most of the autonomists in critical theory that Frye rejects value-judgments from all genuine criticism.[12] In doing this he is taking a genuinely objectivist attitude in that for him literature, like other verbal creations, is a repository of values, but not such that it can stake out a claim for its distinctiveness on the ground of values alone. Take, for instance, his essay "On Value-Judgments" where he rejects the question of value-judgments in these words: "To interpret Dickens is first of all to accept Dickens's own terms as the condition of the study: to evaluate Dickens is to set up our own terms, producing a hideous caricature of Dickens which soon becomes a most revealing caricature of ourselves, and of the anxieties of the sixties."[13] Frye is thus opposed to the forming of definitions with built-in criteria of value, since a great deal of critical theory as well as practice tends to locate criteria of value in a part of the whole and then substitutes that part for the whole. "If criticism exists," Frye avers, "it must be an examination of literature in terms of a conceptual framework derivable from an inductive survey of the literary field."[14]

In order to establish criticism as a science, Frye finds it necessary to treat each literary work as a datum, for, like Kuhn's preparadigm, primitive state of science, the state of criticism too has been one of "naive induction" long since Aristotle first attempted to organize it in the *Poetics*. Indeed, "the absence of systematic criticism," he argues, "has created a power vacuum and all the neighboring disciplines have moved in." To overcome this inchoate and confused state Frye seeks for criticism a "co-ordinating principle, a central hypothesis which, like the theory of evolution in biology, will see the phenomena it deals with as parts of a whole." Thus, like the scientist and the historian of science, the critic and historian of literature must make, in Frye's words, "an assumption of total coherence," for literature belongs to the "order of words" just as the data of the physical sciences belong to the "order of nature." He can thus say: "Everyone who has seriously studied literature knows the mental process involved is as coherent and progressive as the study of science. A precisely similar training of the mind takes place, and a similar sense of the unity of the subject is built up." Conceived in this way, literary works become clinical objects permitting scientific detachment and observation to the critic, and the critic becomes a spectator of the revolving galaxies of the literary universe. And "criticism has an end in the structure of literature as a total form, as well as a beginning in the text studied." [15]

By considering literature itself as the ultimate ground of authority, Frye attempts to mitigate our feeling that all criticism can do is discover the structural elements he has classified and named. It is because on his view literature is the final source of authority and power that Frye contends that criticism fails to function properly when it indulges in value-judgments. Yet his objectivity does not prevent him from exploiting his intuitive resources for profound literary speculation. Indeed, his first principle somehow leads him to his important insight that literature is made out of earlier literature. Frye seems here to be proposing a radical relational definition of literature by means of a sophisticated reconceptualization of the traditional theory of modes and genres. For instance, by conceiving the history of literature in spatial terms, Frye can easily assume a clinical distance that would allow him to develop further categories in which to fix his observanda. This theory of literature and its history might be considered as an application of Aristotle's theory of probability which would allow him not only to perceive patterns but to establish relationships among them and to make prediction possible. One might argue that from his overall context of patterns the artist seems overdetermined, that he is left out as a presence.[16] And coming from the great Blakean that Frye is, this overdetermination would seem to be opposed to the revisionist ardor of the master, for though Frye recognizes Blake's revisionist drive, he would seem, as it were, to betray the master by making his optimism a handmaiden in the service of scientific detachment. Yet even in his book on Blake, *Fearful Symmetry*, he had implicitly made the assumption of total coherence in the order of literature. He had said there: "The quality of art never improves. But it may increase in conscious awareness of the implications of vision as the work of a growing body of predecessors accumulates and is, however haphazardly, preserved. Milton is not a better poet than Sophócles because he follows him in time, but his ability to use Sophocles may have given him a more explicit understanding of what his own imagination saw." [17] But it seems to me that Frye's conception of objectivity is itself constituted by his mode of apprehending the literary field; this, however, is a point that calls for some explanation.

Frye's assumption of the order of literature as analogous to the order of nature has prevented him from recognizing that the very constitution of his field is essentially a poetic act, a genuine making or invention of a domain of inquiry. For, though he would like to treat literature as an objective, autonomous body of knowledge, his genres and modes, despite their schematic nature, are derived from corresponding conceptions of reality. Indeed, the theory of history on which he founds his theory of genres is itself a metahistorical conception which, by definition, is not susceptible to proofs of validity and therefore of so-called objective knowledge. This metahistorical conception is a matter of the insight he has acquired into the nature of literature and thus is at bottom involved with the problem of values. Moreover, underlying his notions of modes and genres is a concept of literary history which, as Angus Fletcher has said, his critics do not seem to have grasped. [18] It is a concept of literary change or transformation brought about in the modes of literary creativity, a concept which makes his genres historical and changing, not immutable objective structures.

The discussion above is intended to suggest that, despite his rejection of value-judgments, Frye is finally not able to avoid an intrusion of values in his criticism. It is indeed because of his specific mode of conceiving modes and genres that Frye, more than any other writer, has recovered for us the significance of romance tradition for literature. [19] This contribution is on Frye's part a perception of value which is not reducible to objectively available facts. Yet because of his failure to reflect on the nature of value-concepts built into his theory of criticism, values become for Frye the values that determine the modes and genres he has articulated in the *Anatomy*. Consequently, when one rejects Frye's theory one rejects it on the ground that, despite its valuational core, his theory conflates values with objective categories for which the knower or the experiencing mind is a mere passive receptacle. His modes and genres can account neither for controversies in criticism nor for generation of meanings in literary response not previously apprehended. For Frye, however, in view of his initial assumption of the total coherence of all literature, these questions are easily solved: if objectivity is the norm, all critical disputes are in principle resolvable by a proper handling of literary evidence which can be brought forward and interpreted by his modes and genres.

THE PRECEDING DISCUSSION shows that, despite their assumed stance of objectivity and neutrality and their assurance about the scientific nature of their inquiries, both Richards and Frye propose for fundamental questions of criticism answers which are radically different. Frye wishes to redefine the relationship of criticism with other disciplines and to establish a sort of harmony between the two in terms of an essential objectivity which he claims ought to inform all inquiries into them.[20] He therefore considers autonomy necessary for achieving such objectivity. Richards, on the other hand, attempts to found a science of criticism on an understanding of values which are noncognitive and which have therefore nothing to do with science or knowledge. Richards, despite his opposition to idealist aesthetics, retains an element of the idealist theory, inasmuch as he insists on the existence of poems in the mind, not in some immutable objective structure. Both critics wish to give art a place of centrality in the endeavors of man. Yet for Frye commentary begins in the text but expands into the whole of literature, thereby involving the mythic archetypes of literature. For Richards poems possess experiential value which is in principle a matter of articulating experience, not of critical exegesis. In their ostensibly scientific endeavors both critics allow, on the question of value and experience, what each seemed initially to oppose. Neither attempt, for all its critical significance, can be said to have established once and for all the logic of inquiry in criticism and critical theory—a situation which calls in doubt the presumed scientific or objective nature of their theories.

Objectivity and Interpretation

IN OUR DISCUSSION of Richards and Frye we noticed considerations of value which govern their theoretical concerns, explicitly in Richards and implicitly in Frye. It would be useful, then, to relate the question of normative considerations to objectivity. Put in simple terms the question is: What does it mean to claim objectivity in criticism, and how does it relate to objectivity in scientific inquiry?

AN ELABORATE AND SOPHISTICATED POSITION for objectively grounded criticism is, I think, distinctively Popperian as it has been articulated and defended by E. D. Hirsch.[21] For Hirsch "the objectivity of interpretation as a discipline depends on our being able to make an objectively grounded choice between two disparate probability judgments on the basis of common evidence which supports them." This *choice* is "compelling only when our probability judgments are sanctioned by objectively defined and generally accepted principles." The critic's responsibility is to know how the various interpretive hypotheses offered stand "with respect to *all* the relevant evidence that has been brought forward." For the "aim of validation . . . is not necessarily to denominate an individual victor, but rather to reach an objective conclusion about relative probabilities." According to this concept of objectively grounded criticism, for which the logic of inquiry is the same as that of science—the testing of hypotheses by means of evidence and logic—"the process of knowledge occurs *on the level of the discipline.*"[22] However, since the evidence already exists waiting for hypotheses adequate to it, Hirsch can go on to posit for the act of interpretation "an analytical dimension which, in contrast to the normative, is logically deductive, empirically deductive, and neutral with respect to values and choices." This dimension enables Hirsch to propose a distinction between meaning and significance. Meaning is for him "a determinate representation of a text for an interpreter," "a principle of stability," whereas significance is "meaning-as-related to something else," embracing "a principle of change."[23]

Why does Hirsch want to say that there is only one single most probable interpretation of the meaning of a poem? He holds a theory of intentionality which, as we saw in Chapter 3, links the poem to its creator, the mind that produced it. He therefore argues that whenever there are two irreconcilable interpretations which "impose different emphases on similar meaning components, at least one of them must be wrong."[24] In proposing this concept of interpretation Hirsch claims to be fighting against relativism, though he does not seem uncomfortable with the relativism implied in his concept, one which involves a historical reconstruction of the meanings intended by the poet. The absolutism underlying his concept is in the principle that asks for a single, most probable interpretation arrived at by a proper mode of criticism, a mode which follows the logic of inquiry common to all intellectual and scientific pursuit. The goal of Hirsch's form of inquiry is the formulation of generalizations with a view to settling disputes about meanings of verbal texts. He conceives these meanings to be in principle neutral, lending themselves to use for developing significance in a number of different ways. As meanings acquired through a scientific weighting of relative probabilities, they are considered to be free from evaluation and judgment.

An important feature of Hirsch's concept of interpretation, I shall now argue, is its dependence on the false assumption that observational categories are independent of theoretical categories. Hirsch, despite his admission that any piece of language is in principle ambiguous, conceives of verbal texts as accessible to observation without the intrusion of valuational elements. It is on this assumption about the logic of inquiry in criticism that Hirsch founds his distinction between meaning and significance. It will be pertinent to ask whether this distinction is warranted, for if we can show that the distinction is not a genuine analytic one, that both are closely interrelated, we can also show that the logic of inquiry underlying that distinction is also questionable for humanistic studies. Hirsch's theory, however, derives its polemical power from pitting itself against Gadamer's hermeneutic theory. But Gadamer's theory, as was suggested earlier, provides a powerful insight into the nature of the human sciences, an insight whose central features can help clarify the question of the nature of literary interpretation.

Like Schleiermacher and other earlier hermeneutic philosophers, Hirsch seeks to bridge the gap between text and interpreter opened by history. In contrast to them, Gadamer reinstates the importance of temporal horizons in the process of understanding texts. "Time is no longer a gulf to be bridged, because it separates, but it is actually the supportive ground of process in which the present is rooted."[25] Moreover, understanding for Gadamer does not involve a method, since it is the mode of being of man's being in the world. Thus if man is rooted historically, how can we ever hope to arrive at a universal logic of inquiry that will define and articulate man's experience? Consequently, those who seek objective, universal knowledge of this experience simply fail to understand man's historically finite situatedness. Given this finitude, man's knowledge is inescapably provisional, and his experience, infinitely open.

For Gadamer "the hermeneutical problem is not one of the correct mastery of language, but of the proper understanding of that which takes place through the medium of language."[26] Such mastery is a precondition for understanding in language; otherwise, one could not even claim to understand a text. Gadamer, we recall, takes the problem of translation as the paradigm from which to develop his analysis of the nature of understanding. There he argued that understanding is inseparably bound up with interpretation, so that the interpreter (or translator) is not an ideally neutral observer with a direct access to the text, but rather brings with him his own horizon of expectations. The interpreter's own horizon seems arbitrary only in relation to the alien nature of the text. It is not arbitrary in the sense that the interpreter can and must rid himself of all preconceptions and prejudgments. To expect that the interpreter be a neutral observer is to expect a logical impossibility, since it demands the idea of an interpreter who does not already possess a language and belong to his cultural context. Gadamer therefore insists that all understanding is inextricably bound up with preconditions and prejudgments.

This bringing of one's own horizon of expectations to bear upon a text is only the beginning of the interpretive process. The process itself, however, is more complex, for it is necessary for the interpreter not to self-consciously impose his own horizon onto the text. It is here that Gadamer's notion of openness to an alien text is fruitful. Because of this openness to the text the interpreter becomes aware, in the process of interpretation, of his own structure of prejudices. Yet the prejudices or fore-structures of meanings which constitute the interpreter's horizon are not at his free disposal. If they were, he could then separate in advance the productive prejudices from the ones that are misleading and false. Rather the separation takes place in the process of understanding itself. When one discovers that some prejudices are false, the discovery is "made from the standpoint of their dissolution and illumination and holds only of unjustified prejudices." But this does not mean that there are no justified prejudices productive of knowledge. In order "to do justice to man's finite, historical mode of being,"[27] Gadamer argues, we must recognize that there are legitimate prejudices.

Gadamer thus calls in question the possibility of the correct interpretation of a text. For if interpretation is necessarily a hermeneutic act which mediates between different life-worlds and brings about a fusion of horizons (*Horizontverschmelzung*), and if interpretation is inevitably caught up in the movement of history, the ideal of a final, valid reading can have no sense. Gadamer's analysis of understanding is a radical one in that it does not explain the hermeneutical circle in terms of the usual description of wholes and parts. Though he agrees that understanding is circular in structure, he denies that it is merely formal in nature. It includes a number of features central to historical understanding. "The circle . . . is not formal in nature, it is neither subjective nor objective, but describes understanding as the interplay of the movement of tradition and the movement of the interpreter." It is the substantive, ontological nature of understanding that makes possible a fusion of horizons. Yet Gadamer insists that since our own horizons are necessarily different from those of the author of a text, no text is completely recoverable. But he does not deny that we should try to understand a text in terms of its own horizonal structure. He merely denies that the attempt can ever achieve a final, valid reading: "The discovery of the true meaning of a text or a work of art is never finished; it is in fact an infinite process." [28]

GADAMER'S HERMENEUTIC THEORY, though working at a high level of theoretical generality and couched in a rather technical vocabulary, can be fruitfully transposed to ordinary critical language. The following discussion does not seek to give a full transposition, but it is at least compatible with Gadamer's theory of interpretation.

A modern reader does not experience certain aspects of Elizabethan drama, specifically its views of good and evil and its superstitions, with the same intensity as an Elizabethan would have. The evil spirits dramatized in an Elizabethan play must have presented a genuine enactment of objective reality in the world for an Elizabethan spectator, whereas for us they represent projections of psychological forces. The terror and mystery we experience in reading Shakespearean tragedy differs from the experience of an Elizabethan insofar as our historical and cultural ambience is different from his. For an Elizabethan the anguish of Dr. Faustus in the face of his eternal damnation had a literal force, whereas for the modern reader it is a metaphorical expression of guilt which is amenable to psychological scrutiny. What intervenes between the two is the difference in conceptual background which inevitably influences the nature of response each has to literature. Thus it is against the Elizabethan world-picture that the rebellion of Satan, the sleepwalking scene of Lady Macbeth, the anguish of Dr. Faustus, the dilemma of Hamlet, the suffering of Lear made particular sense to the contemporaries of Milton and Shakespeare. We can certainly reconstruct the Elizabethan world-picture, as for instance E. M. W. Tillyard has done,[29] but we cannot experience Shakespeare with the same kind of force. On the other hand, our sense of alienation would have been quite foreign to Elizabethan readers, and if they could have understood it, it would inevitably have been interpreted in terms of the conceptual categories of good and evil they possessed for the apprehension of the world in which they lived, not the modern ones that are inextricably bound up with the loss of religious belief in general and the complexities of modern industrial society.

Our understanding of Hamlet's dilemma or Faustus's anguish is an intellectual grasp. We can characterize their experiences and feel their impact on us, but that is not equivalent to saying that we can realize them as the Elizabethans could. This is not to deny either the possibility of imaginative apprehension of literature written at different times or the richness of our experience of it, because that would be absurd. It is not that we are not deeply disturbed on reading *Hamlet* or *Dr. Faustus*, but that the difference in the nature of conceptual categories which inform our life makes for the difference in the experience we have of either play. Moreover, these categories are not so monolithic that all readers at a particular time necessarily share all of them. And this last feature is the one which complicates the scene of modern criticism.

The objectivist assumption, then, that our knowledge of literature increases in some historically continuous, evolutionary terms cannot be justified. A simple example will illustrate this point. A historian of criticism may validly say that Coleridge and Bradley worked within the same critical framework in their discussions of Shakespeare and that Bradley benefited from and advanced beyond Coleridge in his analysis of Shakespeare's characters. But if one says that G. Wilson Knight or Wolfgang Clemen made a significant advance beyond Bradley in the study of Shakespeare, it would be open not merely to doubt; the dispute itself would be unresolvable, except in terms of particular insights and hence a particular mode of response one wants to promote. Coleridge and Bradley tend to study Shakespeare as a great creator of powerful characters, as an artist who shows a profound understanding of human nature; whereas G. Wilson Knight studies

Shakespeare's plays as extended metaphors, as symbols of a poetic vision; and Clemen studies Shakespeare's works as rich configurations of meanings and images.[30] Insofar as we can assimilate Bradley's insights into Shakespeare's characters, and thereby enrich our understanding of his plays as expanded metaphors as configurations of meanings and images, and vice versa, growth of knowledge is possible in criticism; but in principle it is not transferable across different critical frameworks. One can learn from another critical framework by recognizing and accepting some of its insights; but here too genuine learning takes place by readjusting one's own framework, so that the insights, acepted from another framework, are found to be available from one's own. However, this account of criticism seems to postulate different modes of criticism as self-contained languages, each with its own rules of confirmation and coherence, an account which I shall criticize later in the chapter. But I wish to accept it in principle in order to make some preliminary remarks about the nature of rationality underlying the activity of criticism.

If the above account of criticism is correct, then it would be to misdescribe the nature of criticism to say that its objectivity lies in elucidating the meaning of a poem, which is only indirectly and contingently related to its significance. But it is possible to posit a distinction between meaning and significance in a different and minor way. The recognition, for instance, that a generally bad eighteenth-century poem has romantic tendencies is criticism done in terms of significance. One might elucidate the poem's significance for romantic poetry insofar as it did introduce certain elements which had not hitherto been present in contemporary poetry. Retrospectively, our hypothetical poem, despite its overall clumsiness, is a potential carrier of meanings which were later realized in romantic poetry. It is this kind of characterization which enables us to define the poem's significance, and such significance in turn is an important area of inquiry for literary history. Outside this form of separation between meaning and significance, the two are indissolubly wedded together. To assert this is not to say, however, that sometimes criticism is not really done in terms of significance alone. A great deal of T. S. Eliot's criticism consists of a series of value-judgments made in order to define the significance of literary works. Behind almost all his judgments there lies a structure of response on which the judgments are dependent. When one rejects any of Eliot's judgments one also rejects either his apprehension of the poems in question, or the concepts of poems and criticism which underlie his specific critical judgments.

The possibility of rejection of some critical responses to a poem can be theoretically misleading, however. It can tempt a theorist to erect this possibility into a method of critical discourse which will be universally applicable to all poems. Here we touch on the very nerve of critical discourse about poems. If it is granted that literary criticism is a normative discourse, then we cannot expect to discover in poems a structure of laws for which we can claim validity. For rationality of literary criticism depends on our being able to make the contingencies of our literary experience intelligible and should not devolve on the capacity for making universally valid propositions about poems. When the latter is demanded as the criterion of rationality in criticism, the skeptical exposition of a basic irrationalism even in scientific inquiry would be all the more true of literary criticism.[31] Indeed, the demand for this form of propositions is essentially scientistic, with its roots in logical positivism. For instance, despite his advance beyond logical positivism, Popper's principle of falsifiability does not really escape the ontologizing of facts and thus remains trapped by the positivism he has struggled to overcome. It is important to see that the concept of fact in science is a sophisticated and artificial construct which is related to the state of knowledge in the field and which dictates to scientists the conditions of agreement at a given time. Like Popper in his ontologizing of facts, literary theorists who demand objectivity (and therefore validity) as the principle of criticism are also unwittingly sponsors of the same positivism in their ontologizing of poems.

The assumption that methods common to scientific inquiry are also objectively valid methods for criticism is wrong because the standards and conventions of scientific inquiry have their validity within the institution of science. Experiments do decide in science even if the certainty derived from them is provisional, since the results may be discredited in course of time. Einstein, for instance, was aware of not merely unresolved but inherent difficulties in his theory of relativity, though he attempted to prove that his theory was more comprehensive and had greater range of explanatory efficacy than Newton's theory. On the contrary, the kind of question that literary criticism raises is radically different from that raised by scientific inquiry. G. Wilson Knight has a realization of Shakespeare's plays that is different from the one that Bradley has. To take a different kind of example, Northrop Frye will not say that though his theory of myths has unresolved as well as inherent problems for literary studies, he is going to hold it anyhow. Regardless of our acceptance or rejection of his mode of criticism, he would rather claim that there are no real difficulties that his theory cannot overcome. Thus the literary theorist is not interested in seeking coherence with other accepted theories as the scientist is, nor is he interested in aiming either at a formulation of laws or at the comprehensive unification of separate laws as the scientist is. He is nevertheless interested in formulating a theory that will articulate as fully as possible the nature of his response to literature. More important, he is often interested in situating his own theories in relation to other theories, drawing on those that are assimilable, rejecting the ones that propose views opposed to his, thereby claiming privilege for his theory. This claim for privilege, however, should not be confused with a demand for validity, which has a logic and an operational apparatus fundamentally different from those of criticism.

Disputes in criticism do not operate at a level of determining whether something is or is not a fact; rather they function at a level where an interpretation itself constitutes facts. Thus facts worth noticing in a poem are already charged, in the critical interpretation of a poem, with a valued perception. When someone says, "But don't you see this line means x rather than y and that x is a fact which is available to all of us through the conventions of language?" one must not say in reply, "If your investigation were thorough enough you would see the fact that I see and there would be no more disagreement between us about the poem." For to say this is to fail to understand the grammar of criticism. In saying that something is or is not a fact in a poem, I am not describing that "something," for to say something about a poem is to describe a way of talking about it, to show what would and what would not be intelligible to say about it. When critical disputes are conducted in terms of factual evidence, the concept of poems is taken as analogous to the concept of physical objects. But the analogy is deceptive. For instance, common-sense agreement about physical objects is possible by means of ordinary concepts of scientific explanation, observation, experiment, and verification, or falsification; but this kind of concepts is not available to the discourse about poems. Moreover, the possibility of the lack of an objective and immutable structure of words as poems does not occur within any particular framework of critical discourse, but it certainly arises in disputes between different critical frameworks. A phenomenological critic might justifiably say that a New Critic is not reading the same poem as he is, though both are reading the same printed marks. Thus the question of how to decide the identity of poems is closely connected with the question of what it means to talk about poems and what it means to do criticism for each critical framework. For corresponding to the seeming definiteness of the order of words there is no obvious and indubitable manner in which the poem ought to be taken.

Literary Works
and the Ontological Question

THE VIEW THAT LITERARY WORKS have a peculiar mode of existence is a well-known one. While ascribing the predicate *existence* to literary works, this view holds that they do not exist in the same way ordinary physical objects do in nature. To ascribe this predicate to literary works is to confer on them a form of identity which is certainly an experiential identity. For a physical object to exist is to be part of the objective world which human beings as knowing and pragmatic agents can explore and manipulate. Physical objects, moreover, exist in space, have causal relationships with other objects, and possess physical and chemical properties. But the same cannot be said for literary works, because they are not identical with physical objects (except as inanimate, printed marks on paper). Literary works do not possess physical and chemical properties or enter into causal relationships in the manner of physical objects. A copy of *Paradise Lost* can certainly be said to possess physical and chemical properties, and may well hurt someone if thrown at him, but these elements do not constitute its identity as a poem.

This is the view rigorously articulated by Kant when he said that aesthetic contemplation does not involve any concern with the actual existence of the object. And it is the view held by many aestheticians and literary theorists. For René Wellek, for instance, the literary work is neither real nor ideal but a structure of norms; for Roman Ingarden, too, though it inheres in every adequately constituted concretization the literary work is nevertheless distinguishable from it; for Virgil Aldrich the aesthetic object induces a categorial aspection in the agent, since he does not observe the object but *prehends* it.[32] Although there are differences among all these views, they all seem to agree on the essential point that the aesthetic object belongs to a special categorial realm. I shall now argue that, though this is a plausible characterization of the identity of literary works, the ontological question remains a problematical one because of the ambiguous nature of literary experience.

The ambiguity of literary experience is easily illustrated by considering problems that arise in talking about a performance of *King Lear*. We are aware that we are not watching the actors in their capacity as actual human beings; but we are also aware that it is not the characters themselves who are before us but rather actors who represent the characters by performing their roles. What is it that we watch then? The autonomist answer is that, given the disinterested nature of aesthetic contemplation, what we watch does not require us to make any claim about its ontological status. The experience of art creates a hiatus between itself and reality and is therefore fundamentally depragmatized. Though there is an important element of truth in this answer, the answer is nevertheless far from being entirely convincing. For one who opposes the autonomist framework could provide another answer: though we are aware that we are in a theater we still respond as though Lear and other characters portrayed a compellingly real world. Our involvement with his predicament makes us temporarily ascribe to Lear the same ontological status as we do to actual human beings. It is true, as Aldrich says, that during the performance we are transported to another world and there occurs a categorial aspection. But it is also true, contrary to the autonomists, that our involvement in a specific dramatic situation also brings about a temporary suspension of our disbelief. Without this possibility of suspension of disbelief the experience of literature would become radically impoverished. Our response to *Lear* has a peculiar family resemblance to actual tragic situations in life. The resemblance is, of course, peculiar in that in real life one is liable to intervene and help a person in plight, whereas during a dramatic performance our knowledge of ourselves as spectators of dramatic enactments of various life-situations forestalls any urge for intervention. Consequently, though there is a suspension of disbelief it is never total. The suspension is controlled and captures the ambiguous relation art has to life, and aesthetic experience to ordinary experience.

Failure to grasp the ambiguous nature of literary experience is the source of serious difficulties that attend many attempts at defining the nature of literary works. For instance, Roman Ingarden's ambitious theory of the literary work is no exception. Ingarden has sought to give a detailed characterization of the nature of literary works. He holds that a literary work is a heteronomous form grounded in (a) subjective operations in which the work is produced, (b) the ideal concepts and essences, and (c) the "word signs" which preserve and communicate the work to readers. Though the work comes into being in an act of reading, it nevertheless exists apart from the experience of it. Thus the work has a special ontological existence apart from its concretizations. Ingarden further argues that any specific concretization can be contrasted with the work itself in order to determine its adequacy: "The concretization not only contains various elements that are not really part of the work, though allowed by it, but it also frequently shows elements that are foreign to it and which more or less obscure it. These facts compel us to draw a consistent and detailed line of distinction between the literary work itself and its various concretizations."[33] The reader, of course, distinguishes the work from its concretization, and to make this distinction is for Ingarden to intend the work. Consequently, the work provides the criteria of its appreciation.

Ingarden's theory is subject to many serious objections, but I shall mention just a few, since a fuller criticism will require a fuller exposition of his theory. One of the major difficulties with the theory is that it cannot justify its distinction between the literary work and its concretizations. Consider, for instance, Ingarden's argument that "the literary work of art constitutes an *aesthetic object only when it is expresssed in concretization*." But this introduces yet another distinction, namely, that the literary work of art is something different from the aesthetic object, since the latter is the product of a concretization of the literary work. Ingarden seems to be either ambivalent or confused about the grounds for an evaluation of aesthetic experience. For he argues that "the individual differences between concretizations already enable us to establish what belongs to the work itself and what pertains to the accidentally conditioned concretizations."[34] The implication here is that interpretations of a literary work cannot be incompatible or conflicting because all valid interpretations tend to converge toward the growing totality of a coherent interpretation, and all incompatible ele-

163

ments can be simply removed as the products of personal or historical prejudices. If Ingarden had argued that the text offers guidance as to what is to be produced, he would have been right. But the text represents for him the controlling norm which would enable the critic to eliminate differences in interpretations, except for the ones that result from different schematized aspects. Ingarden cannot accept that the meaning of a text is the result of a fusion of horizons, that the text cannot be defined as a static entity, that it is open to a future not contained in the present. Nor can he accept that there occurs a dynamic interaction between the structure of the text and the expectations and experiences of the reader: the former does not impose an absolute structure of norms on the reader, and the latter does not arbitrarily choose to construe the text as he wishes.

The point of my discussion is that the connection between literary works and their material medium is very tenuous, because only as experienced and interpreted texts do they have their value and meaning. This can happen only within the cultural ambience of a community, and hence the importance of the conventions of reading which help us realize a particular text as a literary work. Imagine, for instance, the value of a tragic play about incest in a community where incest is as common as coffee drinking. It is because of the experiential demands that literary works make on us as part of the nature of their identity that we can say that they possess what we might call a peculiar mode of existence. This peculiarity amounts to saying that literary works have no existence independent of the human mind. If one or another human mind is not present, the apprehension of a literary work by that mind is not possible, though the work could be said to exist as a series of inanimate, printed marks.

In more technical philosophical terms that I borrow from Joseph Margolis, works of art can be identified *extensionally* in that they can be linked with the identity of physical objects in which they are embodied. A particular set of printed marks in a particular order makes up the physical (extensional) identity of *Paradise Lost*. But this extensional reference does not constitute its identity as a work of art. It only controls "the threat of common reference and common grounds for interpretative and appraisive dispute."[35] But works of art are particular aesthetic objects in virtue of the *intensional* reference, since they emerge as art in the context of particular cultural assumptions. Physical objects are extensional and therefore context-free, whereas works of art, though physically embodied and hence extensional, are culturally emergent as works of art and hence context-dependent or intensional.

In ordinary critical language, a literary work, like a painting, has to be realized by a contemplating mind, and this is not the same as the scientist's observing a physical object. Scientists employ experimental techniques to remove perceptual illusions in order to see physical objects as, so to speak, they really are. In contemplating a literary work, however, the critic takes the elements as they become relevant to his response, not as they are. Literary works, in other words, are realized in one's response; they do not have their identity outside response, though the material embodiment of a literary work obviously exists outside the response. Consequently, the question of agreement on a particular meaning of a work has to be formulated in this way: When we respond to a poem, do we realize the same work of art? An adequate answer to this question depends on a consideration of elements that contribute to the possibility of identical realization of the poem, for in view of the different and at times incompatible interpretations offered for it, we cannot simply say that all of them are responding to the same poem. Scientists in their disputes agree often enough on what the facts are or how to construe them, whereas critics differ not simply over whether one or another interpretation is correct but over what the facts are. For in criticism facts are what is relevant to a particular realization of a literary work.

On the Nature of Disputes in Criticism

CRITICAL CATEGORIES help constitute the ways in which we conceive the identity of literary works and prescribe a set of strategies which enable us to experience and interpret literature. It goes without saying, then, that because of the difference in critical categories there cannot occur genuine logical conflict among the critical interpretations of a literary work. For the conflict to be a logical one, as M. H. Abrams has argued, "the clashing assertions must meet on the same plane of discourse."[36] Different conceptual frameworks generate different interpretive strategies and do not admit the possibility of a successful critical dispute between them. Nevertheless, there is a deeper and more crucial dimension to incompatible interpretations, one that stems from conflicting insights into art and contributes to the scene of conflict in criticism. To characterize this dimension I shall now attempt to examine two conflicting accounts of poetic creativity and literary tradition proposed by T. S. Eliot and Harold Bloom.

ELIOT'S BASIC CRITICAL CONCERN is with positing a kind of objectivity as intrinsically necessary both to understand "literature as literature and not another thing" and to determine the precise context of criticism.[37] Like Kant, Eliot is asking for a discrimination between the aesthetic judgment and other kinds of judgment. Unlike Kant, however, Eliot argues, "*Qua* work of art the work of art cannot be interpreted; there is nothing to interpret; we can only criticize it according to standards, in comparison to other works of art." This argument is more fully developed in his essay, "Tradition and the Individual Talent," where Eliot grapples with a formidable problem of literary history and creativity that is also a crucial issue for literary criticism. Eliot's theory of creativity there proposes a need for dynamic historical consciousness for the artist if he is to create good art, whereas his theory of criticism deals with and resolves in its own right the problem of criteria for criticism and thus defines the function of criticism. Being committed to a dynamic relationship among specific literary works, Eliot postulates the notion of the artist who is neither a mere blind imitator or a follower of the tradition, nor someone who ignores the tradition to pursue the raptures of the totally new. Such a conception of tradition involves the "historical sense which is a sense of the timeless as well as the temporal and of the timeless and temporal together. . . . [The historical sense] makes a writer most acutely conscious of his place in time, of his own contemporaneity."[38]

It is clear that Eliot's method does not give a definite criterion with which to appreciate and judge poetry, and this is because in forming taste for poetry one is confronted with complex and unpredictable kinds of experiences. It therefore becomes necessary for one to make adjustment in every new context. The absence of clearly formulated criteria, however, is not a defect in his theory of criticism, since his theory is a concept of taste which applies differently to different poems and yet retains its essential underlying form. Eliot's method thus depends on the experience of literature, on the insight into literature that one has acquired. The absence of ready-made rules to articulate his method only underlines the complexity of contexts of life, of contexts of poetry. But that does not mean that there are no rules to give order to one's apprehension of the great diversity of poems. For if the diversity of contexts of life and the complex nature of interaction between the past and the present make for the diversity and complexity of poems, then for Eliot no clear and indubitable definition of poetry can be given. Eliot therefore differs from the New Critics and others who propose definitions of poetry. On Eliot's view, in developing taste for poetry one develops an ability to apply one's insight with consistency and suppleness to a great diversity of poems. This method differs significantly from the method of Arnold, which offered the ideal and immutable touchstones for poetry.[39] For Eliot even the touchstones undergo change. It is clear that he grasped the principle of aesthetic relativity, though this fact has not been generally noticed because of the brief judgmental pronouncements which make up most of his criticism.[40]

Bloom, on the other hand, offers a concept of art and criticism that is radically opposed to Eliot's. According to Bloom, art battles against art and also engages in an antithetical battle against nature. The romantic and postromantic modern poet "quests for an impossible object," for although the modern poet is necessarily a latecomer, he insists upon his own priority.[41] This agonistic relationship of the poet with his predecessor, who has done his work for him and thus has potentially rendered him poetically impotent, Bloom develops into his meditation on the six revisionary ratios by which the latecomer poet "misprisions" his predecessor, thereby creating his own poetry.[42] Bloom's theory of creativity is also a theory of criticism in that, for him, "criticism teaches not a language of criticism . . . but a language in which poetry is written, the language of influence, of the dialectic that governs the relations between poets *as poets*."[43]

Eliot's concept of poetic creativity is essentially serene and envisions new poems as joining the simultaneity of the existing order of literature and as modifying that order. Bloom's concept, on the contrary, is self-consciously agonistic, predicated upon violence and struggle by the emerging individual talent as that talent wrenches and distorts and misreads the strong precursor in order to create a space for itself in the crowded and exhausted realm of poetry. Eliot, insisting on comparison and analysis as the basic tools for criticism, perceives criticism as an activity designed for the "common pursuit of true judgment." For Bloom, in conscious opposition to both Eliot and Frye, strong criticism necessarily insists on its exclusivity and uniqueness and is predicated upon *power* that enables a strong critic to offer a radical (mis)interpretation of poetry.[44] Unlike Eliot, who insists on continuity in tradition, though tradition is always modified through subtle interchanges between the past and the present, Bloom insists that continuity is a demon, the Covering Cherub, whose "baleful charm imprisons the present in the past, and reduces a world of differences into the greyness of uniformity." Given this power of the precursor, the latecomer poet's only recourse is to leap and "locate itself in a discontinuous universe," for "discontinuity is freedom."[45]

BLOOM'S is a self-consciously provocative theory, one that many critics are likely to find not simply extravagant but false. It will be useful to raise some objections that Bloom's critical opponent might bring up and to imagine how Bloom might answer them. The critic who feels that this theory is simply false would first challenge Bloom on his own ground: he might say that not all romantic poets in their most successful poems are ridden with a sense of anxiety and the burden of tradition. Even if he grants Bloom his narrower claim, that the romantics were in general burdened with anxiety about their poetic creativity, he might still contend that the original anxiety that at first drove the romantic poet to write his poem disappears in the process of writing the poem. For the genuine poem may have only a contingent relationship to the poet's anxiety, but we cannot claim it is the constitutive element in the poem. Bloom might consider this to be the easiest objection with which to deal. Whatever one's latitude of interpretation, one cannot deny that the problem of greatness which began to be felt in the eighteenth century does indeed become for the romantics the problem of dealing with the poetry of the past. Bloom might reply that if the romantic poet does not leave any traces of real struggle with his precursor that is because "this absence can deceive us into accepting a new presence."[46]

The critic might shift his ground somewhat and raise a new objection: surely there are great modern poets who write without a genuine feeling of anxiety about the burden of tradition. Bloom can maintain his theory only by arbitrarily excluding such poets as Pound, Eliot, Robert Lowell, and Williams. If Bloom were to do responsible criticism he would have to include all these poets and then see if his theory could be upheld. His critic might adduce the evidence of eighteenth-century poetry, which has little to do with the romantic's burden of anxiety. Bloom would readily answer that these poems are at best mere period pieces, not genuine poems. For it is Bloom's contention that all genuine poetry, at least after Milton, cannot escape the historical-psychological dialectic that he has articulated. The poets who are "strong" have indeed always felt the pull of this dialectic; their strength derives from their struggle with their precursor-poets and their eventual "misprisioning" of them. If eighteenth-century poetry is not great, Bloom might say, it is because its writers too readily submitted themselves to expressing "what oft was thought." And yet, he might add, the poets like Pope at their best engaged in an act of self-expression. If Pope's poetry is good, it must be the result of his self-conscious struggle with the burden of tradition. After all, the fact that Pope was not conscious of the deep drama of psychic defenses he was carrying out does not necessarily mean that he did not really experience it. The struggle that his writing does express is often too overlaid with the clear and simple commonplaces of his culture to be recognized by his conscious self. That Pope or another great poet may have left an apparently convincing account of his method and intention is no logical obstacle, since his lack of awareness of his struggle is not in any way counterintentional to the struggle actually experienced and overcome by him in his work. For instance, Bloom says: "My own experience as a reader is that poets differentiate themselves into strength by troping or turning from the presence of other poets. Greatness results from a refusal to separate origins from aims. The father is met in combat, and fought to at least a stand-off, if not quite to a separate peace." [47]

As for the modern classicist poets, Bloom can argue that their poetry, when it succeeds, is good poetry because they have not escaped the dialectic of anxiety and misreading that he has articulated. Indeed, the difficulty of writing for the modern poet, insisted upon by Eliot, [48] showed an awareness of the burden of tradition on his part. Bloom might add that Eliot was certainly right about this difficulty, but that he failed to give a proper explanation of it, for it is precisely in the burden of tradition and the anxiety of having been anticipated and coopted by the precursor that this difficulty manifests itself. The modern poet's struggle consists in devising a strategy that will liberate him from captivity to the precursor.

The critic might now make some fundamental criticism: what Bloom contends may be true in some cases, but it might also be extravagant and devious guesswork. After all, notice the contortions that Bloom must go through in order to substantiate his theory. The objector might clinch his argument by questioning Bloom's concept of interpretation itself: apart from the drama and extravagance of his theory that gives critics some borrowed glory from poets, it miscon-strues the communal nature of criticism, the interpersonal norms of communication which make dialogue and even conflict fruitful among critics. Bloom's interpreter is a solipsist who, given his concept of the exclusive nature of each "strong" interpretation, cannot provide valid criteria for distinguishing either between strong and weak interpreta-tions or between different strong ones.

This is of course a powerful objection, though it need not entirely disqualify Bloom's argument for one who shares his insight. Bloom can point to the fact that the activity of criticism is generally one of revaluation and reinterpretation of literature. Almost all significant in-terpretations, he might argue, are necessarily motivated by the desire to replace previous interpretations, because those interpretations are found by later critics to be either inadequate or fundamentally misguided.

FROM THE ABOVE DISCUSSION there emerge certain features about dis-putes in criticism which I should like to note here. Both the objector and the defender make their arguments with an awareness of the is-sues involved, but the debate remains interminable, for the critic is not like a patient in the psychoanalytic situation who can be brought to give up a wrong perception of things. But it is difficult to deny that Bloom's theory is extremely arbitrary. When stretched beyond its plausible applications, which are difficult to determine clearly, the theory forces its defender to distort or ignore recalcitrant facts and to read into these facts meanings which may seem to contribute toward the coherence of a theory but which are sustained by a false interpre-tive ingenuity. And what is more, the defender has an elaborate the-ory of what facts are relevant to a critical interpretation of a poem and how to construe them.

Bloom's theory and his criticism most directly stemming from that theory are vulnerable because, like all universalizing theories, they make a claim that cannot be sustained. Dependent upon a well-defined historical period of post-Miltonic romantic and postromantic poetry, his theory must make sweepingly general value-judgments, a strategy which is intended to make the theory immune to criticism. The entire modernist line of Pound and Eliot must be rejected since its acceptance would jeopardize the anxiety-based concept of poetic creativity. The central weakness of the theory is in the attempt to substantialize what is at best an illustrative analogy derived from Freudian concepts of defense mechanism and family romance. And in Bloom's literalization of metaphorical analogies there is a lesson for both criticism and its theory. We soon come to realize that categorial structures of other disciplines, while they can energize reflection in criticism, cannot simply be transposed to it. Where they do seem successful in good critical performance, their efficacy is contextually dependent on specific poems, not applicable to all poems. Moreover, it is important to ask whether, where they are successfully applicable, good critical performance is not possible without adopting those structures. Thus criticism, despite its deepening and enrichment by means of concepts from other disciplines, claims its own intrinsicality.

Can we now say that the conflict between Eliot and Bloom is not a genuine one? I think the conflict is a genuine one and the dispute here turns on what constitutes a literary work, what its relation to tradition is. If we believe that there can be no serious dispute, we can no longer question or criticize either position. Indeed, in terms of its own assumed definition and purpose, each position has a different logical space and is therefore unassailable, except by those who accept each position's basic premises. On these grounds, a dispute would at best bring about greater logical cogency in each position and explore more fully the possibility of its application. I have contended, on the contrary, that the dispute between Eliot and Bloom is an essential and creative conflict, a conflict between two "essentially contested proposals"[49] for aesthetic life. My criticism of Bloom here does not imply a denial or refutation of his essential insight into the nature of romantic and postromantic poetry. It rather exposes certain serious weaknesses in his logical and rhetorical superstructure. Once this arbitrary superstructure is removed, a theorist or critic who feels the power of Bloom's insight can seek more satisfactory ways to develop and refine its possible conceptual structure. Bloom's central insight, like Eliot's, makes possible a whole way of thinking about poetry. For Eliot the principle of difference is important for poetic creativity but is modified by a principle of continuity. He is therefore asking for a body of recognizable values for which communication and normalcy are conditions of health in literary traditions, and his concept of criticism, with its emphasis on comparison and analysis, is flexible enough to preclude rigid objectivity. For Bloom, on the other hand, the principle of difference is not simply important, it is fundamental to poetic creativity for reasons that are inescapably historical and psychological.[50]

Can we, alternatively, say that the Bloom-Eliot dispute is a valuational one which is not concerned with the factual aspects of their specific judgments and the works criticized, and that it is simply a clash of different emotional attitudes? If we say that this is true, then we will have to say that fundamental critical concepts cannot be further justified, though one can give a psychological account of how people come to hold them. We will also have to say that it is not a genuine dispute but rather mutual incomprehension, since each is governed by emotional attitudes which are incommensurate with the other's. Resolution of critical disputes will then depend on how clever one is in manipulating psychological and nonrational means of persuasion. There is no doubt, however, that neither Eliot nor (even) Bloom would accept this characterization of his mode of critical argument. Critics in their disputes attempt to describe, interpret, and judge literary works, regardless of their views about poems as objectively available structures. Bloom and Eliot are no exception. Neither critic's arguments are simply expressions of his emotional attitudes, and though they do not display the logic of discourse that informs scientific inquiry, they are genuine arguments and are amenable to logical scrutiny.

We can criticize, for instance, a number of Eliot's specific judgments, even if we accept the general mode of his critical practice and many of his critical judgments. We can articulate the complexity underlying his critical practice, and a recognition of that complexity need not logically compel us into accepting those of his judgments which are overhasty and extreme. Moreover, we can point up the richness of literary history, which makes some elements of romanticism inescapable for Eliot and renders some of his general literary propositions questionable. Similarly, despite my criticism of Bloom's theory, I have argued that the insight that informs Bloom's theory is a significant one, because his theory is consistent with the romantics' attempts to redefine the nature of poetry in order to make a place for their own poetry. Poems for the romantics were not simply public objects but rather possessed a private significance, and the function of criticism resided for them in critics' endeavors to grasp the complexity and richness of a poet's inner vision. In Bloom's radicalized version of romantic poetics all good poems not only possess this private significance, but rather derive it from the anxiety that drives the latecomer poet to "misprision" his precursor. On this view the history of poetry becomes a history of intrapsychic conflicts among poems, and the history of criticism a history of conflicts among interpretations. As I have suggested, when Bloom's view is taken in terms of its extreme logical consequences, the terms *poetry* and *criticism* are not merely interchangeable; they cannot be distinguished. Neither can one decide what is, and what is not, "strong," since any criteria offered are subject to "strong" antithetical criticism. Thus if both Bloom and Eliot can be criticized it does not mean that either's theory can be conclusively refuted, for the dispute between them turns on fundamental questions concerning the nature of poetry and the proper way to apprehend it. To be able to criticize both and to be able to recognize the moments at which a dispute among them becomes irresolvable is to grasp a profound relationship between reason and value, logic and rhetoric. It is from the interdependence between these two that the concept of criticism both derives its complexity and reveals its unstable, changing, and dynamic nature. In the rest of this chapter I shall try to clarify and develop this characterization of the concept of criticism. I begin by elucidating the relation of tradition to critical understanding.

Tradition and Critical Understanding

THOUGH THE CONCEPT of tradition has been felt as important at least since the rise of romanticism, it assumed a position of centrality for the theorists of the human sciences rather recently. Here again it seems to me that Gadamer has provided what is perhaps the most suggestive general discussion of the concept of tradition. It is valuable because of its theoretical scope: while it may seem closer to Eliot's concept of tradition it is not radically antithetical to Bloom's. No doubt Gadamer's discussion derives from its close dependence on his hermeneutics and does not seek to offer an account designed to elaborate and confirm a specific literary theory. Tradition, he argues, is the source of authority and change, stability and transformation, and without it no experience can make sense. He therefore cautions us that since "we are living in a state of constant overstimulation of our historical consciousness," radical thought or art deludes itself by believing that it is constantly overthrowing tradition's hold on it. For even revolution has meaning in the context of tradition.[51]

Gadamer, of course, does not construe tradition as a simple process of continuity, but rather defines it as the ground of a complex interaction between continuity and change. Thus if a change accounts for the novelty of new literary works, it also shows a new work's relation to the tradition which persists in it in modified and dynamic form. Gadamer's explanation of the hermeneutic act illustrates the complex patterns of interaction that make up the nature of tradition:

> Every age has to understand a transmitted text in its own way, for the text is part of the whole of the tradition in which the age takes an objective interest and in which it seeks to understand itself. The real meaning of a text, as it speaks to the interpreter, does not depend on the contingencies of the author and whom he originally wrote for. It certainly is not identical with them, for it is always partly determined also by the historical situation of the interpreter and hence by the totality of the objective course of history.[52]

Thus both objective history and objective interpretation are exposed as illusory, and literary interpretation is firmly tied to literary history. To interpret a literary work, in Gadamer's view, is to realize its place in the tradition, and hence to grasp that the interpretation generates the history of the text. Moreover, the historical character of literature and the literary character of history do not simply intersect, but reveal the intricate family relationships subsisting among the human sciences.

It is a condition of experience for Gadamer that we already possess a horizon "in order to be able to place ourselves within a situation." This does not require that we eliminate our own horizon, for it is together with alien horizons that our horizon constitutes "the one great horizon that moves from within and beyond the frontiers of the present, embraces the historical depths of our self-consciousness." The interpreter, in other words, always approaches the testimony of the past under the influence of the present; it is therefore "necessary to inhibit the overhasty assimilation of the past to our own expectations of meaning." The hermeneutic task consists in neither mere psychological empathy nor an imposition of fixed criteria on an alien text; it rather calls for a listening to the past "in a way that enables it to make its own meaning heard." The past and the present, then, are not monolithic structures; otherwise, they could be conceived in terms of distinct sets of fixed criteria. But there is no isolated horizon of the present, just as there are no distinct historical horizons:

> Every encounter with tradition that takes place within historical con-
> sciousness involves the experience of the tension between the past
> and the present. The hermeneutic task consists in not covering up this
> tension by attempting a naive assimilation but consciously bringing it
> out. This is why it is part of the hermeneutic approach to project an
> historical horizon that is different from the horizon of the present.
> Historical consciousness is aware of its own otherness and hence dis-
> tinguishes the horizon of tradition as its own.[53]

Tradition, far from being a monolithic whole that remains change-less or is some sort of inert presence of accumulated ideas, comprises a body of anticipatory judgments and prejudices that comprehends the nature and range of possible alternative responses to a given historical situation. Though it is projected onto new cases which it seeks to comprehend in terms of its own categories, it also experiences modifications that belie any argument that tradition seeks instances confirmatory of its own norms. The nature of these modifications could be such that the lines of continuity seen in the present would undergo radical changes at a future time which would generate a new pattern of continuity.

Because tradition is a preservation that, like revolution, is freely chosen, Gadamer argues that it needs "to be affirmed, embraced, cultivated."[54] The authority it embodies is not opposed to freedom and reason, since in the absence of these two conditions authority cannot claim for itself recognition and knowledge. Authority, Gada-mer suggests, "cannot actually be bestowed, but is acquired and must be acquired, if someone is to lay claim to it." Tradition is, then, the ground of the validity of authority. Nevertheless, the peculiar power of tradition's authority derives from the fact that it is not limited by the constraints of reason. If reason strictly dictated the conditions of authority, tradition or its authority could not be distinguished from reason. Gadamer here offers a remarkable criticism of both the En-lightenment and romanticism. The error of the Enlightenment lay, ac-cording to Gadamer, in having set up "a mutually exclusive antithesis between authority and reason," an antithesis which brought about a general devaluation of tradition in favor of reason. For romanticism, on the other hand, tradition "in large measure determines our institutions and our attitudes." But romanticism, despite its reinstatement of the authority of tradition, erred by conceiving tradition "as the antithesis to the freedom of reason" and "as something historically given, like nature." Gadamer, then, contrary to the ideologues of both the Enlightenment and romanticism, conceives tradition in terms of an element of freedom because the justification it has cannot be provided by the condition that reason may seek to establish. The element of freedom allows for both renewal and modification of tradition and denies finality to any interpretation of the past or the present.[55]

An objection[56] that for Gadamer reason is arbitrary and irrational misunderstands his position, for his insistence on the authority of tradition does not deny the use of reason but rather facilitates a proper functioning of the hermeneutic process through history. For instance, the concept of originality becomes meaningful in relation to the models of authority provided by tradition. Because of its claim to reason and freedom, tradition does not impose its exemplars as models for repetition and imitation, for it is a condition of learning that the exemplars become the means of insight into the nature of one's activity. The exemplars, far from being a threat to one's activity, participate in a process that teaches one how and where to call into question their authority. Any simplifying objection that for Gadamer tradition is the force and guarantor of continuity can be overcome by a recognition that every new age has the burden of understanding itself in relation to tradition, and this is a process that changes both of them. The change could bring about certain fundamental discontinuities between the new age and the one preceding it; this results partly from the fact that the new age's understanding of the past could differ fundamentally from the understanding of tradition that the preceding age might have acquired.

For Gadamer everything that can be understood falls under the project of hermeneutics. Consequently, the ideological distortions that Habermas or Foucault might want to reserve for analysis to the critique of ideology also belong to the domain of hermeneutics.[57] The preconceptions and prejudgments, brought to light by hermeneutical reflection, include elements rooted in economic and political interests. The critique of ideology, in other words, becomes meaningful to the extent that it comprehends its own hermeneutic process. As Gadamer argues, authority certainly rests on knowledge, but knowledge cannot be reduced to some body of unassailable truths. Hermeneutic reflection, then, does not require subjection to a particular tradition, but underlies participation in any tradition. Moreover, being historically situated, understanding is necessarily limited, partial, and based on preconceptions and prejudices that are taken for granted. There is therefore no point to the talk about getting behind the "real" conditions underlying a specific historical situation, for ideology is not impervious to hermeneutics. It is simply that hermeneutics makes no pretense to the possession of truth or the eventual outcome of historical events as does the critique of ideology. Thus Gadamer does not attach importance to the ability to disclose false consciousness, but values instead the process of becoming conscious of (and evaluating) preconceptions. One comprehends, he would argue, structures of preconceptions, one's own as well as others', by trying to understand others' points of view.

The Concept of Criticism

GADAMER'S HERMENEUTICS is a philosophy of interpretation, not a theory of criticism. Its importance resides in the internal connection it shows between theory and practice, for it articulates the nature of understanding and its indissoluble relation to experience. In explaining the historical rootedness of understanding Gadamer provides conditions for what knowledge means in the human sciences and what can be meaningfully said about historical and literary texts. His theory does not claim to supply appropriate conditions for specific concepts of criticism. It therefore cannot be confined to a particular theory of critical practice which may prescribe a set of interpretive norms or validate a particular concept of criticism.

This is as it should be, because the concept of criticism is an essentially contested concept. Its most important peculiarity is that disputes about its nature are in principle endless. Each disputant seeks to articulate the special function that the concept fulfills, and each maintains that his is the correct or proper use of the concept of criticism. He tries to defend it, with "convincing arguments, evidence, and other forms of justification." [58] It is not just a fact of the history of criticism that concepts of criticism have been disputed, that new ones have been proposed, the old ones recharacterized. If we examine them carefully, we shall find that the endlessness of critical disputes is a part of their very nature. Being embedded in history, they are finite and therefore changeable in character. And since contingency is an unavoidable feature of history, there is always room for the modification and renewal of old concepts as well as for the development of radically new concepts. This is fully consistent with Gadamer's hermeneutics, since this characterization of the concept of criticism does not commit the historicist fallacy. In other words, the account offered here does not seek to restrict the legitimate scope of a particular concept to its alleged historical origin.

The concept of criticism, then, is a disputed concept and helps explain the controversies that characterize modern criticism and its theories. Often taking highly partisan stands, literary theorists tend to select a part of the total complex of meanings and values of literature and defend that part as the intrinsic and defining feature of literature. Once a literary theorist has reached a decision about that feature, he then proceeds to present and defend it provocatively, (1) by denying and refuting his opponents' theories, and at times, if necessary, (2) by accommodating them. In the second case, where he accepts his opponents' theories, he could go on to show them as deriving conveniently and more legitimately from his own theory. Thus his theoretical endeavor would be directed at privileging his concept of poetry against all rival concepts in the field. This strategy is usually pursued by a given partisan theorist with great polemical skill and persuasive power, and it often enables him to reinterpret and revaluate literary history and the history of criticism. This, however, does not mean that he cannot be criticized or shown wrong in one or many of his arguments, that some concepts masquerading as literary cannot be shown to be simply erroneous.

Moreover, it is not true that different modes of criticism are cut off from all the other forms of cultural life, that literary criticism comprises different critical language-games such that they have no relation to each other and little relation to things outside criticism. Different critical modes cannot be described as self-enclosed systems, each with a coherently articulated set of rules which are constantly refined by its adherents' critical activities. If they can be so described, how would one know that a certain response, though correct in terms of the rules of a system, is not just a mechanical, pointless response rather than a proper one? One wouldn't, since the response is in compliance with the self-authenticating rules of the system. Apart from the extreme self-authenticating, subjectivist construal of the concept of criticism, such a definition of different critical language-games implies not merely a simplistic but a wrong understanding of the relation a critical language-game has with other critical language-games and with cultural activities outside criticism.

The concept of modes of criticism as isolated and self-contained language-games misdescribes the institution of criticism. Romantic literature has its distinctiveness, for instance, insofar as the romantics disagreed with their neoclassical predecessors on the issue of literary creativity and the concepts of self and society. To explain the difference between the romantic and the neoclassicist is to do no more than emphasize the fact as well as the significance of their fundamental difference. But neither romantic nor neoclassical literature or criticism exhausts the concept of literature or the concept of criticism. While recognizing the richness of different literary traditions, it would be absurd to treat every fundamental disagreement or discontinuity as leading to an isolated and self-contained literature. This would populate the history of literature with an indefinite number of modes of literature with radical discontinuity separating them, and so too with criticism. However, the concept of criticism is a disputed concept; one cannot conclusively establish any single characterization of literature as the proper one. But this does not mean that just any concept can be set up as a competing concept. This brings us to the next stage in our discussion: an attempt to explain the logic of inquiry in criticism and critical theory.

The Logic of Inquiry in Criticism

THE USE of one or another conceptual structure requires certain criteria, however unsystematic and informal they may be. These criteria are not inaccessible, though they need not be defended in formal, theoretical terms. It is a conceptual confusion to think that since one can formulate critical criteria one can logically validate one's fundamental framework and thereby found literary criticism on a logic of inquiry which also operates in science. Acceptance of a fundamental critical commitment is not the same as the acceptance of a hypothesis or the holding of an opinion, for one can come to see that the hypothesis or opinion is ill-founded, that it needs to be abandoned or radically altered. But this cannot be done with fundamental critical commitments. These commitments are not statements which are subject

179

to change, confirmation, or disconfirmation in the light of further experience. However, if one conducts criticism in terms of a hypothesis, then one adopts procedural operations consistent with the hypothesis, examines all available relevant evidence, and modifies, confirms, or disconfirms the hypothesis. But as we have already seen, this misdescribes the nature of criticism. The distinction between a critical commitment and a hypothesis rules out the operations fundamental to scientific inquiry. No eventuality need cause a critic to abandon fundamental commitments, unless his convictions loosen or he finds another commitment more meaningful.

If a critical commitment could be equated with a hypothesis, it would be possible to wait both for more evidence to collect and for a more adequate scientific apparatus to evolve. But this kind of expectation, of course, misconceives the activity of criticism. Each fundamental commitment allows for formulation of "hypotheses" that demonstrate the value of the commitment by the range and depth of response to literature that the commitment makes possible. But a commitment is not an expectation about what will be the case in the future; rather it is a form of critical life.

Fundamental critical commitments regulate and guide one's critical response. Normally such a commitment operates implicitly. But when one faces literary works that are somehow too radical and cannot be handled with ease, one's commitments are often made explicit in order to talk about those works. When a literary artist is an apparent anomaly in the context of literary traditions but one allows him a place of centrality in literature, then too it becomes important to elucidate and defend his art by fully articulating the commitment. I am thinking here of F. R. Leavis's critical defense of Lawrence's art. One can endorse Leavis's basic commitment and give an explanation of Lawrence's novels that will be more satisfactory than the one given by Leavis; or, alternatively, one can provide an explanation that is governed by a critical commitment that is radically different from Leavis's. But if someone rejects Leavis's criticism and judgment of Lawrence, he need not necessarily condemn Lawrence. In a sense both critics can see the same facts but differ because they do not see them in the same way. Both may also see the presence of certain aesthetic, cultural values, but differ on the significance of these values. Thus the so-called facts that are noticed but dismissed as valuationally unimportant by Leavis must be made to appear to him in a new light if he is to change his position.[59]

The criteria of criticism that an aesthetic decision would seem to yield do not foreclose on new and radically different literary works. And if our aesthetic decisions do not lead to clear and systematic formulation of critical criteria, it is because the contingencies of literature force us to readjust previously formulated criteria. This is why, I think, Eliot admonishes critics to examine the old in the light of the new and the new in the light of the old, for he suggests in the essay mentioned earlier that a new literary work alters our sensibility and in doing so alters our valuing of the literature of the past. This sort of enrichment accounts for the growth of knowledge in criticism; it is not like the growth of knowledge in science, which, on the accounts of both Popper and Kuhn, is ultimately linear. It follows from this argument that the criteria of what is and what is not meaningful to say about a poem are to be found within criticism, since their value resides, not in an external imposition of them on one's reading of a poem, but rather in making possible particular critical responses to the poem. For critical criteria are necessarily, though implicitly, present in particular critical performances. When critics explicitly formulate criteria, they do so in order to answer certain questions and difficulties which arise; they may also hope to bring out the coherence and value of the critical mode they advocate; and finally they may want to give a defensive account of their professed criteria in relation to other competing criteria advocated by other critics.

I should like to prevent any impression that the logic of inquiry in criticism proposed here is equivalent to Kuhn's logic of inquiry for scientific research. In Kuhnian terms one might say that criticism takes on qualities of normal science when there are a number of critics working within a mutually shared paradigm. When several critics are working within, say, the phenomenological, structuralist, or New Critical paradigm, their activities might appear to be a sort of normal criticism. This characterization presents serious problems, however, since it can deceive the literary theorist or critic into believing that there are problems awaiting solutions. Literary criticism is not a problem-solving activity in this sense. If in the forties and fifties there prevailed a feeling that criticism had for the first time become "literary," it was because for the first time a serious and sustained attempt to examine literary works as verbal structures was made on a major scale.

It would seem that while the disappearance of initial divergences in science are often caused by the "triumph of one of the pre-paradigm schools,"[60] in criticism divergences do not disappear, though, as happened in America in the forties and fifties, they may become temporarily suppressed. More important, in science a theory can be tested, according to both Popper and Kuhn, whereas in criticism a theory cannot be proved better than its competitors *in that sense*. The difference between the two activities—of science and criticism—is precisely in the specific mode of inquiry that underlies each activity. Science is characterized by some concepts of correspondence and coherence, however defined, whereas criticism (as well as literature and the arts) is characterized by the form of aesthetic life each major critic (or artist) promotes as a satisfactory one. Whether a particular major critic explicitly theorizes or not, significant criticism is nearly always characterized by attempts to build the field anew. In explicit theorizing, such an attempt may involve, as with Frye, starting from first principles and justifying the use of each concept used, whether borrowed or invented. It may also involve, as with recent discussions of intention in criticism, attempts to expose critical concepts and categories offered as genuinely "logical."

It is clear, then, that propositions and theories of criticism cannot be treated as experimental facts or hypotheses like propositions and theories of scientific inquiry. Critics attempt to refine and improve their propositions and theories, but these refinements are not like those of scientific inquiry. Critical propositions function as insights, as fundamental aesthetic commitments, which can be better elucidated and defended, but no restatement of them is logical or scientific like the formula "water is H_2O." Refinements and improvements of propositions and theories of criticism are not improvements of the commitments underlying them but fuller explanations of them. We thus reach a notion of progress in the humanistic discourse which is governed by logical dynamics fundamentally different from the ones governing the discourse in scientific inquiry.

Moreover, inasmuch as criteria and literary works are interdependent in critical response, there is no doubt that one can enrich and readjust one's response and that one can also enrich and readjust one's critical criteria, thus allowing for growth in knowledge and understanding of literature. Whether Popper's principle of falsification is correct or not, and whether Kuhn's concepts of normal science and paradigms are adequate or not, both recognize advancement in scientific knowledge. I should like simply to assert here that in *that* sense of scientific inquiry there is no linear growth of knowledge in literary criticism. It is possible to compare "two paradigms with nature *and* with each other" (Kuhn) and to test different theories in order "to probe deeper and deeper into the structure of our world" (Popper).[61] It is *not* possible to compare two different interpretations of a poem with the poem *and* with each other in the same way. For the interpretive act constitutes the poem in its response and thus does not have the poem as a naturalistic datum existing outside the act of criticism.

It is true, however, that there is considerable conflict among the philosophers and historians of science over what constitutes the nature of scientific inquiry. But there is nonetheless general agreement as to what will count as a scientific problem, what will count as a satisfactory resolution of it, and the kinds of data that will be permitted as proper evidence. Thus, despite the controversy over the nature of scientific inquiry, there does obtain general consensus among members of the scientific community concerned with a particular set of problems and puzzles. But ever since Plato and Aristotle no such consensus has been reached among critics and theorists of literature. Thus explanations in criticism differ from those provided in science essentially because critics disagree, not simply over what are the laws of creativity or literary changes that they might invoke to explain literary works, but also over the question of the form that a "scientific" or "systematic" explanation in criticism ought to take. Some critics and theorists have argued that natural scientific and literary critical explanations share the same formal characteristics, whereas others have simply denied that literature is amenable to systematic or scientific study. We cannot dismiss these disagreements as peripheral or inessential in the belief that there might be concealed and more serious agreements in the actual critical explanations that critics give of literature, for the dispute turns on what will count as a genuine critical explanation of a literary work or of a given context of literary creativity. Such disputes are necessarily based on conflicting presuppositions about the nature of literature and criticism, which generate different *and* competing conceptions of the form of critical explanation, each of which claims validity as literary criticism.

If critics and critical theorists recognize that concepts of criticism are "essentially contested concepts," they will learn to overcome the narrow-minded and fanatic critical outlook which often characterizes their endeavors. For they will then cease to hold that their specific concepts are indubitably true for all, and thus they will learn respect for the aesthetic decisions of critics who presumably are opposed to their own concepts. While it is possible that two critics in disagreement fail to understand each other and are therefore not engaged in a genuine dispute, it is important to see that there do occur genuine disputes in criticism, that two critics in dispute holding different concepts can and do know what they are in dispute about and what they are rejecting. And this latter argument seems to suggest that they are participating in the operations made possible by the institution of criticism. Yet in the sense that a Popperian scientific statement "must remain tentative forever,"[62] a critical response to a literary work cannot be considered tentative; the critic is necessarily interested in offering it as an indubitably proper and true response. For if he did not, he would then have to accept the notion of progressive and linear increase in knowledge of the work, though within that context the poem (or its truth), like Popper's scientific truth, must forever remain outside our reach. We would then have the concept of critics' ethical responsibility to the literary work; and the work would dictate to critics principles of its decodation which would slowly but certainly help them get closer to its essentially inaccessible reality. However, we have already criticized this concept of poems by showing the mutual dependence of literary works and the criteria of criticism.

The fact that there can be different aesthetic insights for interpretation of literature and that they can lead to genuine disputes in criticism has two important ramifications. One is that, despite the fact that disputes may be informed by valuable insights into literature and human experience, their proponents may all be forced to reexamine their positions. Such a reexamination is likely to enrich and deepen one's understanding of the modes of reasoning involved in critical interpretations and thereby may help one avoid schematic categories for the apprehension of a given literary work. The other ramification is related to the first. It is that disputants may realize, as a result of their dispute, that the inapplicability of physical modes of inquiry does not entail rejection of objectivity as such for criticism, because otherwise the dispute would be grounded in subjective preferences and could not properly be called a dispute. These ramifications argue against the claim of the self-confirming nature of different critical languages, for it is only in terms of a rejection of the presumed autonomous and incommensurate nature of critical languages that one can say that one or another interpretation is weak or inadequate, that one or another critical language is weak or inadequate.

It is important to notice that, through the history of criticism as well as the history of philosophy, significant changes have occurred in both as a result of reaction against the conceptual hardening of one or another mode of thinking. Changes in criticism occur, for instance, not just because one mode of thinking has dominated the field too long, though that is true, but also because the dominant mode has become so categorical that it has ceased to recognize its relation of mutuality with literary works. Consequently, the reaction does not come simply from those who reject it; it also comes from its adherents who attempt to reorient and reassess it in order to bring out its value which presumably got distorted by the initial excessive schematism in its first adherents' articulations of it. The resurgence of romantic studies in recent criticism and of neoromantic trends in recent literature and arts is a good example of this quasi-dialectical movement in the history of the concepts of art and criticism. To take another example, the emphasis on content and individuality in nineteenth-century literature led, by reaction, to a rise of classicism in modern literature and arts; the reaction was so strong initially that Ortega y Gasset even advocated "a dehumanization of art."[63]

Because of the close relation between criteria and literary works, criticism is neither a natural science nor a branch of a formal discipline but a hermeneutical discipline, and it necessarily fails to satisfy a blueprint which makes the natural sciences, or the modes of inquiry from the social sciences, exemplars of rational inquiry. When these modes are presented as exemplars of inquiry for criticism, either criticism will be misconceived and distorted by being pressed into the deductive or the inductive mold or it will be misdescribed as not being a genuine mode of reasoning, and it will accordingly be rejected altogether, since it fails to fit into either of these two molds. Critical theorists who try to defend criticism by misdescribing it as essentially scientific and logical, and theorists who attack criticism because they recognize that it is neither scientific nor logical have all been driven to their similar though opposite mistakes by another, more serious mistake which both groups share. They have failed to recognize the role and importance of modes of reasoning which are neither inductive nor deductive but rather a priori; and these modes of reasoning are nondeductive and involve logical connections which are nonnecessary. Fascinated by the neatness, simplicity, and elegance of scientific theory and its practical applications, critical theorists often have been captives of a craving for unity, simplicity, and generality. They have

supposed that all experiences, all good criticism, and all valuable literary creativity must be describable in inductive or deductive modes of
reasoning in accordance with one's chosen paradigm of inquiry. Thus
they have often overlooked and misrepresented the complex nondeductive and noninductive modes of apprehension which govern
criticism at its best.[64]

In criticism when the skeptical questioning of a dominant critical
mode begins to make serious impact, it is usually the case that such
questioning has promoted explicitly or implicitly another mode of
criticism, another fundamental commitment. To expand briefly on
this point, changes in modes of criticism occur primarily in two ways:
they may occur in one's critical practice, and they may also occur for
the entire climate of criticism. In the first case, because the commitment which was once the enabling ground of one's criticism has now
lost its grip and given way to another, one has reoriented one's critical
practice. The changes in the second case are more complex and are
related, in fundamental ways, to the changes in the culture as a
whole. Changes of this sort occur rather slowly and are not wholly
attributable to one or another individual's efforts, though they may
crystallize more fully in the work of one thinker than in the works of
those who more or less obscurely and unwittingly pave the way for
major changes in the culture. To give a simple but important example
from literary criticism, Wordsworth championed the self-expression-
ist doctrine of poetry but also retained such elements of the neoclassical theory as the moral aspects of the poet's function. However,
romanticism gradually but decisively made a major shift of emphasis
from community to the individual.[65]

Humanistic and aesthetic discourses do not aim at a conception of
truth towards which the entire community of minds is moving. For
science I would insist, with Popper, that diachrony is inescapable; I
would also insist, with Kuhn, that one ignores synchrony at the risk
of great loss in knowledge. For humanistic discourse, on the other
hand, the past is neither disconfirmed nor the only repository of values. It is the province as well as the prison-house of the individual
talent. And criticism is rational to the extent to which critics observe
the interdependence between critical criteria and the literary works
they study. A major critical performance can be methodologically
sound, though never quite fully articulated or logically defensible, except on its own terms. And these terms will always be governed by a

fundamental commitment which can be logically scrutinized and rejected but never refuted by any logic of inquiry. It cannot be refuted because it is impossible to arrive at universally agreed upon standards that establish a logic of inquiry. Literary interpretations can of course be seriously criticized. Some of them could be shown to be downright wrong, confused, inadequate, or silly, and others could be shown to be more plausible or convincing. To admit that a literary interpretation can be criticized is not to say that one can also propose a determinate structure of reasoning which all literary interpretations must follow in order to claim legitimacy. Epistemologically, then, major critical practice is never so precarious as the sciences are in terms of both Popper and Kuhn. The reason for the epistemological soundness is that fundamental critical commitments can never be falsified, though they may cease to attract attention. Yet disagreements in criticism imply that disputants agree at least on one thing—that they are making claims about what is objectively true of a poem. And although all criticism is undergirded by conceptual structures and therefore by aesthetic commitments, critical disputes in principle ought to involve the opponents in examining whether their conceptual structures are good or adequate, whether their specific interpretations of poems are good or adequate. Once we recognize the mutual dependence of criteria and literary works, we may also recognize that our conceptual structures are inadequate or that they have become, as John Wisdom puts it, "a network which confines our minds"[66] and not instruments of critical vision.

CHAPTER SEVEN

Deconstruction and Criticism

> *This is an age without passion: it leaves everything*
> *as it is, but cunningly empties it of significance.*
> *Instead of culminating in a rebellion, it reduces the*
> *outward reality of all relationships to a reflective*
> *tension which leaves everything standing but makes*
> *the whole of life ambiguous.*
> Kierkegaard

As I have argued in Chapter 6, the concept of criticism is a changing and dynamic concept and cannot be reduced to a statement of essence which can be captured by any one theory of criticism. Criticism is therefore the arena of contest where different theories of criticism compete for supremacy by trying to exhibit their presumed greater efficacy for interpreting literary works, and where each theory explicitly or implicitly claims for itself the proper credentials for both grasping and putting to effective use the concept of criticism. Moreover, I argued that while some of the theories can be shown to be confused, erroneous, silly, or downright wrong, the theories that possess genuine insights into the concept of criticism are necessarily partial and limited and require sophisticated defense and characterization. Increase in sophistication and complexity in a theory, however, does not mean that the conflict and difference among literary theories can be overcome by an eventual critical harmony, because to believe that as an unquestionable possibility toward which all criticism and its theory must move is to self-complacently believe that one has acquired a perspective that transcends the finite and historical nature of one's understanding.

If my discussion thus far makes sense it should enable us to examine critically what purports to be the most radical form of contemporary criticism, "deconstruction." I want to focus on two related versions of deconstructionist criticism: one is that developed by Paul de Man, and the other is a whole series of antisystematic, antimetaphysical studies by Jacques Derrida. De Man and Derrida seem to agree on certain fundamental notions about the nature of language and the problem of reading literary and philosophical texts, notions that they employ in order to articulate and defend their thought. Though there is a convergence between de Man and Derrida, it is Derrida who has developed the radical implications of the thought of Nietzsche and Heidegger, and it is mainly Derrida's thought, supplemented by de Man's, that their followers have sought to transpose to criticism. Though I focus on de Man's entire critical career, my discussion will engage only his specific notions about language, literature, and criticism. My discussion, however, of the relevance of Derrida's thought to criticism will apply to the early as well as the later phase of de Man's criticism.

Paul de Man and the Allegory of Reading

THERE ARE THREE phases in de Man's critical career that need to be carefully examined. The first phase culminates in his well-known essay "The Rhetoric of Temporality," the second in his collection of essays in *Blindness and Insight*, and the third in the essays written since 1971, some of which are collected in revised and altered form in his recent book, *Allegories of Reading*.[1] The significance of the first phase derives from de Man's radical reinterpretation of romanticism, one that puts into question several traditional interpretations of romanticism, specifically those proposed by M. H. Abrams, William K. Wimsatt, and Earl Wasserman. The second phase conducts a series of critical discussions of several major contemporary critics and theorists, offers some generalizations about the nature of both literature and criticism, and proposes a theory of literary history. The third phase takes its inspiration from the thought of Derrida and attempts a series of deconstructive readings of several philosophical and literary texts; its primary contribution is the theory of interpretation it proposes. It is my purpose to show that, despite the differences among these three phases in his critical career, the form underlying de Man's theory and practice remains unvarying and problematical.

189

De Man's earliest position is existentialist, deriving largely from the early works of Jean-Paul Sartre, and contains some elements of the thought of Nietzsche and Heidegger.[2] De Man criticizes the early romantics for philosophical mystification or error in their literary works[3] and offers an observation that will provide the essential ingredient for his revisionist reading of romanticism. Romanticism, construed in traditional critical terms, privileges symbol and castigates allegory, because the first seeks unity between thought and being, sign and referent, word and concept, whereas the second attempts a mimetic representation of the world. The symbolic drive wishes to establish an identity between "the substance and its representations," a relationship in which "the intervention of time is merely a matter of contingency." For the allegorical drive, however, the relationship between *signifiant* and *signifie* (its meaning) "necessarily contains a constitutive temporal element." The necessity derives from the fact that the allegorical sign must "refer to another sign that precedes it." Yet the preceding sign does not contain the essence of coincidence between subject and object, because "it is of the essence of this previous sign to be pure anteriority" ("Rhetoric of Temporality," p. 190). De Man, in seeking to reverse the opposition between symbol and allegory, wants to question the valuation prized by the traditional interpreters of romanticism and at times offered by the romantics themselves. He thus argues that symbol, far from being opposed to allegory, is in fact indistinguishable from it. The traditional definition of symbol is essentialist and represents what Sartre would call "bad faith": it yearns for a condition of being that human beings cannot authentically acquire. The symbolic drive, consequently, is a refusal to accept man's condition as a form of predicament in which man must live beyond hope and beyond nostalgia. Seen as allegory, however, symbol would free itself from its essentialist bad faith, for it is in the nature of allegory to disclose the unbridgeable gulf between word and thing, sign and referent. Moreover, allegory, as de Man defines it, affirms its cultural and historical nature, and becomes the authentic discourse of the *pour soi*, a discourse that recognizes that human being cannot be like natural being, that natural being, though ontologically independent, has no necessary privilege over human being (pp. 188, 194, 195).

Reversing, then, the traditional schema of the dialectical relationship between subject and object, de Man argues that the dialectic inheres in "the temporal relationships that exist within a system of allegorical signs." This dialectic is "a conflict between a conception of the self seen in its authentically temporal predicament and a defensive strategy that tries to hide from this self-knowledge." The romantic poets find their "true voice" when they experience moments of negative self-knowledge, ones that bring them to realize that human being is not continuous with natural being, that, though natural being is ontologically secure because of its possession of spatial permanence, human being forever remains caught within the temporal nature of its exisence (pp. 190, 197). Thus the rhetoric of temporality constitutes the profound and original moments of romantic poetry and liberates the romantics from self-mystification induced in them by their own desire to find ontological security for human being by a fusion or continuity with natural being. "Wide areas of European literature of the nineteenth and twentieth centuries," writes de Man, "appear as regressive with regard to the truths that come to light in the last quarter of the eighteenth century" (p. 191). If literature derives its value from its awareness of the condition of human being which forever identifies man's transcendental homelessness, the function of criticism would seem to reside for de Man in an identification of those moments of awareness which disclose man's temporal predicament, moments which are truly constitutive of literature. For de Man this identification would require a vigilant observation of the self's proclivity to fall into mystification or error.

It is clear, then, that de Man's important concern is to identify and question philosophical regression in romantic literature, romantic thought, and their interpretations by modern critics and historians. This concern entails a belief that certain philosophical views are unquestionably correct, and its corollary that they are constitutive of literature in its genuinely serious and profound moments. If the romantics gave priority to the self, then for de Man it is part of the periodic confusions occurring in romantic poetry.[4] De Man's interpretation thus intends to be a philosophical disclosure of two opposed strands in romanticism and to isolate that which is finally enduring and which truly deserves the name of literature. However, this project is subject to serious theoretical criticism. De Man conceives criticism to be an act of philosophical interpretation, though he construes it in an extremist and simplified sense. As he conceives it, philosophical interpretation identifies and questions bad or supposedly "exploded" philosophical views in literary works and shows where and when a literary work possesses "authentic" philosophical content. But this cannot help de Man toward a genuine critical appreciation of the power of romantic poetry. For there arises the crucial question of the propriety of subjecting, in the name of literary criticism, a particular philosophical view to criticism from a presumably more enlightened philosophical one. The question, in other words, is whether literary criticism or interpretation ought to be concerned with both making philosophical criticism of literature and offering the criterion of "authentic" literature in terms of a presumed correct philosophical view. There is no reason to deny the value of philosophical interpretation of literature, but there is every reason to question the propriety of criticizing (in the sense of rejecting) a specific philosophical view believed to be implicit in a poem. De Man's method seems to imply that he has a better philosophical logic and view. In point of fact, however, he commits the fallacy of historical progress. His shrewd qualification that the late eighteenth century had developed the view he finds authentic does not really obscure the existentialist conceptual framework that operates in "The Rhetoric of Temporality."

Moreover, the question is not whether one ought to take into account philosophical views implicit in literary works. For when one refuses to consider philosophical views implicit in a literary work as a legitimate critical concern, criticism is liable to degenerate into a strictly formalistic approach unconcerned with serious content and attitude. Or, one is liable to create a great tradition in the manner of Eliot and Leavis and to reject the works that espouse heretical philosophical views. De Man, at the opposite pole from Eliot and Leavis, is in the grip of a metaphysical commitment. And he is convinced that he is possessed of the truth about the authentic condition of man's being in the world and in nature. It is this conviction that provides him with the criteria of interpretation and judgment. Suspending the question who has acquired the true insight into the philosophical content of romanticism, one may yet ask whether one's belief in the acquisition of that truth will necessarily help one better appreciate romantic poetry. One could well argue that Wimsatt, Abrams, and Wasserman do not ponder or articulate the ambivalences in romantic poetry. Yet, to the extent that de Man's philosophical commitment dictates what is, and what is not, authentic, he cannot truly claim to have acquired a grasp of the difficulties involved in responding to romantic poetry.

There is no reason to say, however, that one cannot talk about profound moments in literary works and about moments when some literary works seem poor in conception or weak in execution. But this
grasp occurs in the hermeneutic process of realizing a literary work.
Experience, stability, consistency of critical response, capacity for
grasping nuances of literary expression, and a host of other elements—
these features of the hermeneutic process help one experience the
power and seriousness of a literary work; and it is this process that
helps one discover a failure of artistic skill, a weakening in conception, or the poverty of imagination operating throughout or at a
given moment in a literary work. When de Man elevates allegory over
symbol because the latter is the product of an "ontological bad faith"
("Rhetoric of Temporality," p. 194), he gives us a strictly metaphysical
reading that stems from his explicit philosophical commitment. Inasmuch as he wishes to practice and advocate criticism in terms of a
specific philosophical world-view, de Man has failed to take into account an important consideration: with respect to different metaphysical systems or belief-structures, one cannot legitimately say that
one's own perspective is intrinsically superior to any other because
each provides its proponent with a set of criteria in terms of which to
make sense of phenomena and to take responsibility for what one
says, means, and does. To compare one perspective with another in
order to arrive at a more enlightened perspective is more often than
not to commit the fallacy of historical progress. One who commits
this fallacy, of course, does so in order to guard against relativism. Yet
relativism is never properly avoided by a complacent assertion of the
superiority of one's own beliefs, since the latter stand often prompts
one, as it does de Man, to find one's own beliefs in the works one
admires. The myth of historical progress, however, constantly needs
to be exposed, not only because it breeds a false sense of philosophical superiority in the later ages, but more crucially because it is precisely this myth that underlies the quest for certainty which has been
the temptation of epistemology from Plato through Descartes, Kant,
to positivists and some exponents of analytic philosophy. De Man
writes, in all three phases of his criticism, from the vantage point of
certainty.

It is in order to avoid the myth of historical progress, or of the unquestionable validity of an insight that is supposed to help prevent
one from falling into regression, and to avoid relativism, that I have
sought to appropriate Gadamer's notion of a fusion of horizons. To

experience this fusion one does not assume the intrinsic superiority of either the past or the present; one simply engages a process by which the work acquires its contemporaneity in one's experience without superimposition of one's philosophical views. Again, this does not imply a denial of the value of sophisticated philosophical interpretation and analysis in literary and cultural criticism; it simply denies value to philosophical views as prepackaged conceptual structures. When poems become compelling because of their capacity to yield philosophical views that later ages may have acquired, the whole process of criticism is forced into a deductive and predictable mold of thinking, for a critic holding a specific view will find it in some poems and criticize others for their condition of mystification or philosophical naiveté because they do not embody the presumed enlightened view. This is de Man's strategy of criticism.

Consider for a moment de Man's method of interpreting poems. He quotes Wordsworth's lines from *The Prelude*: "The immeasurable height / Of woods decaying, never to be decayed / The stationary blasts of waterfalls." And then he interprets the lines thus: "Such paradoxical assertions of eternity in motion can be applied to nature but not to a self caught up entirely within mutability. The temptation exists, then, for the self to borrow, so to speak, the temporal stability that it lacks from nature, and to devise strategies by means of which nature is brought down to a human level while still escaping from 'the unimaginable touch of time'" ("Rhetoric of Temporality," p. 181). This response is a characteristic feature of de Man's mode of reading. He takes from a literary work a line or a moment that he considers significant and then derives from it an apparently unquestionable proposition. In this case the proposition is about the mutability of the self. Insofar as this is a major proposition (and it is an obviously existentialist one), it cannot withstand philosophical scrutiny. To call the self unstable, or "caught up entirely within mutability" in an absolute existentialist sense is both to forestall possibility of any meaningful action and to abandon acceptance of responsibility by the existentialist agent. Consequently, if, in an abstract sense, history becomes a welter of meaningless or absurd actions, in a real sense there is no possibility of any viable connection among events in one's life. Yet neither consequence need follow from a rejection of the idealist conceptions of history, self, and human action, though it is probably true that these conceptions are rather sanguine and simplistic. The extreme existentialist posture in de Man's notion of the self is merely an inversion of this sanguinary idealism, and is at bottom not seriously distinguishable from it.

The concept of mutability that de Man holds is an extremist metaphysical notion which forces him to valorize those moments in a poem that seem to express it. This concept, however, is a radicalized version of the concept of change and voids itself of any value by its extremism. The concept of change itself makes sense against the background of stability and consistency. In itself, when construed in extreme terms, it leads to dissolution of the entire fabric of cultural concepts. This fabric, as I suggested in Chapter 6, is not held together by some form of internal harmony or unity among cultural concepts but in a relation of dialogue and conflict which contributes to the difficult process of qualification and recharacterization of all our cultural concepts. When Sartre proposed the "progressive-regressive" method it was in order to mediate between existentialism and Marxism.[5] For the notion of the self proposed in his early thought was, in its extreme form, incompatible with revolutionary action or hope, and it represented a serious theoretical impasse for any significant historical reflection. De Man's notion of the self's captivity in "mutability" operates as a rigid a priori concept which undermines his critical practice by turning it into a metaphysical discourse. It is, of course, a tribute to de Man's logical rigor and honesty that he allows the impasse implicit in his concept to manifest itself at the level of his practice. The resolute adherence to the consequences of his commitment will continue, as we shall see, to lead his work to the exploration of further impasses, not just for the theory and practice of criticism but in principle for all discourse.

We have questioned, then, de Man's philosophical commitment and the method he employs in order to reinterpret romanticism, and we have suggested the ways in which de Man's characterization of romanticism can be questioned and shown to be arbitrary. Yet there is little doubt that romanticism, when construed through an interpretation of romantic poetry, will appear to be highly complex, ambiguous, and heterogeneous. But is subtle response to poetry conceivable strictly in terms of the radical philosophy of a Sartre or a Derrida? Why not accept that romantic poetry is ambiguous, that its power derives from its ambivalences and self-contradictions as from other features, that though it may seem to offer one or another comprehensive schema of propositions, its ambivalence—rather than being reducible to some intrapsychic warfare among poets as Bloom would have it, or to a Sartrean stance of authenticity as the early de Man would have it—is the product of a genuine quandary of a poetic age that had lost the certitude of its predecessors, that there is a new and desperate attempt in romantic poetry to understand nature and the human self, that this attempt traverses a whole range of relations? When there are no longer socially sanctioned norms available to a poet like Wordsworth, when the inherited forms of writing poetry seem integrally connected to the norms that have lost their efficacy, it is inevitable that he should search for forms of literary expression which may help him articulate the novelty and strangeness of his experience. It is no wonder that, with the foundations of the Renaissance poetic and cultural inheritance shaken, Wordsworth should give expression to the contradictions and ambivalences of his feelings, that he should seek to anchor his own self in the permanence of natural objects, and that he should worry over being caught in the process of change that reveals his difference from natural objects. It is against the knowledge of the self's deficiency that some of Wordsworth's best poems raise a song of thanks to memory and imagination which may provide a temporary stay against the ruins of time. Thus if memory and imagination are the agents of consolation, they are also the agents that heighten one's sense of the self's losses. Consequently, the best of Wordsworth's poems are certainly structured by a profoundly paradoxical response, and the burden of criticism is to find ways that would facilitate the process of hermeneutic reflection without reducing it to the implications of a preconceived conceptual structure.

BECAUSE THE NEXT TWO PHASES of de Man's critical career overlap and are in principle subject to the criticism leveled at his first phase, I shall treat them together. In *Blindness and Insight* de Man discusses a number of major contemporary critics and arrives at one crucial conclusion: "Critics' moments of greatest blindness with regard to their own critical assumptions are also moments at which they achieve their greatest insights." For his readings of these critics reveal to him that "not only does the critic say something which the work does not say, but he even says what he does not mean to say" (*Blindness and Insight*, p. 109). De Man's statement that the critic "even says what he does not mean to say" involves a complicated conception of the nature of

assumptions and its relations to literary works. One might want to explain this conception by saying that what one says in the process of
interpreting a literary work is liable to go against the strict logic of
one's assumptions. Yet de Man would not accept this explanation because he is interested in constructing a general theory about the rhetoric of critical theory and practice. His interest is certainly a legitimate
theoretical concern, one that ought to be carefully scrutinized. The
shape of his theory emerges most clearly in his essay on Derrida,
where de Man asserts "the interaction between critical blindness and
critical insight . . . as a logical necessity dictated by the very nature of
all critical language" (p. 111). This is a radical view of the nature of
contradictions in criticism, since de Man does not merely say that critics sometimes contradict themselves or that they occasionally say
things that go against their enabling assumptions. Such contradictions
can be overcome with greater awareness of the meaning of what one
says and of the implications of one's assumptions. De Man's view, on
the other hand, characterizes critical language as inherently limited.

One might inquire as to when one is justified in saying that the
critic says "something that work does not say." The answer, of course,
is simple: only from the perspective of an insight into the work. Yet
the answer cannot be simple if one recalls our earlier argument that
conflicting or incompatible insights into literature lead critics to interpret it in conflicting or divergent ways. De Man's mode of proceeding
throughout *Blindness and Insight* seems to suggest that literature possesses an insight into the patterns of its own duplicity and that by an
uncanny reflective power he too possesses that insight, which other
critics can gain only when they unwittingly violate their own stated
assumptions. Thus whereas critical language is inherently limited,
de Man's own language must claim for itself an essential fusion with
literary language. Whether or not de Man would accept this implication, which is logically unavoidable for him, the more serious
consequence of his view of criticism is that no interpretation can ever
claim to have grasped the meaning of the text it interprets: "the possibility of reading can never be taken for granted" (p. 107). The traditional project of reading a literary work for the meaning it embodies
or helps one experience is thus seen as an impossible one. This has
continued to be a crucial point in de Man's work, and extends even to
deconstructionist criticism, since it is caught in the antithetical project
of doing what cannot be done: deconstruction attempts to perform

"what it has shown to be impossible to do. As such we call it an allegory."[6] For de Man, then, the project of criticism is to be conceived as one that seeks to articulate the impossibility of reading. To characterize and defend this nature of reading literature is to seek to release critical language from the delusion of a finality of meaning and hence to reestablish the essential oneness of his language with literary language.

De Man's conception of criticism depends on his conception of literary language. The point is clearly made in the following statement:

> That sign and meaning can never coincide, is what is precisely taken for granted in the kind of language we call literary. Literature, unlike everyday language, begins on the far side of this knowledge; it is the only form of language free from the fallacy of unmediated expression. All of us know this, although we know it in the misleading way of a wishful assertion of the opposite. Yet the truth emerges in the foreknowledge we possess of the true nature of literature when we refer to it as *fiction*. [*Blindness and Insight*, p. 17]

Thus literary language derives its complexity not simply from its projection of multiple meanings of what it seems to say but from its awareness of the philosophical implications of operations of language. Literary language is metalinguistic in that, aware of its own falsehood, it exercises such a complex control over readers that it duplicitously leads them to say what they implicitly know to be untrue. A literary text "can tell its story as a fiction knowing it full well that the fiction will be taken for fact and the fact for fiction; such is the necessarily ambivalent nature of literary language." Literary language not only accounts for the "rhetoricity" of its own mode, it also "postulates the necessity of its own misreading" (*Blindness and Insight*, p. 136). De Man, then, formulates this idea in a statement that purports to be a definition of the constitutive principle of literature: "any text that implicitly or explicitly signifies its own rhetorical mode and prefigures its own misunderstanding as the correlative of its own rhetorical nature" is "literary" (p. 136). Because fiction names the void of reality and at the same time claims knowledge of its own fictional nature, it escapes the inherently fallacious nature of all man's concepts and structures that seek to capture reality. For de Man this quality of fiction "characterizes the work of literature in all its essence" (p. 17).

It is important to remember that de Man's concept of the impossibility of reading is a logical or conceptual impossibility, not an empirical one, just as Cleanth Brooks's notion of the heresy of paraphrase is a conceptual, not an empirical notion. In other words, empirically every act of interpretation cannot help paraphrasing or reading a text, but conceptually no single interpretation can exhaust the richness of meaning a poem embodies (Brooks), no single reading can claim to arrive at a determinate reading of a literary work because the work necessarily enacts the process whereby any determinate meaning is put into question by the antithetical meaning that cohabits with the determinate meaning (de Man). The form of the concept of criticism in Brooks and de Man, despite the difference in viewpoints, would seem to be the same, since they seem to agree that criticism is a metaphor for the act of reading, that one can never claim a reassuring finality for the interpretation one has proposed. Brooks's concept has its support in the organic theory of idealism, whereas de Man's concept derives its support from the revisionist and problematized idealism of Nietzsche and Heidegger. De Man, following Heidegger, construes the act of criticism as a dialogical concept: "The completed form could never exist as a concrete aspect of the work that could coincide with a sensorial or semantic dimension of the language. It is constituted in the mind of the interpreter as the work discloses itself in response to his questioning. But this dialogue between work and interpreter is endless" (pp. 31–32). Thus if for Brooks literary works are forever inexhaustible because of their tensional or ironic nature, for de Man literature, far from possessing the plenitude of a full being or meaning, embodies as its essence an awareness of the absence of plenitude.

In the work written since the publication of *Blindness and Insight*, de Man has pushed his critical practice and theory into a far more radicalized and skeptical stance. His essays on Nietzsche and Rousseau, for instance, leave no doubt that de Man has now boldly embraced the final logical consequences of his position. The concept of fiction available to de Man in *Blindness and Insight* because of its peculiar dependence on the antithetical concept of reality is no longer valid, for de Man would now seem to consider the distinction itself to be the result of a self-mystification. If language is fundamentally metaphorical, then the critic can no longer talk about the "constitutive" or "essential" quality of literature, except in terms of the figurality of all language. Neither can one posit any distinction between criticism and literature.

De Man's increasing preoccupation with rhetoric and its implications for logic, reason, and thought emerges most clearly in his essays on Nietzsche. The exemplary contribution of Nietzsche resides for de Man in the shift that he brings about in the study of rhetoric from the methods of oratory and persuasion to a theory of figures and tropes. It is Nietzsche's contention that tropes constitute the nature of language rather than being mere superadditions to it which one can subtract at will. De Man therefore argues that Nietzsche makes a "straightforward affirmation that the paradigmatic structure of language is rhetorical rather than representational or expressive of a referential, proper meaning."[7] Thus if language is originally figural or rhetorical, then the idea of a primitive, literal or unrhetorical language makes no sense. The rhetorical nature of language undermines the concept of truth, since the relation between referential and figural meaning is rendered ambivalent and problematic. A direct result of this idea for all interpretation is that instead of the assurance of unambiguous referential meaning desired by traditional philosophy and criticism we are faced with "vertiginous possibilities of referential aberration."[8] Thus thematic interpretation is exposed as a fundamentally misguided effort, since a rhetorically self-conscious reading recognizes the necessity of a reading that will articulate the abyssal possibilities of "referential aberration."

De Man's reading of Nietzsche has thus led him to overcome the existentialist antithesis between fiction and reality and the nostalgia for authenticity implicit in that antithesis. The shift in de Man's view, however, is not a radical break with the view in *Blindness and Insight*, though literary language no longer has the privilege granted in that book. Yet de Man's recent view—that rhetoric both founds and subverts all human discourse—is a further radicalization of the implications of *Blindness and Insight*. His insistence on the rhetorical nature of language only helps him develop his notion about the impossibility of reading literature into the final theoretical impasse: "Rhetoric is a *text* in that it allows for two incompatible, mutually self-destructive points of view and therefore puts an insurmountable difficulty in the way of any reading or understanding."[9] Discussing, for example, *The Birth of Tragedy*, he argues that the presumed radical interpretation of Dionysus as the authority of truth cannot be affirmatively stated, because the constant antithetical interplay of constantive and performative statements, of Apollo and Dionysus, in Nietzsche's text, forbids the possibility of any resolution of meaning.[10] The significance of a rhetorically aware reading, then, resides for de Man in the reader's capacity to grasp language as it is constituted by the moment of *aporia*, the moment that renders the meaning of a text fundamentally undecidable.

If in *Blindness and Insight* de Man had allowed a presence in the text of the intentionality of language as well as of the intentions of the author, now in a study of Rousseau's autobiographical work de Man develops a notion of textuality based on his reading of Nietzsche's theory of praxis: "Far from seeing language as an instrument in the service of a psychic energy, the possibility now arises that the entire construction of drives, substitutions, and representations is the aberrant, metaphorical correlative of the absolute randomness of language prior to any figuration of meaning."[11] The shift here in de Man's thought is from his earlier concern with literary language to language in general. Since the constitutive feature of figural language is its disruptive randomness, literature can no longer be distinguished from criticism or have priority over it. Neither can philosophy be distinguished from literature "in terms of a distinction between aesthetic and epistemological categories." For de Man's deconstruction of the figurality of language has disclosed "a shared lack of identity or specificity" for philosophy and literature.[12]

If all language is originally rhetorical, if rhetoric underlies the endlessness of the tension between constative and performative statements, then all presumed philosophical, historical, or literary texts do not simply permit but encourage misreadings. "If one wants to conserve the term 'literature', one should not hesitate to assimilate it with rhetoric. . . . The deconstruction of metaphysics, or 'philosophy' is an impossibility to the precise extent that it is 'literary'" (*Allegories of Reading*, p. 131). In other words, the privilege traditionally accorded to literature can be preserved by identifying literature with rhetoric. The term *literature* no longer retains its traditional valuation, since even philosophy (traditionally defined as dealing with the universal) resists deconstruction because it is always already self-deconstructed because of the motions of its rhetoric, which sustain the subversion of the *telos* of logic and grammar. Thus philosophy is "literature" precisely to the extent that it is caught in the moment of *aporia*. A text, any text, should be read "not in terms of explicit statements . . . but in terms of its rhetorical motions," since it cannot simply be reduced to intentions or to identifiable facts.[13] Thus every interpretation de Man might offer would always be a disclosure of the metaphorical subversions of all thematically or philosophically "coherent" meanings, another disclosure of the cancellations and narrative feints, of the endless reversals and substitutions taking place in language. To be seriously engaged in philosophical or literary discourse is to do nothing other than to attempt a characterization and recharacterization of the subversion of all textual authority. To be serious in any other way is to be naive or to be captive of Western ontotheological metaphysics. The only valid authority consists in according privilege to the critical consciousness indentured to a recognition of the subversive necessity of all linguistic expression.

MY CRITICISM of de Man's last two phases will be brief, for his deconstructionist phase is in principle subject to the criticism I offer in the next section, whereas *Blindness and Insight* is subject to the criticism already offered of his first phase. In *Blindness and Insight* de Man finds almost all criticism traversed by a pattern of blindness and insight, where blindness stands for logical, rational thinking, and insight for the force of intuition and imagination. De Man thus sets up an opposition between reason and intuition or imagination; or more accurately, he finds the critics he discusses influenced by a pattern of dualism in which reason is opposed to imagination and logic to rhetoric. This pattern allows him to disentangle what he considers genuine insight from misunderstanding or blindness in the work of a given critic. But de Man cannot validly regard misunderstanding as intrinsic to critical language or thinking, in opposition to the luminosity of literary language, because insofar as he judges others as making mistakes, or saying unwittingly insightful things, he is faced with conceiving his own discourse as free from the fallacy of all mediated expression. The reason he is able to disclose errors in others is that he must implicitly think of his own discourse as "literature," free from the liability of critical language to fall into error or self-mystification. It is conceivable that de Man would not make such an egregious claim. His claim, then, to knowledge of the true insight into the nature of the language of both literature and criticism must be a metatheoretical one; his theory therefore must be assessed as a metatheory, a discourse about the theory and practice of criticism.

The first question to pose before his theory is whether de Man could possibly observe the interaction between critical blindness and critical insight without being entrapped in a form of blindness engendered by his own critical language. It would be useful to guess what answer he might give. He cannot say that he has achieved a kind of transcendental critical neutrality, that he holds no a priori standpoint, for he already holds the view that fictions name the void of reality. But he might answer that his theory of critical language is the product of a complex double reading of the critics he examines and the works they interpret. Yet this answer is not available to de Man, because he already holds a literary theory and that theory is a direct logical extension of his metaphysical doctrine. His own words will illustrate the point: "The consciousness does not result from the absence of something, but consists of the presence of a nothingness. Poetic language names this void with ever-renewed understanding. . . . The human mind will go through amazing feats of distortion to avoid facing 'the nothingness of human matters'" (*Blindness and Insight*, p. 18). Thus de Man not only holds a specific critical perspective but could not conduct his discourse without one. In terms of the logic of his theory the insight de Man would acquire into literature would annihilate the premises that led up to it. If his stated assumptions were thus annihilated, he could not legitimately seek to establish them by examining Derrida's commentary on Rousseau. But he does. The only argument available to de Man is that his critical language resides, as it were, in the very heart of literary language, and is free from the limitations that he persistently exposes in other critics.

It is clear by now that de Man believes that he has acquired the unquestionable perspective on literature and criticism, one that enables him to establish an unproblematical relation between literary language and his own critical language. But this claim would contradict one of his major statements in *Blindness and Insight*: "There are no longer any standpoints that can *a priori* be considered privileged. . . . All structures are, in a sense, equally fallacious and are therefore myths" (p. 10). It seems to me that the major enterprise of *Blindness and Insight* has by now begun to collapse. De Man holds a literary theory and derives it strictly from a metaphysical doctrine, he refuses privilege to any standpoint but does not see his refusal as a problem for his own theory, and he holds a theory about critical and literary language but does not see it as an obstacle to his own critical language. What might be the source of de Man's own blindness? Why is it that despite his rather remarkable power of theoretical reflection he remains so persistently blind to the implications of his own thought? These questions cannot be answered by seeking to disclose the pattern of blindness generated by his own critical language, because to attempt to do so would be to take for granted the truth of his theory. (De Man's theoretical tactic is shrewd in that he shows other critics as seriously confused or in error, but if someone shows his own work to contain a pattern of blindness it would only confirm his own theory.) A satisfactory answer to these questions will reveal that de Man's difficulties have their source in a confusion over the nature of a priori commitments.

Without repeating our earlier discussion of the nature of a priori commitments, we still need to reflect on the implications of the ways in which they are held. Some theorists hold them in a dogmatic fashion in that they consider them to be privileged insights into the nature of literature, language, culture, or thought. One who holds an a priori commitment in this way considers himself to be holding a metatheory that is in possession of truth and authority in a given field of inquiry. Contrary to his sobering generalization which would deny such a posture, de Man holds his own a priori commitment as an indubitably true metatheory about literature and reality: fictions name the void of reality and know themselves as fiction. There is another way, however, of holding an a priori commitment, and that consists of a penumbra of prejudgments and preconceptions, a kind of critical atmospherics of literary or philosophical presuppositions that enables one to enter into dialogue with a literary or philosophical text. When an a priori commitment is held in this way, it facilitates critical practice. De Man's basic propositions, however, instead of helping him inaugurate response to literature, predetermine it; they become strict hypotheses which he then sets out to confirm in his critical practice.

The criticism offered here thus suggests that de Man has no legitimate grounds for implying that his a priori commitment is more correct than that of the early romantics or the New Critics or Georges Poulet. His claim would make the experience of literature impossible, except as elaborations of the truth of his stated commitment. The conception implicitly held by de Man of the nature of operations of a priori commitments leaves no room for the possibility of confusion or error in the interpretation of a literary work. Confusion or error becomes at best the product of a critic's assumptions, and insight the product of the critic's unwitting violation of his assumptions. The form of his adoption of a priori principles is such that unless he realizes that they cannot operate in that way except detrimentally to the practice of criticism or philosophy, de Man could at best change his specific principle in order to adopt another. And this is precisely what happens in the two phases that follow the phase of his existentialist commitment.

Since de Man's specific analyses are products of the highly prescriptive nature of his theory, it follows that they may not be free from the difficulties that attend the theory. I want to illustrate this claim by probing de Man's reading of the American New Critics. De Man undertakes a "re-examination of the assumptions on which the position of autonomy was founded, for it is not at all certain that this position has been well understood by the American formalists" (*Blindness and Insight*, p. 22). And he chooses to examine the New Critical stand on intention. De Man argues that Wimsatt's rejection of intentionality "leads him into contradictory assumptions about the ontological status of the work of literature" (p. 24). For though Wimsatt construes the poem as an act which by definition would accommodate intention, he hypostatizes the poem as an object. This hypostasis suppresses the intentional character of the poem and requires as a condition of critical description that "the status of literary language [be] similar to that of a natural object." Wimsatt's hypostatization rests on "a misunderstanding of the nature of intentionality" (p. 25). For the New Critics, by describing the poetic imagination in terms of the organic analogy, failed to realize its inherently intentional structuring nature. Consequently, their practical criticism, as it articulates the radical oppositions of significations, explodes the analogy between nature and poetic language. De Man grants that the New Criticism "perfected techniques that allow for considerable refinement in catching the details and nuances of literary expression." But this is because they "pragmatically entered into the hermeneutic circle of interpretation, mistaking it for the organic circularity of natural processes" (pp. 29, 27). The New Critics rejected intentionality because they feared that introducing "the principle of intentionality would imperil the organic analogy and lead to a loss of the sense of form" (p. 28). Moreover, the discrepancies between their theory and practice prevented them from integrating their discoveries of the distinctive structures of literary language into a unified, totalizing conception of form. The result was an ambivalence in American formalism such that "it was bound to lead to a state of paralysis" (p. 32).

It seems to me that de Man's reading of the New Critical autonomist principle is a seriously distorted one. As we saw in Chapter 3, Wimsatt and Beardsley do not deny intention as an element in a literary work; they rather question the legitimacy of a criticism that seeks to interpret the work by searching for intention outside it. Contrary to de Man, then, the New Critics did not reject intentionality but rather implied a distinction between intention and intentionality, for which the former is authorial statement outside a literary work and the latter a structural element within the work. It is true that the New Critics and even Wimsatt and Beardsley, to ensure objectivity to critical discourse, tend to talk about literary works as objects. It is also true that the organic analogy is part of the romantic problematic, and that the connection between art and biology is necessary for Kant to provide coherence to his philosophical system. But the success or failure of the concept of poetic autonomy does not depend on the organic analogy that initially helped the autonomist principle find expression. To say that the New Critical autonomist thesis depends on the organic analogy is to confine the legitimate scope of a critical concept to the historical context of its emergence. De Man, of course, would not allow for such a restriction because, besides being a gifted theorist who also happens to be thoroughly ahistorical, he believes in the possibility of a totalizing theory of literary form.

The totalizing theory that de Man sketches is at best a restatement in Heideggerian phenomenological terms of the New Critical concept of the literary work, for he argues that "the elucidating commentary simply tries to reach the text itself, whose full richness is there at the start" (*Blindness and Insight*, p. 30). As I argued in Chapter 4, the drive for objectivity in criticism (construed on the analogy of physical objects) was the reason for the New Critical misunderstanding of the concept of interpretation. De Man, on the other hand, has adopted a sophisticated concept of interpretation, but that adoption does not take him beyond the limitations of the New Critical concept of the literary work. Consider, for instance, de Man's statement of the relation between poetry and criticism: "Poetry is the foreknowledge of criticism. Far from changing or distorting it, criticism merely discloses poetry for what it is" (p. 31). The difficulty that attends the New Critical theory comes back to haunt de Man's theory: if there are different and conflicting interpretations, how are we to talk about the ontological status of the literary work? Are disagreements or differences to be conceived as the products of personal or historical prejudices of a critic, as Ingarden considered them to be? And if they are, can we be sure that they do not penetrate to the core of the interpretation that has pushed closer to the self-understanding of the work? The statement that "criticism discloses poetry for what it is" may be a charter for critical freedom, but it cannot be distinguished from critical confusion. Like Heidegger in his essay on Holderlin, de Man conceives poetry as the language of authenticity and assigns to it a quasi-transcendental status.[14] De Man's statement does not allow for the difficulties of talking about poetry which preoccupied the New Critics in their best endeavors. And de Man is in error again when he says that the New Critical rejection of intentionality hardens "the text into a sheer surface that prevents the stylistic analysis from penetrating beyond the sensory appearances to perceive this 'struggle with meaning' of which all criticism, including the criticism of forms, should give an account" (*Blindness and Insight*, p. 27). This stricture would apply to most stylistic criticism, but to apply it to the New Critical practice is to reduce that practice to a sterile formalism. For the New Criticism, for all its theoretical inconsistencies and contradictions, is a criticism performed in terms of irony and attitude, and its concern with form is for interpretation and evaluation of the quality and disposition of content in literary works.

IF IN THE DECONSTRUCTIONIST PHASE of his criticism de Man has forsaken the earlier claim to the true insight into the nature of literature and criticism, it is only in order to replace it with a new and more extreme insight into all discourse. Though I shall discuss deconstruction at length in the next section, I want to conclude this section with a few remarks on the stance of authority that controls de Man's deconstructionist work.

It seems to me that de Man's work involves a conflation of two opposed categories, for though he cannot validly distinguish criticism from literature and either from philosophy, he must theorize in a mode that makes specific propositions. Moreover, he intends his propositions to embody a specific unquestionable content. Consequently, there occurs a serious discrepancy between de Man's views and his own writing: language is for him constitutive of referential aberration and opens an endless play of tension between the constative and performative statements, yet his own language cannot be that. His language is referential, descriptive, objective, detached, and finally authoritative. He thus conducts his own discourse in the mode of truth that he has logically denied to all others. His discourse is a metacommentary which allows for neither dialogue nor conflict but rather issues in a series of declarative statements. De Man's work, in other words, presupposes the process of critical argument which his mode of thinking consistently prevents him from entering. By importing certain strict philosophical views into criticism de Man simply does not enter criticism as a shared practice. The result of his method is that his criticism of others cannot be taken as in any way intelligible. For he cannot recognize that the interpretive problem arises not because language autonomously engages its own deconstruction nor merely because an interpreter necessarily brings a structure of preconceptions and prejudgments, but because the interpreter may unselfconsciously impose this structure and hence do violence to an adequate interpretation which is the goal of understanding. De Man's case seems rather peculiar in that he self-consciously imposes his structure of prejudgments and cannot admit that his mode of proceeding does violence to the very process of understanding.

If his mode of interpretation had helped him to become aware of the structure of his prejudgments he could have then allowed for an openness necessary for proper hermeneutic reflection. If he had interpreted Rousseau or Nietzsche in a way that would preserve the writer's alien character, he could still have brought it into an intelligible relation with his own life-world. To engage interpretation in this manner is to grasp the finite and historical nature of one's understanding. But this limitation (which from a Heideggerian point of view would also constitute a condition of freedom and creativity) would go against de Man's aspiration to talk in the universalist mode, and it would recognize the importance of historical reflection. De Man, however, conceives the complexities of interpretation in such a manner that it has no place for historical reflection. In the preface to *Allegories of Reading* de Man says that he "began to read Rousseau seriously in preparation for a historical reflection on Romanticism but found [himself] unable to progress beyond local difficulties of interpretation" (p. ix). No one can question the sincerity of de Man's admission, for *Allegories of Reading* everywhere dramatizes the paralysis of understanding engendered by rhetoric. What is nevertheless open to question is that de Man should have entertained the idea of historical reflection on romanticism. For "The Rhetoric of Temporality," which may seem to suggest elements of a historical reflection, already demonstrates a dissolution of the very possibility of this idea. In that essay de Man not only privileges allegory over symbol, but discloses symbol to be indistinguishable from allegory. The essay finally shows irony itself to be the culminating condition of allegory. De Man had then begun the process of dissolution of distinctions and denied the possibility of historical reflection some time before Derrida came on the scene with his deconstructionist message.

One cannot help wondering why even some of de Man's opponents call his critical theory and practice "exemplary," what grounds one could give for a term of such high valuation. Yet the reason is simple: de Man has the courage of his convictions, and the courage consists in his resolute attempt to disclose the paralysis of meaning that he believes rhetoric engenders in all language. Densely written, all of de Man's essays vigorously assert and characterize his position. From the existentialist stance of his early criticism de Man moved to a Derridean position as soon as he found it a comprehensive radical statement on all of man's cultural endeavor. And it would be logically consistent for him to move to a more radical position in philosophy if one were available. De Man maintains his stance with imperturbable authority because he does not believe that his theory or criticism can be seriously challenged or criticized. It is this element of his stance which makes his radical colleagues and followers admire him and makes his opponents silent in dismay. But there is no reason for either uncritical adulation or dismayed silence. Both stances bifurcate criticism into orthodoxy and radicalism and prevent serious discussion from taking place. The next section will make an attempt toward a serious critical questioning of deconstructive criticism.

Jacques Derrida and the Metaphysics of Deconstruction

IN CALLING Derrida's project of deconstruction metaphysical at the outset, I want to indicate the lines along which my discussion of Derrida and specifically of deconstructionist criticism will move. By arguing that discourse cannot be conducted except within or at the boundary of the metaphysics of presence, Derrida has insisted on the need to develop concepts or nonconcepts antithetical yet, by a parasitical relation, close to this metaphysics. I shall argue that Derrida's critique of Western philosophy, despite its genuine radicalism, remains bound to the elaboration of theoretical reason and its various subconcepts in the philosophical texts that he seeks to deconstruct. My stronger argument will be that the alternative to theoretical reason and its various conceptual models cannot be provided by deconstruction but rather by a critique of theoretical reason elaborated in certain elements of Nietzsche's thought, in Wittgenstein's later works, and in some elements of Heideggerian hermeneutical theory developed by Gadamer. The alternative to the metaphysics of presence, in other words, is not Derrida's project of deconstruction because Derrida is perhaps its most distinguished heretical offspring; rather it is the elaboration of practical reason which would seek to restore the connection between language and its complex and often contradictory concepts on the one hand, and on the other, the forms of life evolved in specific historical contexts. Consistent with my discussion in Chapter 6, I shall not defend the rigidly objectivist concepts of culture promoted in one or another way by the metaphysics of presence, nor suggest the necessity of interpretive impasse, almost interminably (though often with great imaginative resourcefulness) offered by Derrida.

I shall instead argue that the deconstructionist project was engendered by the metaphysics of presence, though the necessity of deconstruction inheres in the paradoxical mode of attraction and repulsion felt toward that metaphysics by Derrida and (through him) by his followers. I shall also argue that a concern with practical reasoning need not lead to a total rejection of the whole network of concepts developed by various forms of theoretical reason. To take the example of literary criticism, one can study the history and theory of criticism since Plato in order to elicit valuable insights from it even when one discloses the ways in which some of the insights have become distorted because of one or another critic or theorist's compulsion to subsume them under rigid principles of epistemology and metaphysics. Critical inquiry, I shall argue, need not result in either the elaboration of theoretical reason (conceived as the quest for foundations) or the critique of that reason (conceived as the program for undermining that quest) because the second is at best an inversion of the first and logically requires it for its sustenance. The first pursues the ideals of certainty and objectivity, simplifies the concepts of interpretation and communication, and is in a sense mystified. The second, in contrast, occults the concepts of interpretation and communication and takes mystification itself as the goal of understanding. Neither alternative explains the complexity of relations that characterizes the major concepts of criticism and culture.

DERRIDA'S CONCERN is to examine a number of major philosophical texts, in order to expose what he considers to be the project of Western philosophy, its metaphysics of presence. This metaphysics is the project of Western philosophical reasoning, which has sought to establish that meaning is something self-present, that truth, self, origin, center are concepts that possess secure ontological essences. Derrida probes Plato, Rousseau, Hegel, and Saussure, among others, and interrogates them for their systems of valorization, and argues that the major texts of classical philosophy and semiology offer themselves as logically constructed arguments that purport to account for everything by *re-presentation*. "It would be possible to show," Derrida says, "that all the names related to fundamentals, to principles, or to the center have always designated the constant of a presence – *eidos*, *arche*, *energeia*, *ousia*, . . . conscience, God, man, and so forth."[15] He puts into question all of these founding concepts of Western thought by arguing that the detour of signs is inevitable. Consequently, the presumed relation between the sign and meaning, far from being natural, is inevitably arbitrary. The concepts they offer claim "a reassuring end to the reference from sign to sign" by conceiving an identity or proximity between the sign and the signified.[16] Derrida questions both this presumed relation and the metaphysics of presence authorizing that relation.

Derrida's double strategy of analysis and questioning emerges most clearly in his relatively early, though seminal, essay, "Differance." His coinage of the term *differance* is a play upon the French *différer* and helps elucidate what he characterizes as the ceaseless play of sign-substitutions which can never be traced to any ontological resting place. If one meaning of the term "indicates difference as distinction, inequality, or discernibility," the other "expresses the interpretation of delay, the interval of a *spacing* and temporalizing that puts off until 'later' what is presently denied, the possible that is properly impossible."[17] For classical semiology a sign represents that which one cannot possess; it is "a deferred presence," since it is conceivable only *on the basis* of the presence of the present that it defers and in view of the deferred presence one intends to "reappropriate."[18] Differance, however, provides a critique not only of classical Western semiology but also of phenomenology: "there is no presence before the semiological difference or outside of it."[19] Derrida's argument is not that the transcendental signified is forever absent but that it "is never absolutely present outside of a system of differences."[20] Consequently, mimesis, truth, representation, center, origin, self—these concepts are not rejected but rather problematized. While all of these terms and concepts seem to suggest the sense of ontologically secure essences, their possibility resides in their inherence in the system of differences. This possibility, in other words, is not a temporary deferral known to be realized in full self-presence but rather inheres in the impossibility of their ever acquiring ontological certitude.

Thus differance is a nonconcept or anticoncept, one that would resist reduction to essence. It is a grammatological term that helps Derrida clarify and elaborate the task of deconstruction. Derrida calls differance more primordial than Heidegger's "ontological difference," because it is "less conceivable than the difference between Being and beings."[21] Heidegger continues the quest for the proper word, the unique name, and calls it Being, which, though crossed, is nevertheless not distinguishable from a kind of "transcendental signified." Derrida's differance, on the other hand, does not retain this element of the transcendental signified. He thus tries to accomplish what he accuses Heidegger of having failed to do. Differance "commands nothing, rules over nothing, and nowhere does it exercise any authority. It is not marked by a capital letter. Not only is there no realm of differance, but differance is the subversion of every realm. This is obviously what is threatening and necessarily dreaded by everything in us that desires a realm."[22] Derrida's negations cannot be characterized as a form of negative ontotheology for which neither Being nor God could be named. For Derrida linguistic signs do not contain any "transcendental signified" but are the result of a "system of differance." Differance, then, is paradigmatic of his interpretive strategies, because it points to the play of differences which defers possible presence by showing it to be always absent. The relation between word and meaning or word and experience is never one of identity, proximity, or presence, since the meant object is never present in a word. One never encounters the object of signification; it is always absent. The object of signification is always the trace of a presence that never could be self-present.

Nearly all the other fundamental nonconcepts such as "trace," "supplement," "dissemination," that Derrida develops have essentially the same formal (non)attributes that characterize differance. His elaboration of the "trace" will illustrate the point. The sign is always determined by the trace of that which is forever absent; there is no possibility of its ever finding its full being. A trace never appears as itself but is the movement which makes anything that we could phenomenally call a visible trace. A trace necessarily occults itself when it appears and is therefore always a repetition with a difference. The notion of trace, then, exemplifies the process of something becoming other than itself. The trace is not a norm of control but simply an entry into the play of significations.[23]

Derrida's questioning of the metaphysics of presence has ramifications for virtually all of his interpretive endeavor. This metaphysics, as for instance in Rousseau, Saussure, and Lévi-Strauss, has tended to castigate writing as unnatural, usurpative violence, a castigation that valorizes speech as both innocent and in proximity to the plenitude of meaning. In questioning this system of valorization Derrida does not aim at making a simple reversal in order to install writing as innocent. Instead, he argues that "there is an originary violence of writing because language is first . . . . writing." Writing is being used here in a special, technical sense, as the place where the play of significations is in play.[24] Thus if words have no fixed meanings, and if language is freed from the fallacy of a fixed origin, then the idea of an authorizing subject or consciousness is voided of the value traditionally accorded to it. For to attribute a subject or an ego to the marks is to introduce the notion of determinate meaning and the presence of a specific set of concepts, both of which limit the free play of interpretations. This notion of the absolute freedom of interpretation from any intersubjective norms of control or agreement Derrida elaborates by exploring the radical implications of Saussure's influential theory of the nature of linguistic signs. Signs, according to Saussure, can be identified not by any positive attributes, because they have none, but rather by their difference from other signs within a particular linguistic system.[25] Such differential relations are in principle infinite, since, for Derrida, each term differs from other terms and authorizes the ceaseless production of meaning.

Moreover, major philosophical texts, in spite of their stated intentions and their metaphysics of presence, are already subverted, because writing, exceeding the meanings intended, always escapes any scheme designed to make it serve the goal of a representation or meaning. By allowing for an infinite generation of meanings through its undecidability, writing is originary or primary rather than derivative or secondary. Consequently, the texts that Derrida examines are not philosophical in the traditionally understood sense, since his disclosure of their infinite generative capacity for meaning has rendered suspect the usual distinction between philosophy and literature. The performative violence of writing precedes all generic distinctions between literature and philosophy, philosophy and psychology, and so on. These distinctions, he argues, are maintained by a failure to understand the nature of metaphor, which is traditionally conceived to be a secondary element, a trope of resemblance, within the larger traditional distinction between language and any presence. Thus in "White Mythology: Metaphor in the Text of Philosophy," Derrida says that metaphor is "classified by philosophy as provisional loss of meaning, a form of economy that does no irreparable damage to what is proper, an inevitable detour, no doubt, but the account is in view, and within the horizon of a circular reappropriation of the proper sense."[26] Metaphor is granted some propriety in philosophical discourse, but only as a means of reappropriating the proper meaning. Derrida seeks to undermine this conception of metaphor by arguing that the proper is itself an undecidable term. If the proper is that which is literal as opposed to figurative, then philosophers cannot avoid considering the metaphorical an obstacle to clarity. If the proper is that which is appropriate, one cannot help invoking the opposition between proper and improper, but this opposition or distinction works within the epoch of metaphysics. Moreover, the whole distinction is problematical and can be comprehended only by a deconstructionist reading of it. "The metaphorization of metaphor, its bottomless overdeterminability, seems to be written in the structure of metaphor, though as its negative side."[27]

If all expression is inescapably figurative, what strategies of interpretation are available to the cultural writer today? Derrida seems to offer only two: "to attempt the sorties and the deconstruction without changing ground, by repeating what is implicit in the founding concepts and in original problematics, by using against the edifice the instruments available in the house, which means in language as well"; and "to decide to change ground, in a discontinuous and eruptive manner and by affirming absolute rupture and difference."[28] To choose the first would be a Heideggerian project which Derrida has shown to be a captive of the metaphysics of presence that Heidegger sought to deconstruct. And to choose the second exclusively would be to fail to recognize that one cannot escape the metaphysics of presence but must remain at its border.

Thus Derrida's endeavor is directed toward a radical questioning and "erasure" of the usefulness of traditional thought, its concepts of origin, center, truth, knowledge, meaning, and self. Such a questioning involves a denial of the possibility of deciding what is traditionally construed as a text, since a text, Derrida argues, exists in a complicated network of intertextuality which is its relation to all other texts. Moreover, Derrida construes all philosophical texts to contain misleading or repressive strategies which tempt their readers to propose their determinate meanings, their conceptions of reality, for instance. It is Derrida's contention, however, that all texts violate their own stated intention and possess a power that he calls dissemination.[29] Dissemination, a bursting through of all intended semantic horizons, makes a text fundamentally undecidable. Because a text is constantly moving in the direction of this undecidability and makes possible an infinite free-play of interpretation, it is impossible for us to possess any determinate concepts of reading or understanding. Texts, on this view, are palimpsests of heterogeneous textual materials that refuse any unitary or determinate reading. Consequently, the process of interpretation is in principle infinite. Yet Derrida does not simply say that philosophy and psychoanalysis and the semiotic project, all constituted by the Western ontotheology, are like literature in their susceptibility to the endless play of significations. He also makes the reverse proposition that literature, traditionally assumed to be "the *arche* and *eidos* of order,"[30] not only participates in this metaphysics but is, like philosophy and psychoanalysis, without its presumed transcendental signifier.

A STANDARD DERRIDEAN PROCEDURE for the practice of criticism would be to examine what a writer's work explicitly attempts to do and show that, because of the fundamental undecidability of all texts and by implication of all words, the ideas and intentions, techniques and conventions are always already subverted. Another procedure would be to inscribe a presumed alien text within a so-called autonomous text and show that the second contains the alien text and is therefore already self-deconstructed. One reason advanced for the inevitability of deconstruction is that the traditional distinction between concept and figure has no justification. As J. Hillis Miller puts it, "there is no conceptual expression without figure, and no intertwining of concept and figure without an implied story, narrative, or myth. . . . Deconstruction is an investigation of what is implied by this inherence of figure, concept, and narrative in one another. Deconstruction is therefore a rhetorical discipline." Miller's characterization of deconstruction as a rhetorical discipline is, of course, modest, but it should not be allowed to conceal the claim that deconstruction as a radical hermeneutical theory prescribes the conditions of what counts and what does not count as proper interpretation in criticism. This claim is a logical consequence of Miller's acceptance of Derrida's presuppositions about language and text. "Since all referentiality in language," says Miller, "is fiction, the aboriginal trope or turning away from the abyss, the blind spot, the referentiality of language is its fall, its unconquerable penchant toward fiction. All words are initially catachreses. The distinction between literal and figurative is an analogical deduction or bifurcation from that primal misnaming." Because of this primal misnaming, all interpretation, all reading is necessarily misinterpretation.[31]

Deconstructionist criticism, then, seeks to interrogate words, the most unexpected ones, for their "antithetical and irreconcilable meanings."[32] As the critic discloses the "undecidable play between proper and improper uses of language" he leads the reader to experience the inevitability of the "labyrinthine *mise en abyme*."[33] The simplest example to take here would be Miller's deconstruction of the word *parasite*, a word Wayne Booth used in order to show the necessary dependence of deconstructionist criticism on "obvious" or "univocal" reading. Miller tries to show that *parasite* has no univocal meaning and covers a heterogeneity of concepts and words that seem antithetical. *Parasite*, in Miller's words, "has no meaning without its apparent counterpart. . . . At the same time both word and counterword subdivide and reveal themselves to be fissured already within themselves and to be . . . an example of a double antithetical word."[34] *Parasite* has no decidable meaning and already carries within itself the complicated network that entails the uneasy but inevitable cohabitation of metaphysics and nihilism, forever suspending the certainty of meaning desired by traditional criticism. "All poetry and all language are *mises en abyme*, since all language is based on catachresis."[35]

Thus if all distinctions are problematical, and language cannot afford words with meanings that may grant the possibility of communication and dialogue, criticism is faced with radically redefining the concept of text. There are no genuine conflicts except in the inevitable sense of antithetical relationships among meanings of words, nor is there a historical context or recognizable semantic horizon for a given text. There is only one determinate context: the vast network of textuality which is the antagonistic relationship between occidental metaphysics and nihilism, which all interpretation must articulate in order to disclose *mises en abyme*. The idea of cultivation of sensibility traditionally assumed to result from sustained reflection on literature has no meaning, nor is the concept of evaluation meaningful because of its hierarchization of texts. All words being catachrestic, all texts, whether psychoanalytical, historical, literary, or philosophical, share the same rhetorical "form"—the disposition of elements in any text—which criticism, itself part of the same network of textuality, discloses. One might want to argue that since all texts are always already self-deconstructed there is in principle no logical necessity for criticism to undertake the task.[36] However, a self-deconstructing text, because of the movement of trace, occults its own self-deconstruction and therefore some kind of task of reading is necessary. Interpretation is rendered necessary in a special sense in that it has to be written in the margins of a text to reveal the folds of its own concealment and duplicity with regard to its own deconstruction. Nevertheless, even criticism hostile to deconstruction is doing, though at a naive level, deconstruction, because it cannot escape the dynamics of textuality that this mode has revealed; its hostility springs from its ignorance of the nature of language. Finally, the concept of someone's coming to change his perception of literature has little point to it, since rhetorical self-consciousness cannot help but confirm the deconstructionist insight into language. Deconstruction has reached something close to the finality of comprehension about the nature of language and reading; it may become further radicalized but cannot be qualified, or modified, without being intellectually aberrant or regressive. To be converted to another position, to come to an awareness of error or mistake in one's position, to experience the loosening of the hold of one's conviction—these things have no meaning to one who has arrived at the deconstructionist insight.

MY INTENTION is not to question the inevitability of Derrida's conclusions, for as M. H. Abrams has said Derrida's radical conclusions are not wrong but, given his assumptions, "infallibly right."[37] Nor is it my intention to deny the power of his interpretations, for though the consequence of his work remains the same and the form of his constantly innovative and resourceful readings is essentially unchanging, Derrida, despite the growing number of imitators he has attracted, remains inimitable. Nevertheless, I want to examine the importance of deconstructionist assumptions for the theory and practice of criticism. I shall do this first by briefly discussing Miller's deconstructionist practice and then by focusing on the questioning of the concepts of intention and self in poststructuralist thought. Both phases of my discussion will provide grounds for considering the relation of theory to practice and for examining the implications of certain kinds of preoccupation with theorizing.

Let me begin with a consideration of a statement Miller makes: "Each scholar is only one of a long line of tillers of the soil; he justifies himself by destroying the scholars who preceded him. The publication of his findings is suicidal in the sense that he is offering himself up to be destroyed in his turn by the next scholar." [38] I have chosen this sort of general statement because I am interested in discussing certain explicitly radical ideas Miller seems to propose. Miller's statement may at first appear as a sobering statement on the value of criticism or scholarship, but its real import conjures the vision of a romantic's anarchist utopia, seemingly offering the thrill of a truly radical posture. For this posture criticism becomes the scene of a bizarre mortuary where new generations of critics are busy destroying and burying the older generations' work, and at the same time making preparations, through their newer work, for their own eventual self-destruction. In point of fact, however, the idea is quite uncomplicated and resembles de Man's apparently more cautious statement that the history of criticism is a systematic narrative of error. As a characterization of the surface phenomenon of criticism, both observations are generally true because there is no such thing as unassailable knowledge (except on trivial questions such as the authorship of *Bleak House* or *Paradise Lost*). However, when the importance of criticism is conceived in terms of a critic's success or failure in "destroying" previous criticism, it misdescribes the activity of criticism. For though new interpretations and interpretive assumptions do at times come into being by taking positions antithetical to the established modes of critical practice, the difference at the level of constitutive principles makes the dispute not genuine but rather a matter of historical change. When the dispute does become genuine, it is often because the contending insights have acquired greater understanding of one another and have acknowledged the necessity that drives each to propose a competing theory for the practice of criticism.

The advantage Miller claims for his position is that the poststructuralist scholar is aware that some day his work will be destroyed by another radical scholar, and that it is in the teeth of this knowledge that he must grind away at his necessary, and necessarily futile, labor. But the advantage is superficial, since it privileges an empty form of awareness. It cannot recognize that the history of criticism is a pattern of agreements and disagreements, of competing theories that undergo qualifications and modifications, that within this pattern there occur fundamental incompatibilities because of differing conceptions of the concept of literature, that in principle humanistic concepts can never be refuted, though in their reconfiscations by later critics they tend to get modified. Neither absolute discontinuity nor unproblematical continuity characterizes the history of criticism; rather, patterns of continuity and discontinuity exhibit the form of the concept of criticism which, I have argued above, can never be reduced to any one competing concept.

Like de Man, however, Miller would not countenance any objections other than the one his deconstructive method prescribes. "The only way," he asserts, "persuasively to challenge deconstructionist readings would be not to construct an alternative theory but to show the inadequacy of the particular readings associated inextricably with whatever is 'theoretical' in such work." Miller thus insists that the challenge would show the inadequacy of a particular deconstructive reading by proposing another reading. The rival reading would not be really rival but only confirmatory of the deconstructive method. In other words, there can be no genuine challenge to deconstruction because a good rival reading would only expunge from the other reading its mystified theoretical notions. It is Miller's contention that "the readings of deconstructive criticism are not the willful imposition of a subjectivity of theory on the texts but are coerced by the texts themselves." The logocentric metaphysics of literature and philosophy makes it unavoidable that all of the texts should coerce themselves in the same manner. For Miller it is only the subjectivity of a theory, itself the product of a failure to comprehend the process of deconstruction naively at work even in its own text, which causes the aberration of differences in nondeconstructive readings of literature.[39]

There is in Miller, as in other deconstructionists, a conviction of great critical neutrality which, he seems to argue, enables him to share and articulate the deconstructive process already embodied in texts. What is strange in Miller, as in de Man, is the confidence which blinds him to the extremist doctrinaire manner in which all his deconstructive readings proceed. Without this manner Miller could not possibly argue that the value of literary works consists in the testimony they provide to deconstructive intuitions into language, self, truth, meaning, origin, authority, and reading. Take, for instance, Miller's discussion of the problem of reading *Lord Jim*. Miller starts out with an unexceptionable statement that the novel contains "self-interpretive elements" but goes on to add that it embodies "a self-sustaining motion of an unending process of interpretation" which readers are enticed into sharing. He cites a principle of interpretation from Foucault's reading of Marx, Nietzsche, and Freud, one that insists that it is not only impossible to go back to "an unequivocal beginning" but that all genetic explanation is always caught up in a process of interpretation which opens the abyssal labyrinth of signs referring to other signs. Miller then straightforwardly asserts, "Thematically and structurally *Lord Jim* is an example of this absence of origin, center, or end." He thus adopts this principle of interpretation as a means of putting into question Coleridge's logocentric theory of the organic unity of the work of art. *Lord Jim*, like the cosmos, has "no beginning, no foundation outside itself, and exists only as a self-generated web." [40] This way of proceeding, it would seem to me, is symptomatic of a significant problem for contemporary American criticism: despite its repeated and repetitive attacks on the New Criticism, it is not able to evade the precursor idea that works of art are autonomous. Deconstructionist criticism, of course, radically changes the idea, since it abandons poetic autonomy for the autonomy of all language.

Now, the difficulties, specifically the inconsistencies and contradictions, that attend the New Critical theory need not worry one who is concerned with the New Critical practice at its best. The best deconstructionist practice, however, is logically restricted by the necessity it cannot evade for confirming its presuppositions. If de Man must tie the New Critical theory of poems to its organic analogy, Miller must tie it to its logocentric heritage. But they do not realize that these connections are historical and therefore contingent, and do not strictly determine the power of the theory. There is no doubt that the New Critical commitment to poetic autonomy could not transcend its own historical limitation, one which derived from the compulsion the New Critics felt for conceiving art as antithetical to science. Their theorizing became erroneous and self-mystifying because they could not propose discriminations as distinctions without at the same time conceiving them as oppositions. The deconstructionist endeavor, on the other hand, aspiring to a goal of higher theoretical generality, errs by failing to realize that nothing is properly put into question without knowing how to make discriminations, without experiencing the complexity that attends art's relations to fable and science, myth and history. The complexity inheres in part in the necessity for criticism to distinguish art from other cultural endeavors, and in part in the difficulty that attends efforts to propose unquestionable distinctions.

Like most theorists, Miller has a strict commitment to his theory, and proceeds to apply it to *Lord Jim*. "Can this description of the form of *Lord Jim*," he asks, "be sustained by close examination of the text?" The question, of course, is rhetorical and announces his decision to confirm the description of the novel's form he has sketched. Since the description is also one that characterizes the form of "most works of literature," [41] it is an a priori principle. And as an a priori principle it prescribes the conditions of what can and cannot be said. It is no wonder that Derrida's basic propositions are taken by Miller as well as by other deconstructionists as a sort of paradigm to be mastered and applied to literary works, and that deconstructive practice should elaborate the same synchronous saga of rhetorical motions that, according to its principle, endlessly unfolds in all narratives. Nevertheless, when Miller does say truly insightful things about specific literary works, it is because his strict deconstructionist commitment does not always predetermine his response. Contrary to this concept of interpretation, I have argued that both reader and text represent an unavoidable interpretive axis and that a literary work is realized in an act of understanding. Neither proposition implies that the work contains an autonomous process of its own interpretation or that it can have a fixed set of meanings. As Heidegger put it in "The Origin of the Work of Art," interpretation makes possible a preservation of the artwork. [42] The reception theory of the artwork implicit in Heidegger does not amount to saying that any interpretation can ever claim the finality of meaning. It only means that the fusion of horizons taking place in the act of interpretation allows for freedom and creativity and at the same time discloses the kinds of constraint imposed differently by reader and work.

WITHOUT DENYING, then, the radicality of Derrida's thought or of his interpretations, we can subject it to serious criticism. We can ask whether a presumed insight into the nature of *writing* or *language* has bearing on the theory and practice of criticism, and what the implications of response to these questions are. These questions are important because to the extent that in questioning the dominant metaphysical doctrines in Western philosophy Derrida adheres to certain metaphysical assumptions about *writing* and other concepts, his thought must impose a metaphysical doctrine on those who adopt it for literary criticism. For it is not simply that Derrida and his followers hold certain metaphysical assumptions; they centralize these assumptions, thereby necessarily ignoring the peculiar and complex features that characterize humanistic concepts. It is inescapable that, given his initial assumptions, his strict followers should promptly dissolve or rather "erase" the distinction between art and non-art, that they construct a broad category of Western verbal narratives, of intertextuality, and finally that they conceive all expression as necessarily participating in the complex web of intertextuality. A questioning of any rigid distinction between literature and nonliterature would not in itself be radical news, for we have already granted that there are no logically tidy criteria available for justifying such a distinction. Derrida's method, however, has other logical consequences, the most important of which is that all writing, including literature, has participated in the logocentric enterprise of Western philosophy. The function of criticism is therefore to bring out or deconstruct those traces in literary texts that make up their logocentric ground. Derridean critics have thus adopted an a priori principle which involves a conceptual structure from outside the experience of literature, and it is bound to lead them to problematize and erase all distinctions between literary and ordinary language, literature and philosophy, criticism and literature.

For such a questioning of distinctions deconstructionists have a philosophical precedent in a major tradition of aesthetic theory: that of the absolute idealists. Idealists begin with an important insight into art, and part of the value of their work resides in the distinction they seek to establish between art and non-art. But they err in putting their aesthetic insight into the service of their metaphysical and epistemological doctrines. As a result they share with deconstructionists certain absurd consequences which follow from their strict allegiance to their (different) metaphysical doctrines. Take, for instance, the early Croce's aesthetic theory. It is Croce's distinction between intuition and expression that is at the basis of his conviction that linguistics provides the model of what we mean by art. "Expression," according to Croce, "is an indivisible whole. Noun and verb do not exist in themselves but are abstractions made by our destroying the sole linguistic reality, which is the sentence." Hence translation is impossible, and each proposition irreducible. "Language is perpetual creation. What has been linguistically expressed is not repeated, save by reproduction of what has already been produced. The ever-new impressions give rise to continuous changes of sound and meaning, that is, to ever-new expressions." Owing to this nature of language, by the utterance of any new words "we generally transform the old ones."[43] Thus Croce conceives of all linguistic usage as a "rule-changing" rather than a "rule-governed" operation.[44] Modeled on this conception of language, works of art are uniquely singular entities, untranslatable and unparaphrasable. It will be T. S. Eliot, not Croce, who would draw the implication, from this organicist epistemology of idealist philosophy, that each artwork redefines every artwork that preceded it because the totality of aesthetic works constitutes an organic and living whole which undergoes modifications with the birth of every new artwork.

Croce's theory is riddled with difficulties. His denial of the communicative efficacy of language leads him to ignore what Kant also failed to take into account: the social character of our concepts. By defining the notion of expression very broadly Croce has ended up by denying all distinctions among our apprehensions of different forms of linguistic expression. Since one cannot claim to intuit something without at the same time expressing that intuition, and since every intuition is expression, any expression is necessarily a work of art insofar as it is intuited. Moreover, Croce's argument that the artist does not know what he is expressing till he has expressed it is simply a tautology derived from his idealist principle. The statement amounts to nothing other than saying that we do not know what we are intuiting until we have intuited it. Croce's conclusion is therefore unavoidable: "The limits of the expression-intuitions that are called art, as opposed to those that are vulgarly called non-art, are empirical and impossible to define. If an epigram be art, why not a simple word? If a story, why not the news-jottings of the journalists? If a landscape, why not the topographical sketch?" That it is extremely difficult and perhaps even impossible to define art and to mark it off convincingly from nonart no one would deny, but to say that every expression is by definition a work of art is to do nothing more than to prove one's extreme allegiance to one's metaphysical doctrine. It is to the absurd consequences of such allegiance that Richards and his collaborators on *The Foundations of Aesthetics* retorted, "If a word is a work of art, why not a comma, which expresses a distinct impression of a pause?" [45]

However, Croce's theory only brings to the surface a tendency that is fatally present in all idealist aesthetics. For instance, Hegel, too, had argued that every sensuous manifestation is a manifestation of the Absolute and that every sensum is therefore in principle a work of art. [46] Even Kant, who gave the idealists their most important doctrine of art—the autonomy of aesthetic experience—is not free from the absurd consequences that follow from his desire to construct a thoroughly consistent philosophical system. At first he wants to keep cognitive and aesthetic experiences separate, but he also wants to maintain a close relation between the cognitive and aesthetic experiences. He links them together in order to argue that just as cognitive judgments are universally communicable, the state of mind during aesthetic experience too is universally communicable. By establishing this link Kant hopes to maintain, on the one hand, subjective universal validity of aesthetic experiences and the accord of the cognitive faculties with cognition generally, and, on the other hand, their separation from cognitive experiences which claim objective universal validity. This is out of Kant's desire to overcome both aesthetic skepticism and radical subjectivism in aesthetic judgments. But if such communicability of the state of mind were to be truly universal, experts in the cognitive inquiries should also be the experts in aesthetic inquiries, and the question of cultivating sensibility in order to experience works of art more fully would have no meaning.

In spite of the polar opposition between their metaphysical doctrines, idealist aesthetic theory and deconstructionist critical theory share some "logically" parallel absurdities. Idealists argue that at every moment and in every thing, all of reality is operative, though its manifestations can be multiple and apparently different. Moreover, by insisting on the uniqueness of artworks, they characterize art in terms of perfection. Their metaphysical doctrine, however, has already characterized everything as art and trivialized the ideal of perfection. This ideal has meant that a work of art is so totally integrated that a slight alteration in it radically changes the work and brings into being a new whole. Deconstructionists, on the other hand, would argue that in every gesture, word, and sound are operative the latent dynamics, the violence, of *écriture* and that as a result all expression necessarily participates in the complex web of intertextuality. For all expression has its being in the complicity with all other texts from which it pretends to differentiate itself by its claim of a separate identity. This identity, however, is only a substitution that contains that which it claims to replace. Deconstructionists thus put into question the distinction between art and non-art, and they conceive of a broad category of Western verbal narrative which contains nihilism as "an inalienable alien presence within Occidental metaphysics, both in poems and in the criticism of poems."[47]

The deconstructionist, like all other metaphysical theorists, solves problems of criticism with the help of certain metaphysical principles. He does not derive his a priori principle from the activity of literary criticism itself, but from Derrida's reflections on the nature of language. His principle imposes a form of thinking on all narratives. In breaking down or problematizing all distinctions, the deconstructionist proposes an antisystematic criticism which is itself programmatically systematic. And thus, despite his claims for radicality, the deconstructionist also attempts to fix the logic of verbal narratives, even though his criterion is heterogeneity rather than unity.

The deconstructive impulse, however, represents just another moment in the history of criticism which shows a recurrent temptation critics have felt for authoritative knowledge from philosophy. In the past philosophy was considered the queen of the sciences, and the philosopher did not restrict himself to a narrow field of inquiry but rather took the whole of reality for his province. He could not only distinguish art from non-art but also provide an explanation of art in the scheme of things. The fascination for philosophy becomes all the more compelling to artists and critics when, for instance, the idealist considers beauty as one of the three manifestations of reality, the other two being goodness and truth. That such a prospect for their activity has been an exhilarating temptation for both critics and artists is confirmed not just by those who seek metaphysical systems for art but also by some of those who attack such systems. Both drives are the consequences of the guidance critics seek from philosophers for systematizing their critical endeavors. The deconstructionist position that the whole of literature is a logocentric textual network ceaselessly dismantling its own drive for presence, unity, or meaning, and the idealist position that all of reality is present in every gesture or expression are in a sense philosophy's revenge upon criticism. For deconstructionist criticism is simply a movement toward the negative pole of the extremist idealist aesthetics and is no more than an inversion of the aesthetics of unity and perfection: any verbal narrative, rather than being mind-dependent or judged by a principle of unity, is necessarily heterogeneous as well as constantly self-deconstructing and self-deconstructed. "Deconstruction," in Miller's words, "is not a dismantling of a text, but a demonstration that it has already deconstructed itself." [48]

There is no reason to deny that the deconstructionist endeavor is truly informed by a desire to interpret literary works, and that their recourse to Derrida's method of reading is intended to make criticism vital and dynamic. It is an entirely legitimate goal, since critics have always sought help from philosophers, psychologists, and others— in order to make their sensibilities conceptually more acute. Often enough, however, such help proves to be detrimental, for coming from a conceptual structure that is alien to the experience of literature it ends by dissolving this experience into one general kind of experience. The kind of help one can get from a philosopher who is engaged in problematizing all of man's cultural endeavors breeds a false sense of freedom and creates a false sense of philosophical profundity. After all, the temptation to participate in the disillusionment of a whole culture by presiding over a dismantling of its philosophical and literary traditions is an irresistible one. The dream of being a psychologist of human nature, a metaphilosopher of all philosophy, and a thoroughly self-conscious and undeluded critic of literature and culture is a snare that waylays all critical activity and perhaps explains the tremendous sense of liberation and confidence among critics who follow this mode of criticism. For reading literature forces us to ask questions that encompass all of life, and as I said in Chapter 6, it is possible to select an aspect of our experience of literature and aggrandize it so thoroughly that all other aspects are then conceived to be obvious or unimportant.

Nevertheless, it is undeniable that philosophers and critics from Plato on have often made rigid, unjustified, or questionable distinctions (not to be confused with discriminations) between mind and language, language and reality, philosophy and literature, literature and criticism. The pertinent question to raise here is whether their questionable distinctions also imply a lack of genuine insight into literature or philosophy. If there is no indubitable connection between the two then it is possible to say that their distinctions could involve insights which need to be conceptually articulated. Consider some of the traditional notions of criticism. No one would deny, for instance, that Plato did possess a profound insight into the affective powers of literature. That his epistemological principle led him to reject literature and the arts and to give an extreme account of their affective powers does not invalidate his original insight. To take a different kind of example, there are no justifiable grounds for saying that Aristotle's account of literary experience is wrong or historically superseded by the later theories of criticism, because in reading a novel or in watching a play readers or spectators respond not just to the multiple symbolic meanings of words but also, and perhaps more consequentially, to the characters and their situations.

The presumed erasure by Derrida and his followers of all distinctions between literature and philosophy, literary and ordinary language, is part of the structure of deconstructionist presuppositions; this structure authorizes the very procedure that guides the practice of deconstruction. Deconstructionist practice does not merely remain bound to its governing theoretical premises; it rather ceaselessly seeks to confirm those premises. My criticism of deconstructionist practice implies that a recognition of the impossibility of tidy and supposedly unquestionable logical distinctions does not commit us to the false conclusion that humanistic theory is doomed to failure. For the complexity of interpretive operations contextually permit us to employ distinctions which have force within the space of reasoning in a specific critical practice. The reason it is impossible to formulate distinctions founded in logic and reason and believed to be unassailable is that the contingencies of human experience tend to dissolve whatever distinctions are proposed. These contingencies modify theoretical characterizations of the experiences of a new generation of critics who may therefore attempt to refine the available modes of criticism or to propose serious revisions of them. Consequently, there is not just one conceptual structure in humanistic discourse but several, all of which are mutually competing and all of which undergo change through history. The conceptual structures in humanistic discourse are thus unstable and changing. The conceptual structures in the sciences, on the other hand, are *relatively* stable and unchanging and allow for formulation of something like a concept of progress (though from the viewpoint of scientific practice that concept may seem debatable).

A MAJOR SOURCE of the poststructuralist inspiration is the thought of Friedrich Nietzsche, which gives Derrida and de Man some of their radical critical weapons. Among the most valuable of Nietzsche's work are his reflections on rhetoric, on the nature of language and its concealed duplicity. For instance, the following remarks of his have the force of critical axioms for deconstructionists:

> What, then, is truth? A mobile army of metaphors, metonyms, and anthropomorphisms—in short, a sum of human relations which have been enhanced, transposed, and embellished poetically and rhetorically, and which after long use seem firm, canonical, and obligatory to a people: truths are illusions about which one has forgotten that this is what they are; metaphors which are worn out and without sensuous powers; coins which have lost their pictures and now matter only as metal, no longer as coins.[49]

Moreover, for Nietzsche, the referential drive of language is forever doomed to failure, since words originate out of nothing and language can never contain and capture the mind's relationship to reality in any unproblematic way. Nietzsche's contention has radical implications for the theory of interpretation, for he would not only question but reject the usual notions of intention and authorship. For him, "there is no 'being' behind doing, effecting, becoming; the 'doer' is merely a fiction added to the deed—the deed is everything." He therefore says: "One may not ask: 'who then interprets?' for the interpretation is a form of the will to power, exists (but not as a 'being' but as a process, a becoming) as an affect."[50] Nietzsche's thought, then, has not only inaugurated a perception of the fragmentary nature of self and world but located the inevitable fragmentation and provisionality of all concepts in the nature of language. It is this aspect of Nietzsche's thought that is central to contemporary French thought. Jacques Lacan, for instance, has argued that "it is not only man who speaks, but that in man and *through* man the signifier speaks . . . that his nature is woven by effects in which is to be found the structure of language of which he becomes the material, and that therefore there resounds in him, beyond what could be conceived by a psychology of ideas, the relation of speech." [51] According to modern linguistics and ethnology the dynamics that govern discourse are so complex and impersonal that human beings as specific speakers cannot control their discourse to suit their intentions, nor can they truthfully privilege the consciousness or subjectivity which they may hope to manifest through their manipulation of language. [52]

Nietzsche stands in an important relation to this moment of contemporary thought which has sought to characterize the thinking subject as no more than a function in the collective and transpersonal anonymity of discourse. Moreover, no one will deny that Nietzsche's work is complex and fragmentary and has not permitted critical harmony among even his radical interpreters. [53] I want to suggest, however, that the value of Nietzsche's work consists in inaugurating the critique of theoretical reason and that it is this critique that the most important works of Heidegger and the later Wittgenstein, from different viewpoints, consolidate. Derrida, drawing inspiration from Heidegger and Nietzsche, seems to me to occupy a place in this context, but the extent to which he remains obsessively preoccupied with the critique of metaphysics, and the way he elaborates his critique, prevent him from contributing to the elaboration of practical reasoning.

Nietzsche's attack on the distinction between doer and deed is an attack on the reification of doer as an entity, as a permanent and unchanging self, and is ultimately related to his exposure of the epistemologies underlying the thought of Socrates and Christ and its influence on Western culture. By essentializing theoretical reason and by interrogating the logical nature of moral practice Socrates dethroned that practical reason which had organized the precarious but vital Greek life from Homer to the time of Socrates. This was the beginning of the "enormous driving wheel of logical Socratism" [54] which was "bent on the destruction of myth." Christ, on the other hand, by essentializing love, removed the self from its agonistic relationship with nature and other men, a relationship by which it acquires its meaning. In both these essentializing modes reside the "absurd overestimation of consciousness" and the fatal distinction between doer and deed, and their most drastic consequence is the opening up of the gulf between man and the world. As Nietzsche put it in a powerful passage in *Anti-Christ*:

> If one shifts the centre of life—of gravity of life *out* of life into the "Beyond"—into *nothingness*—one has deprived life as such of its cen-

tre of gravity. The great lie of personal immortality destroys all rationality, all that is salutary, all that is life-furthering, all that holds a guarantee of the future in the instincts henceforth excites mistrust. *So to live that there is no longer any meaning in living: that now becomes the 'meaning' of life. . . .* What is the point of public spirit, what is the point of gratitude for one's descent and one's forefathers, what is the point of co-operations, trust, of furthering and keeping in view the general welfare? . . . So many 'temptations,' so many diversions from the 'right road'—'*one thing* is needful.' [55]

When, as with Christ, this world is rejected for the "spiritual," and when, as with Socrates, concrete social-political-moral practices and their mythical bases are put into question, and theoretical reason is privileged as the guiding spirit of human life, the result for actual living, Nietzsche argues, is nihilism. It confirms the separation of doer from deed, person from expression, and it encourages individuals to reject responsibility for their actions. In cultural thought and criticism nihilism brings in a play of response which claims complete arbitrariness as the norm of value.

For Nietzsche the distinction betweeen doer and deed involves a rejection of historicity of human action and understanding, a rejection of the changing nature of human concepts and language. Far from questioning the capacity of language to say what it means, Nietzsche questions the conditions that have held human beings captive to the teachings of Socrates and Christ. And he questions human beings whose "sickness" has infected the language they use. For this language has become diseased and problematical, and it has taken over the life of human beings and lives, as it were, by its own fitful, nihilistic momentum. This is why Nietzsche asserted, "Every time something is done with a purpose in view, something fundamentally different and other occurs." [56] This presupposition, or rather something that his analyses make evident, prompts Nietzsche to ask what Socrates or Christ or Kant did *not* think, what drove them to their denials. That enables him in turn to interrogate and unmask the conditions that make possible their forms of thought, and to expose the errors that have affected the subsequent history of thought.

Thus Nietzsche was above all a moral critic of culture, a critic of the destructive implications of the inherited forms of morality and reason. He took ideas seriously and relentlessly examined their relation to life. The consequence of his analysis was a profound distrust he felt toward thought divorced from life and a deep urge to celebrate life. The aphoristic energy of his writing and the deliberate cultivation of the fragmentary mode of writing provide testimony to his awareness of the crippling denials inherent in the forms of thought and culture dominated by the quest for foundations that informs epistemology and metaphysics.

For Nietzsche, then, the concept of self is a moral concept. His view has a logical connection with the concepts of self and intention I briefly elucidated in Chapter 3. There I argued that the concept of self does not make sense in terms of some ideal notion of absolute autonomy; it acquires its meaning in relation to other persons. I also suggested that to interpret a text is also to ascribe to it an intention, that one construes intention and interpretation together. My elucidation does not entail the metaphysical concept of self as unity or origin or entity, nor does it entail "the absurd overestimation of consciousness" that Nietzsche rightly castigated. It underlines the historical (therefore changing) and intersubjective character of the concept of self which is inescapably involved in, and has its value in relation to, other concepts. This elucidation attempts to exhibit the grammar of self and is not in conflict with Nietzsche's criticism of "consciousness." Nietzsche considered it "essential that one should not make a mistake over the role of 'consciousness': it is our relation with the 'outer world' that evolved it." Convinced that a multiplicity of subjects through an interaction and struggle makes up the basis of our thought, Nietzsche sought to overthrow both theoretical reason, which Socrates had installed at the apex of human activity, and love (interiorization of self), which Christ had exalted at the expense of conflictual nature (Dionysian necessity) of vital being.[57]

The consequences of a stand on the concept of intention are fundamental and affect the activity of criticism in inescapable ways. A rigid adherence to the concept of intention as authorial meaning can lead to an ideal of objectivity which denies the complexity of critical response that must spring partly from a play of one's subjectivity. Such an adherence can lead to the replacement of criticism by historical scholarship, of judgment and sensibility by a search for facts. The formalist rejection of intention, on the other hand, fails to comprehend the historical and changing nature of both literature and criticism, and it misdescribes the nature of literary works by assigning to them a quasi-transcendental, essential identity. A conception of the absolute impersonality of language, cut off from all cultural praxis—this is true of de Man, Miller, and most of the deconstructionists, though Derrida's own work is quite rich in historical insights—has consequences which are inexorable, since all distinctions are problematized in a manner that suspends the very possibility of communication and dialogue.

FOR DERRIDA and his followers language is inescapably infected by the metaphysics of presence, a metaphysics that always lurks within all of man's cultural endeavors. It suffers from a disease that can be diagnosed but cannot altogether be eliminated. Consequently, the deconstructionist endeavor can be construed as a quest for perspective on the assumptions of both literature and criticism. It is a quest that seeks to stand back from what critics normally take for granted, to disclose the unwitting subversive moment in all discourse. It claims to be not simply an endeavor to make critics aware of their method of representation or interpretation, or of the assumptions and conventions they employ in the practice of criticism. The deconstructionist rather claims to have acquired an unassailable universal point of view, a point of view that they may grant can be further radicalized but that cannot be reduced to just one more perspective on language and literature.

What Derrida and his followers refuse to recognize is that the relation of language to the world is not theoretical but practical, and that to admit this is not to deny either the constitutive nature of language or, as Heidegger and Gadamer would have it, the historicality and linguisticality of man's experience. This is the relation that the later Wittgenstein persistently explored. His explorations, of course, do not provide comfortable certainties or a transportable or a summarizable theoretical superstructure, yet in seeking to disclose the grammars of forms of life (and language) Wittgenstein's analysis touches on significant areas of humanistic inquiry. By exhibiting those features of our language that make us conscious of the nature and function of our forms of life, his analysis tries to break the hold that philosophical problems have exercised over our minds. He accomplishes this apparently modest but in reality profoundly enduring task through exhibiting the inner connections between our language and practice. For Wittgenstein there are no theoretical rules for judging whether one has learned or mastered particular rules of language. Instead, the test is a practical one and consists in seeing whether one can successfully participate in a particular linguistic practice, whether one has run against disturbance or distortion in communication.

Derrida, on the other hand, by divorcing the meanings of a word from its use in the practical contexts of life, is able to show the contradictory and bewildering implications of a word or concept. All language, then, becomes not just metaphoric but rather a shifting mirage of metaphors. The consequence of Derrida's strategy, moreover, is not simply a loss of our realization of what we mean; it is also a loss of the concepts of knowledge and meaning in the ordinary context of living. Contrary to Derrida, however, as Wittgenstein would teach us, these concepts can never possess the logical coherence Derrida wishes to question, for our fundamental concepts are neither strictly referential nor strictly performative but rather quasi-performative and quasi-referential. The reason for the impossibility of their ever acquiring convincing theoretical coherence in an abstract sense is that all our concepts derive their value and meaning from the contexts of human practice, the contexts of human beings speaking and interacting in innumerable specific situations. There arises a conceptual puzzle when one tries to think about examples of self, knowledge, meaning, or intention without the context of someone's claiming to say and mean something and to take responsibility for his action or words.

Language, then, like all our concepts, is neither strictly referential nor strictly performative but tends toward reference and performance. When the referential is separated from the performative and professed as the standard of knowledge, the result is positivism in method. When the performative is separated from the referential, and professed as the standard of comprehension, the result is rhetoric. The first leads to formal logic and rigorous inductive and deductive procedures, the second to absolute interpretive freedom. I have argued here that logic and rhetoric, inductive and deductive procedures, and interpretive freedom and constraint, subsist in a complex relationship that defines the nature and function of reasoning in literary criticism; that logic and rhetoric intersect in multiple and complex ways enabling critics and theorists to offer sometimes compatible, sometimes conflicting insights into the concepts of art and criticism.

Criticism comes to grief when it pursues general theoretical systems to talk about both the problems of interpreting literature and its history. The remarkable succession of methodological outbursts from Lévi-Strauss's anthropology to Lucien Goldmann's sociology to Roland Barthes's rather mercurial brand of structuralism to Althusser's Marxism to Derrida's deconstruction is symptomatic of a critical consciousness unable to come to terms with the unavailability of a general theory that will deal with all possible contingencies of literary and cultural experience. The scramble that many American critics have made since the mid-sixties for methodological models, especially those developed in France, is a testimony to the craving not just for generality but for methodological certitude. If this scramble exhibited a certain genuine intellectual excitement or hope for interdisciplinary studies, it also suggested an incapacity to realize that their pursuit for universalist models was from the beginning doomed to failure. Paradoxically, this sense of failure has emerged on the critical scene not as a realization that no general theory can be set up as the valid conceptual structure with which to conduct the practice of criticism, but as a metaphysical notion announcing the impossibility of reading literature. And it has emerged in the idea that the value of criticism is in proportion to its capacity to undermine all concepts of criticism. But the radicalism of this idea cannot disguise its own general, narrow, and repetitive nature. Thus poetic autonomy is forsaken for the autonomy of language, qualitative and provisional differentiations are forsaken for "differance," and both substitutions end by disclosing the sameness of operations performed by all language.

The reason deconstructionists cannot help endlessly repeating the same synchronous tale in all their interpretations is that the limits of what they can say are defined by the concepts they hold. In other words, the concepts they employ determine the limits of their experience. What they see or say is so thoroughly a projection of their presuppositions that they cannot cast doubt on it. Doubting or problematizing has become the necessity of all interpretation for them, but it cannot lead them to doubt, or find problematical, the form of their own doubt. However, neither philosophy nor criticism can succeed without knowing what it is to doubt and to affirm and hence to examine the grounds of its own doubt. If in philosophy or cultural thought doubting leads to radical skepticism and knowledge to unassailable certainty, both are voided of meaning. It would not matter, then, whether deconstruction or objectivist epistemology prevailed. It is the symbiotic relation between these two that makes the traditionalists nervous, angry, or resentful, and the deconstructionists parasitic, theatrical, and self-congratulatory. One is justified in guessing that when the ideal of epistemology no longer has its defenders, the deconstructionist presuppositions will put new life into it because their presuppositions logically require that ideal.

Deconstructionist theorists and critics hold Saussure's notion of the arbitrariness of the sign in a rigid fashion which accounts for their desire to show that all thought and criticism occur in the mode of crisis. Our knowledge that words are not things, that they do not represent the essence of meanings nor provide adequation to the things they purport to represent leads to crisis only for those whose goal is to achieve commensuration among the multiple, complex, and contradictory life-worlds evolved by human beings. As Heidegger argues, traditional philosophy's search for objective knowledge or truth is only one human project among others and becomes self-deceptive when it seeks to discover a privileged access to reality.[58] Reality would, then, become either an interiorization of self which one seeks to fathom by introspection or an external objective world which one seeks to determine by trying to fix the conditions of agreement. Both claim to discover the truth of reality and misunderstand the finitude and relativity that define man's existence.

Wittgenstein, too, teaches us that the order in our language is fragmentary and the meanings of words we use are relative and context-dependent. Nevertheless, the meanings of words we use determine our world in fundamental and inescapable ways, because our world itself is dependent on human practices and conventions. Though our conventions too, like the words we use, are arbitrary, they possess a natural necessity in having constituted the form of life we live. Consequently, human beings are in the predicament of having to use words with often unreliable and contradictory meanings. It is in that world where arbitrary signs must of necessity assume the force of conventions that human beings have to live and create a situation of communication and dialogue. And it is in this situation that they may fruitfully conduct disputes and seek ways by which to understand one another. This knowledge of the nature of our world and our language may contribute to a further increase in self-knowledge, in our understanding that our concepts provide us with no unshakable stability and order, that the concepts with which we seek to understand ourselves and the texts of culture are themselves the products of human convention. But this knowledge need not force us to apocalyptic postures because, as Wittgenstein teaches us, we can after all live in our predicament and indeed take it as the condition of more self-knowledge and greater creativity. Heidegger and Gadamer would call this recognition of the ways in which we interpret and understand ourselves and the texts of culture and take responsibility for what we say and mean a condition of hermeneutic conversation. Such conversation does not depend on the possibility of eventual agreement but on the possibility of continuation of dialogue in which hope for agreement recognizes the fruitfulness of disagreements and differences.

My CRITICISM OF DECONSTRUCTION does not imply that Derrida's method of reading can have no relation to criticism. Insofar as it is a method of reading (just as psychoanalysis is a method of analyzing human experience), it can have an important bearing on any activity of interpretation. I am simply saying that if one strictly adheres to the logical dynamics of Derrida's method, one will bring criticism under a monolithic interpretive mode that cannot account for the variety and complexity of literary experience. For Derrida's attacks on systematic method and his attempts at dedefinition and dethematization are themselves systematically carried out and are not free from a whole set of concepts or "anticoncepts." It is true that concepts of criticism involve one or another a priori principle, but this principle is expressed in each case in the context of actual confrontation with literary works and enables a given critic to apprehend given literary works and to articulate his apprehension in a consistent and intelligent manner.

To do significant criticism the deconstructionist will have to abandon the metaphysical superstructure which involves his criticism in a series of tautologies and predictable responses. And this is certainly possible to do. Consider the case of idealistic aesthetics for critics like A. C. Bradley. The idealist metaphysical doctrine did not prevent Bradley from giving a satisfactory account of the expressionist theory in his "Poetry for Poetry's Sake." [59] Nor did Richards's psychological apparatus prevent William Empson from practicing criticism in terms of the Ricardian notion of complexity of literary experience. It will be difficult, however, to reconstruct the deconstructionist insight into art as long as its proponents continue to carry on their discourse within the declared boundaries of occidental metaphysics and nihilism. A successful reconstruction will involve a more rigorous scrutiny of the aesthetics of unity, perfection, and so on. Such a scrutiny can be based on an understanding that works possessing semantic significance cannot be experienced or understood on the ground of internal coherence alone. But the deconstructionist cannot easily make this argument, nor can he claim radicality for it. For instance, Empson has demonstrated in his practical criticism the importance of this argument without subscribing to the metaphysical doctrine that the deconstructionist puts at the heart of his concept of heterogeneity of texts.

There is nothing invidious, however, in the urge for a radical criticism. Those who follow Marx or Foucault, for instance, have a difficult and necessary task to combine a capacity for sensitive and profound response to literature with the desire for articulating the ideological distortions or power-relations that inform the institution of literature.[60] Let me sketch here the strategy of a vague and amorphous form of criticism that might offer itself as radical. It would not purport to arrive at an authoritative body of theoretical knowledge about literature and its history, but rather to probe the suggestiveness of literature's rhetoric. It would seek to examine what a text does and does not seem to say, what its linguistic silences are. It would seek to investigate the structure of a text, not to establish or resolve its presumed ambiguity, but to understand the form of its constitution of man's cultural and historical being. One of its questions may concern the rhetorical dimensions of a text that, while calling forth its meanings, also bring about its contradictions. And it would seek to understand the forces that bring about changes in literary history and the difficulties that attend our attempts to find satisfactory explanations for those changes. These are the kinds of things that could develop into a form of radical contemporary criticism, and they would no doubt seek their inspiration from Kierkegaard, Nietzsche, Marx, Freud, Wittgenstein, and from some elements of the works of Benjamin, Adorno, Foucault, and Derrida. Deconstructionists like Miller and Joseph Riddel, who have done valuable criticism in their pre-deconstructionist phases, may contribute toward developing a criticism that will be free from subservience to the strict framework of deconstruction.[61] For it would be absurd to think that deconstruction or some other developments in contemporary intellectual life may not force us to ask questions we have never asked before. For Derrida's critique of structuralism can be understood as the rejection of an anemic and life-denying rationalism which takes its inspiration from Saussure and culminates in the confidence of a universal grammar. Similarly, Wittgenstein's relentless probing of our concepts forces us to recognize that the concepts of knowledge, truth, certainty, meaning, understanding, and self have contradictory or ambiguous implications, and that these implications ought not to compel us to find better or more coherent concepts but rather ought to return us to the consideration of the praxis, the "forms of life," in which they acquire their significance. Yet neither Derrida nor Wittgenstein should be taken as providing prepackaged solutions to the difficulties that we encounter in carrying on the task of reading literature and of theorizing about literature and criticism. The questioning that we may learn to do of our concepts of criticism cannot be accomplished by any deliberate transposition of concepts elaborated elsewhere to criticism. For though different disciplines can thrive by realizing the value of their interdependence, criticism (or any other discipline) will stand to gain when its own process of reflection leads it to consider questions and answers elaborated elsewhere.

CHAPTER EIGHT

On Metacriticism

The preceding chapters have attempted what I characterize as "metacriticism." Now I should like to elaborate the theoretical and methodological implications of the concept of metacriticism.

It is safe to say that literary criticism, roughly speaking, is an empirical activity, an attempt at experiencing and interpreting and judging literary works. Critics occasionally find it useful to think about philosophical questions such as "What is a poem?" "What is literary experience?" "What is criticism?" and so on. When reflecting on these questions the critic is necessarily using the modes and techniques of philosophical inquiry. And he makes this incursion into theory with a view to making progress in criticism, just as Lévi-Strauss employs techniques and theories of linguistics in order to deal with problems specific to anthropology. Some critics also engage in philosophical analysis of the problems of criticism and critical theory; they are then functioning as metacritics. Like the advocate of a theory seeking to modify and refine that theory, the metacritic can point up confusion or significance in that theory. Unlike critical theorists, however, who attempt to provide foundations for their presumed correct theories, the metacritic does not intend to provide such a foundation. Metacriticism and criticism as well as metacriticism and critical theory are logically independent of each other, but they are not incompatible. However, this is a point that I hope to make clear in the discussion that follows.

In view of the plurality of the modes of criticism some critical theorists consider it absurd to identify the truth (about literature and criticism) with any one of them. Some would say that critical truth is the sum of all the critical modes, or especially the sum of the central and compatible strains of criticism.[1] Some would consider a sum of all the available positions or of the compatible ones simply absurd since it would involve a conflation of premises which are either mutually incompatible or mutually exclusive.[2] And still other theorists ask whether it is not possible to find a criterion of critical truth which would enable them to avoid identifying it with any one major critical tradition. Somewhat resembling the first group, this last group nevertheless differs from the first in its belief in the possibility of a criterion which is furnished, according to them, by philosophical aesthetics.[3] For such an aesthetic is conceived to articulate and impose its own criterion of what is good critical reasoning and what is bad critical reasoning, and thus though it begins, like metacriticism, with a descriptive analysis of concepts of criticism and their logic, it is implicitly controlled by certain normative considerations. Like metacriticism, philosophical aesthetics purports to examine critical reasoning; but unlike metacriticism, it claims to possess a norm of meaningfulness or goodness. When we press it to show what this norm is, it almost always turns out to be another definition of literature.

Often metacriticism is (or is like) philosophical aesthetics, but it does not propose a particular definition of literature. However, when philosophical aestheticians maintain an essential doctrinal neutrality, then they are functioning as metacritics (or metatheorists). When Harold Osborne, in his excellent book *Aesthetics and Criticism*, examines different criteria of art he is functioning as a metacritic, but when he exposes them as inadequate in order to offer his own criterion (of configuration) he surrenders his metacritical credentials.[4] Thus not all attempts to examine other theories and to show their serious difficulties are metacritical, although they may involve metacritical analysis. This need not imply that critics ought to be doctrinally neutral and engage in metacritical analysis of what they do instead of attempting the formulation and defense of one or another concept of art and criticism.

Yet exaggerated theoretical and critical gestures of defending a position, though they may valuably underline its *point*, often falsify the position either by coopting everything new and seemingly important outside itself as implicitly available from one's own position, or by excluding everything outside itself as irrelevant or unimportant to criticism.[5] These two strategies share a conceptual difficulty with a third strategy: that of weak-kneed or indifferent pluralism that conceives every position to be essentially right on its own grounds.[6] The difficulty stems from the failure to recognize that while many positions may offer important truths about literature some of them may misrepresent and misdescribe the business of criticism and critical theory. Genuine metacriticism does not offer an indubitably true theory of criticism, for its objective is to enable us to understand the basis of literary criticism, by seeking to countervail parochial attitudes in criticism and at the same time by developing fuller and finer responses to literature and criticism. It helps us perceive the complexity of the form of critical life. Metacritical investigation is not directed toward poems themselves; it does not replace criticism. It is directed toward the possibilities of poems and criticism. It reminds us of the sorts of statements made about poems and criticism, and about their relation to other aspects of culture.

Metacriticism also examines the premises of critical response and critical methods and relates them to what is or can be known, thought, and said. Metacriticism cannot therefore avoid a certain amount of skepticism if it is to inquire into what is sayable about constructs of words offered as literature, and to probe into the nature of experience made possible by given forms of criticism. But it is not interested in changing critical concepts. Critical theorists often show how certain concepts break down in order to replace them with their own theories; metacriticism may suggest how even "exploded" concepts of criticism can work.

Some modern analytical philosophers and aestheticians, especially equipped for metacritical analysis, have repudiated theoretical endeavors in the criticism of literature and the arts. Their repudiation of theory, however, is a repudiation of the search for a universal theory or real definition of art. They seem to me right, since the form of aesthetic life is not such that it can be captured by the logical demand for universality and coherence. This, I think, is the point of Morris Weitz's argument that "logic has as much to learn from aesthetics as aesthetics has from logic."[7] Consider, for instance, theorists who seek real definitions for art. They cannot account for the conflict that characterizes the concepts of art and criticism. For either they must broaden their definitions so that they become too general and vacuous, or they must narrow them so that many putatively aesthetic works are characterized as non-art. The first alternative leads to a dissolution of the conflict over the concept of art, whereas the second contributes to the conflict, though because of a fanatic commitment to the task of proposing and defending a definition it does not recognize that fact.

The analytical philosophers who repudiate general theory and real definition thus seek to exhibit the complexity of the *form* of aesthetic life. They therefore ask the question, What kind of philosophical account does the concept of art call for? This is an important question, and it should not be conflated with the apparently similar questions about the concept of physical objects. It is here that, following Wittgenstein's advice, we must determine the depth grammar of the concept to be examined. What is the case in the context of art is not established in the way it is established in the context of physical objects. But a conflating of these two kinds of questions often occurs, and in order to avoid it philosophers such as William E. Kennick and Morris Weitz either dismiss a great deal of inquiry into the nature of art as simply a mistake or admit its value only in a subordinate manner.[8] They argue that definitions of art, contrary to their purported claims, do not provide necessary and sufficient features because they *cannot* provide such features. What is then denied is theory as "real" definition, poetics as a universally valid theory. But this denial does not entail a further denial of criteria of criticism. However, the reason some theorists seem to offer their criteria as "real" definition is that they offer them as the proper mode of experiencing and interpreting art. The criteria one offers represent an insight in terms of which to carry on one's activity of criticism. Nevertheless, as I have argued, criteria can be criticized, or examined for their adequacy. If, for instance, one criticizes Aristotle's definition of tragedy, one may argue that the experience of tragedy is too complex to be defined satisfactorily in terms of pity and terror. For what do we say of those tragedies that evoke neither emotion, or evoke them singly? Are the terms *pity* and *terror* definable in any straightforward sense? Moreover, if they are not sufficient conditions of tragic experience, are they necessary? Yet one who believes in the power of Aristotle's definition could counter that his definition does not equip us with rigid standards, but rather provides us with flexible categories and speculative instruments which enable us to apprehend works of art.[9]

But how does one determine the depth grammar of the concept of art? Admonishing us to pay attention to the philosophical grammar of what is said, Wittgenstein makes a distinction between surface grammar and depth grammar. He suggests that when we compare the depth grammar of a statement with its surface grammar, "we find it difficult to know our way about."[10] Now, it would seem that critical theorists too often pay exclusive attention to the surface grammar of critical statements—which leads both to the proliferation and refutation of critical theories and to the sense of crisis that prevails in the discipline in general. But then one might ask, How is one to understand "depth grammar" and how is it revealed? On Wittgenstein's terms we show the depth grammar of a concept or proposition by asking what can and cannot be sensibly said about it. In order to do this one must take account of the context in which that concept or statement operates. For it is an understanding of the operation of a concept in the context in which it has its force and meaning that we can say and mean one thing rather than another, and see what does or does not make sense to say or expect about it. Thus, for instance, when someone rejects Aristotle's theory of imitation, metacriticism questions the grounds of the rejection and asks if Aristotle's theory has really been understood. Theorists at times have rejected Aristotle's theory on the ground that it is a copy theory of art. But as I discussed briefly in Chapter 2, Aristotle's theory is a highly complex theory of representation. If we carefully examine it we should see that for Aristotle mimesis is not an imitation of either the external or the internal world, but it is an intentional embodiment of reality that deals (like philosophy though in a different mode) with universals. This is not to say there are no legitimate grounds to criticize Aristotle. One can say, for instance, that Aristotle's concept of literature cannot account for the fact that literature can and often does dramatize contingencies of life.

Analytical aestheticians who have learned from the later Wittgenstein and Austin ask questions that seek clarifications of concepts of criticism. The questions they ask do not entail a rejection of critical criteria and critical theory. In the beginning, however, when Wittgenstein's influence began to be felt, some analytical philosophers did take an extreme position. John Passmore, for instance, has said that while criticism of the different arts is possible, aesthetics as a general theoretical inquiry into all the arts is simply impossible, and so castigated the whole endeavor of aesthetics as "dreary."[11] Stuart Hampshire, to cite another example, has said that the whole endeavor to construct a poetics is bogus, for the questions that this requires are not real questions at all, since the answers are outlandish generalizations which have no relevance to criticism. Criticism for Hampshire, as for Kant, deals with the "unique" work of art.[12] The rejection of a general theory of all arts finds its philosophical support in Wittgenstein's dictum against the "craving for generality" (as well as from Kant's aesthetic theory). It is true that there are important differences among different arts as well as different works of art. Although no one would now argue for an identity of fundamental features among different arts, only a crippling notion of the "unique" would prevent one from seeing an overlap of features among, say, representational painting, sculpture, and literature. Consequently, the problem with which Lessing grappled was genuine, not a pseudoproblem. Often the overlapping features among different arts are described analogically, as when one says that a poem has the form of a sonata; such statements are critically useful if not stretched beyond a point.[13] However, this extreme position, as we saw above, does not characterize all analytical discussions of art.

Moreover, we should note an important feature of the help that analytical philosophy can provide to critics and critical theorists. It does not offer a set of doctrines and definitions of art, but it can certainly equip us with a method of analysis. And its contribution differs in significant respects from the ones made by both the metaphysician and the traditional philosopher of art. The metaphysician claims to give insights into art by relating it to his presumed insight into the ultimate nature of reality, mind, or language. The traditional philosopher of art, on the other hand, claims to give a definition of art, one that purports to characterize the necessary and sufficient properties of art. The analytical philosopher rejects both modes of talking about art by exhibiting the features of reasoning involved in talking about art. By adopting the analytic method, we can then attempt to exhibit the complexity of the form of aesthetic life which cannot be captured in either metaphysical systems or neat, economic definitions.

To do critical analysis in this way is to abandon both the grandiose assertions of the metaphysician and the comfortable certainty of simplified formula. And it is to recognize that aesthetic insights in the work of such thinkers as Aristotle, Kant, and Coleridge are not integrally connected to their metaphysical systems. Indeed, they must be separated in order to avoid a systematic imposition of metaphysical systems on the activity of criticism. For instance, to the extent that the New Critics succeed in making a defense of the autonomist concept of art, they do not adopt either the Kantian or idealist philosophical system. Moreover, the considerable sophistication in recent Anglo-American analytic aesthetics, though indebted to Kant, depends on an avoidance of Kant's conjunction of biology and art, which is a logical requirement of his philosophical system. William Empson too, as was said before, accepted Richards's principle of the complexity of literary response without adopting his psychological apparatus. Finally, to cite one more example, Jonathan Culler has given a rigorous defense of the structuralist poetics without rigidly basing it on the principles of structural linguistics.[14]

THE CONCEPT OF LITERATURE is a complex concept, and to develop an understanding of it is to be able to handle a diversity of literary works and to identify features that are relevant to carry on one's critical practice with force and insight. And to grasp the complexity of the concept of literature is to realize that literary works do not share common features among them so that one can describe their necessary and sufficient qualities. The critic who has grasped this complexity does not look for the same set of experiential features in all literary works, but rather knows how to apprehend the diversity of their contexts, however indeterminate and shifting these contexts might be.

Though what we consider important depends on the insight we have acquired into the nature of literature, the concept of literature stands, like many other human concepts, for many different things. Take, for instance, the variety of the uses to which the concept of form can be put: the Aristotelian notion of form is different from the New Critical notion of form, and Georges Poulet's criticism too involves a different mode of conceiving it. The more remarkable fact, however, is that all these three uses are also different from the ordinary notion of what we call "shape." With regard to literature, then, the situation becomes enormously complicated. The variety of works it denotes are sufficiently vast so that no one class of literary works can be legitimately taken over as the standard general representative of all literature and then used in order to judge whether new or different instances of works offered as literature are indeed literary.

Once we recognize this diversity, we will also recognize that there is not just one valid criterion of literature or art but rather many different criteria. The tendency among critics, however, is to generalize on the basis of their insights into a limited area of literature and to claim one or another insight to hold universally valid for all literature. This craving for a universal theoretical principle is of course found in all fields of human inquiry. Thus it is, for instance, that Plato considers the moral criterion more important than the aesthetic one and therefore subordinates art to morality, whereas hedonists give supreme importance to the criterion of pleasure in everything. In literary criticism, the picture reveals the same pattern of competing theoretical principles which are often adequate and even sufficient for studying a certain class of literary works but which are generally offered as necessary criteria. The New Critics, for instance, give the place of centrality to irony or paradox for appreciation and judgment of poetry, whereas the romantic critics consider the problem of greatness and the nature of the self in literature as the most crucial issues in talking about literature. And Pater, convinced of the nature of beauty as the finer accommodation of words to the vision within, emphasized style as the criterion of beauty in literature and the arts. Although each of these criteria can provide an important insight into some works of literature, no criterion by itself is adequate as a principle by which to apprehend all literature. Because no criterion is adequate by itself, critics often end up violating their explicit theoretical principles in their practical criticism. For instance, A. C. Bradley, who defended an idealist-formalist principle of poetry in his Oxford lecture, "Poetry for Poetry's Sake," also argued for the intellectually convincing nature of Shakespeare's characters in his famous *Shakespearean Tragedy*.[15] Pater, despite his criterion of style for elucidating the value of literature, recognized that the adequacy of expression could not explain the function of content in literature; he therefore included the criterion of truth in his criticism.[16]

It is because of the craving for generality that critics and theorists tend to say that "all good literature is . . ." "all good criticism does . . ." or "all good poetry is . . . ." What all of these accounts are missing is that literature can be many different things, that there is room for many different critical decisions or criteria and that critical theory, despite its close connection with the reading of literature, is not essentially an empirical inquiry. The criterion one uses is a matter of the insight one has acquired into literature and manifests itself in a series of intuitively mastered procedures. In other words, a criterion is an a priori categorial structure and is not given in experience but rather is contributed by our mind or the language we use. Since there are general criteria which make possible the kind of experience we have of literature, there is a contest among different criteria. What we say about a poem is therefore not a private matter, nor is it simply temperamental. For we offer our interpretations of a poem for all who want to read that poem as a valid and convincing experience of it.

Every significant human concept is complex and contextually implies different sorts of things. As Wittgenstein has shown, we "are unable clearly to circumscribe the concepts we use; not because we don't know their real definition, but because there is no real 'definition' to them. To suppose there *must* be would be like supposing that whenever children play with a ball they play a game according to strict rules." [17] To have understood a particular concept in humanistic discourse is to have developed an ability to do something in a particular way. And in order to develop such an understanding it would be unnecessary to look for a clear and indubitable distinction between, say, literary and ordinary language. For if it were possible to make such a distinction, it is strange that throughout the history of critical endeavor we have not yet articulated one that is unchallengeable.

When the craving for generality becomes overriding in humanistic discourse, critical theorists propose and defend partisan concepts of criticism. For instance, a romantic critic would say that poetry is self-expression, a New Critic would say that poetry is an ironic dramatization of contradictory elements in human experience, and Arnold would say that poetry is a criticism of life. There is little doubt that each concept is limited. The romantic concept cannot properly apply to a great deal of neoclassical poetry without arbitrarily distorting it; the New Critical concept has to reject a great deal of romantic poetry because its holistic principle cannot adequately explain the ambiguities of that poetry; and Arnold's principle is inadequate to deal with self-conscious and playful art. The built-in inadequacy of each concept accounts for the contesting and changing nature of conceptual structures in humanistic discourse.

WE SHALL not be able to describe the complex patterns of literary works and literary history if we are committed to a monolithic critical scheme according to which form or emotion or self or absence or myth is central and essential to literature, and all else is peripheral and inessential. To characterize any one element in this way is to pursue a mode of inquiry that carries the elements of its own limitation and eventual dissolution. Yet those who have conceived form or emotion or self as central to literature and therefore to criticism have gained insights of undeniable value. For instance, the emphasis on personal feelings and self led to the emergence of romanticism, and the emphasis on form at the end of the nineteenth century and the beginning of the twentieth led to greater attention to those formal features which the aesthetic and critical consciousness of the preceding period had seemed to ignore. Thus, although unitary theories of art are destined to fail in their attempt to fix the logic of the concept of art, they bring out certain features of art which enrich our experience.

As we attend to the variety of the modes of criticism and to the overlapping and criss-crossing between criticism and other forms of reasoning, we begin to grasp the complexity that characterizes the institution of criticism. Metacriticism concentrates our attention on the connections and parallels and complexities that are often ignored by critical theorists in search of neat distinctions and tidy criteria. This is not to deny that formulation and defense of one or another theory is important, but rather to deny the quasi-solipsistic isolation of the modes of criticism. Metacriticism thus places an unfashionable emphasis on the objectivity of critical inquiry without degenerating into the rigidity that objectivity suffers in the hands of positivists. It resists both the positivistic relegation of criticism and literature to the realm of mere likes and dislikes, or pro and con attitudes for not conforming to the shape of either logic or science, and the irrationalism of the defenders of some critical modes who have accepted the positivistic principle that all forms of reasoning must be either quasi-logical or quasi-scientific and who have therefore ceased to hold that criticism at its best is a reasoned mode of inquiry. Intelligent metacriticism should succeed in resisting and exposing the extremes of skepticism, reductionism, and subjectivism in criticism, and thus restore to it a confidence that at present seems to be possible only in clichés of anarchic self-adulation.

Conclusion

UNDERLYING THE OBJECTIVIST DEFENSE of interpretation is the notion that what criticism is about perennially is the adjustment of differences, the production of effective interpretation, and the increase of correct perception of the critical process which eliminates ideology as well as the whimsy of subjective response. Proponents of such a conception of objectivity clearly believe that this kind of criticism is one which depends less on illusion and sees things as they are (as Arnold advocated). This view of criticism is closely bound up with the epistemological presuppositions of objectivist criticism and its inability to recognize the historical, conceptual, and individual specificity of critical responses to literary works. These three elements make up the texture of critical response, and yet, as I have argued, they do not preclude rationality but make it central to the logic of criticism. It is this relation of rationality to criticism which makes for the genuineness of critical disputes and at the same time makes them endless in principle. As a result any genre of literature and any concept of criticism, even if it has been put into question, can be reconfiscated, though given historical and other changes, it will be considerably different in its later articulations.

Proponents of a common logic of inquiry in criticism generally contend that when different interpretations of a poem are brought into relation with the relevant criteria of assessment, most of the interpretations would be shown to be arbitrary, erroneous, illusory, or exaggerated. As Wittgenstein argued tirelessly in other contexts, this sort of conclusion results from a deep-seated philosophical prejudice, the dominant feature of which is to subsume all different modes of inquiry under one mode. What constitutes an intelligent and successful mode of inquiry in the sciences is taken by those theorists to constitute the valid mode of inquiry in all contexts.

It is important to recognize that it does not make sense to ask for the grounds of fundamental aesthetic decisions. When one asks for evidence or grounds for such decisions one is construing these decisions as hypotheses requiring confirmation. But these decisions are never the same as hypotheses. We learn a mode of response through examples, teaching, rethinking. As we refer to specific features of a critical response, we begin to recognize the specific grammar of aesthetic life that informs its criticism. Aesthetic decisions, never clearly formulated as unchanging verbal yardsticks, make up the criteria that enable critics to decide what is relevant in discussing a text, but the criteria are not subject to assessment and refutation in the sense theories in the sciences are. To construe criteria of criticism or fundamental aesthetic decisions as objects of assessment would be to take them for hypotheses which may or may not be true and thus to falsify their mode of operation in criticism.

The following example should clarify the above point. Suppose that a critic says that a poem is the poet's way of sublimating his fantasies and achieving wish fulfillment through his poem; the function of criticism is to articulate the process of sublimating these fantasies and thus relate the poem firmly to the poet's psychic substrate. We may ask the critic whether he thinks that all genuine criticism leads to the explication of the complex of defense mechanisms and the specific relations among them. If he answers in the affirmative, then the commitments involved in criticism become testable hypotheses. Critics who do not follow psychoanalytic procedures are considered confused or seriously mistaken. The psychoanalytic critic can also say that nonpsychoanalytic critics are reasoning wrongly, since they ignore what he considers to be the true mode of critical response. In this way he brings criticism under a logic of inquiry where the concepts of explanation, hypothesis, and evidence are construed in terms of inquiry in the exact sciences.

But critical activities have a different meaning and are characterized by a form of rationality that is not definable in terms of the concepts of hypothesis, evidence, testability, and refutation. Fundamental aesthetic decisions are not testable hypotheses but ways of responding to literary works. But this is not to say that aesthetic decisions cannot be criticized; this is the level at which the logic of critical disputes reveals a peculiar depth. Holding different and conflicting conceptions of art, critics often reject some putatively aesthetic works as not artistic. Thus, for instance, Eliot and the New Critics criticized many romantic poems; for Arnold, Dryden and Pope took place among the classics of prose; and for some contemporary critics, such as Bloom, Eliot and Pound become anathema. Yet it is not that the disputants do not know what facts there are to be known about, say, the poetry of Eliot or Shelley; they rather conduct their dispute over the relevance of certain facts to criticism.

To characterize critical disputes in this way is not to say this is *the* way criticism functions. It is rather to show how specific aesthetic decisions that spring from genuine engagements with some kinds or periods of literature enable their proponents to speak with insight. When a particular decision is theoretically elaborated as a universally valid theory, talk about literary works is characterized by explicit and excessive proclamations of value-judgment or by rigid impositions of schematic theories. Yet the conflict over "What is good art?" "Why is it good?" or "What reasons can we give for our judgments?" is endemic to criticism. Moreover, since the rise of romanticism, a body of universally acceptable conventions is no longer available to artists and critics. And some of the greatest artists and thinkers of the last hundred and fifty years have radically questioned the deepest values that formerly sustained Western culture. It is in this radical context, even if somewhat altered by the return to objectivity advocated by both the New Criticism and structuralism, that the dispute over fundamental questions of criticism turns.

A particular form of criticism does not cease to become meaningful when it is questioned. For, as I have said, different forms of criticism compete for supremacy, but the competition cannot be settled by logical proof or further evidence; it is in principle beyond any final solution, though specific questions and answers do often enough get modified, rejected, or resolved. What is more important, there often occurs a renewal of competition through growth in sophistication and complexity in the position that is questioned. To recognize this nature of forms of criticism is to cease to seek tidy and logically compelling criteria for distinguishing literature from nonliterature, aesthetic response from moral evaluation, literary language from ordinary language, and to avoid valorization of one form (in this case literature) against other forms of cultural activity. There is no acid test for either literature or criticism, though both are such that they exhibit a complex internal structure and indefinite, blurred boundaries. This conception of criticism admits that what is literary may vary widely and in surprisingly radical ways and yet fall within the general rubric of literature.

My argument about forms of criticism does not lead to a sharp separation between critical discourse and other kinds of humanistic discourse. For, as I have said, it will not do to construe criticism as a sort of technical language, cut off from the language spoken by the members of the cultural community. Forms of criticism could not be what they are if it were not partly because of the factors independent of them. To see this reciprocity between criticism and cultural life outside it is to see where and when one or another form of criticism lapses into dogma and ceases to have vital relationship with the life of a culture as a whole.

Nevertheless, advances made in other fields and general increase in knowledge have the capacity to do harm as well as good for criticism. It is often said that literary critics should adopt conceptual and explanatory models from such disciplines as linguistics, psychology, and anthropology. However, models developed in, say, linguistics grow out of considerable regularities in the discipline, and even so these models are heuristic tools and do not command the assent of all linguists. These models are often recharacterized in order to cope with new data. And they are questioned or rejected if they fail to be logically and experimentally successful with difficult or anomalous elements, or if a more satisfactory model becomes available. The adoption of a model depends essentially on what it can explain, and what a model can explain depends on the state of the discipline. While it may recharacterize familiar and generally understood phenomena, it is not for such recharacterization that a new model is valuable. Its value consists mainly in explaining problematic elements and integrating the explanation with previously accessible phenomena.

There is no a priori guarantee then that a model from another discipline will yield useful results in criticism. And the decision to adopt an external model, while it will be fundamental in determining the criticism one practices, can be seriously misleading. The adoption, for instance, of a Freudian psychoanalytical model determines what is pertinent for criticism. Yet the decision to adopt a model from an external discipline is not the same as a fundamental aesthetic decision. For criticism generates criteria of intelligibility from its own practices. For instance, someone with no understanding of the tradition of the Elizabethan sonnet or revenge tragedy would gain little from Freud's theory of defense mechanism. Or, in order to understand what is going on in, say, Leavis's criticism, one would have to learn the nature of critical performance. Only someone who has grasped the concept of criticism can criticize Leavis intelligently, agree with some of his responses, recognize some of his claims as rigidly dogmatic. But no development *outside* criticism can make criticism any easier; it may make writing intelligent criticism more difficult. There is no doubt about the help that psychology, or structuralism, or phenomenology, or linguistics can bring to criticism, yet we cannot develop from them simple techniques that will replace the complex maneuvers into which criticism normally forces us.

However, the internal consistency of rules in a particular form of criticism does not give force to the criticism. Criticism does not consist of a number of autonomous languages, immune to serious logical criticism. To construe criticism as such would be to deprive criticism and disputes about concepts of art and criticism of significance, since each critical language would, then, possess its own rules of meaningfulness. It is the institution of criticism, I have argued here, which is itself the condition of the possibility of meaning for different concepts and strategies of criticism. Within this institution there are clusters of concepts which have a contestatory relationship, whereby each claims maximum explanatory efficacy and valuational richness in dealing with literary works. Each cluster of concepts has boundaries, sufficiently unclear and overlapping so that precise definitions and demarcations are seldom allowed.

The institution of criticism shows a multiplicity and complexity which is not reducible to the basic premises and certitudes of one or another form of criticism. For there are competing ways of construing the concept of literature, ways which show that criticism is a complex hermeneutical activity. Nevertheless, competing critical claims do not mean that the only solution to this conflict is outright skepticism. If it were a genuine solution, the concept of conflict itself would not be intelligible. On the other hand, the concept of criticism construed as incommensurate "frameworks" would also replace the concept of conflict by the concept of difference. Both alternatives trivialize the concept of conflict which is integral to both literary history and criticism.

A recognition of the complexity of critical procedures should prevent us from seeking to establish rigid or false distinctions between literature and history, literature and science, literary and ordinary language, literary experience and ordinary experience. These distinctions are false because they are generally construed as oppositions, a construal which does not really explain the activity of criticism. And yet, as Aristotle said, we cannot help making distinctions if we are to make sense of things; and we generally succeed in making these distinctions in the activity of criticism. We therefore need to recognize that we can commend artworks without importing dubious notions of restoring our precognitive levels of experience, or executing complex interpretive strategies through the rules of language, or of literature's primacy over all other modes of human experience. Insofar as the notion that experiencing literary works is valuable has any force it is implicit in the concept of criticism we possess, but no one concept of criticism is a standard concept which is indubitably valid over against the others. Thus the history of criticism is unstable, like the history of culture itself, and its concepts are mutually contesting. All of these concepts are inadequate if they are offered as universal propositions and many of them make possible a powerful realization of certain aspects or certain classes of literary works.

If literary criticism were solely a matter of facts, it would amount to the objectivity of historical scholarship; but that kind of objectivity does not solve questions involving insights into literature because in criticism the question of fact merges with that of value. If, on the other hand, criticism were merely a matter of validity, the problem would be a purely formal one, a question of logic. Criticism requires aesthetically rich and cultivated sensibility with psychological perspicacity; it requires an experiential grasp of the nature of forms as they undergo change through history, and not merely a grasp of forms as generic envelopes.

The concepts of criticism and critical theory offered here are intended to avoid the mistakes of a positivism which, however sophisticated its arguments and however subtly concealed its bias, insists on seeing literary interpretations as experimental hypotheses leading to a better and more correct interpretation of a literary work. And they are offered to avoid the difficulties of a methodological pluralism which, however carefully concealed its own dogmatism and however vocal its claims of generosity to other methods, insists on treating criticism as autonomous and self-validating languages. Neither position can account for the conflict that characterizes modern criticism: the former errs by a longing for indubitable knowledge, the latter by a turning of disagreement into difference. What we need to see is the greater complexity involved in what constitutes a fact, what is evidence or validation for literary criticism.

Appendix

On the Logic of Inquiry in Science

THE NATURE OF SCIENTIFIC INQUIRY is not easily characterized. Consider, for instance, Hume's well-known theory of knowledge, which contends that induction is an independent psychological principle which is incapable of being inferred from experience or from logical principles, although without induction science itself would be impossible. This idea has long been an embarrassment to philosophers of science, since it makes a paradoxical assertion that there is no logical foundation to the whole activity of science and that it is nevertheless internally consistent and practically useful. The philosopher's burden is therefore to provide a rational foundation for science, a task which Kant carried out with considerable rigor in the *Critique of Pure Reason*. Though Kant has made a permanent contribution to the philosophical analysis of the form of the concept of scientific inquiry, his own conceptual validation was for Newtonian physics. However, the discoveries of modern science and recent investigations into the theory and practice of science have brought out features which have complicated the problem of characterizing the nature of scientific inquiry. One crucial and insistent problem would seem to be the relation of observation to theory: that is, whether observation is fully constitutive of theory or whether theory not merely modifies but also constitutes what is observed. Another question is, If theory and observation are inextricably intermingled, what is the nature of both scientific knowledge and change in that knowledge? I shall sketch, and briefly comment on, answers to these questions given by two major philosophers of science, Karl Popper and Thomas Kuhn.

Since 1934 Popper has attempted, as did Kant before him, to overcome the philosopher's embarrassment posed by Hume's principle.[1] His earliest and most trenchant formulation of the question of scientific inquiry is perhaps this one: "How and why do we accept one theory in preference to another?" (*Logic of Scientific Discovery*, p. 108) Popper's question already implies his recognition that the history of science represents a nearly endless spectacle of replacement of one theory by another and that none of them is absolutely true. He therefore concludes that "science never pursues the illusory aim of making its answers final, or even probable. Its advance is, rather, toward an infinite yet attainable aim: that of ever discovering new, and deeper, and more general problems, and of subjecting our ever tentative answers to ever renewed and ever more rigorous tests" (p. 281). He then rejects the traditional view of the scientific method—induction—as a myth and substitutes for it his principle of falsifiability. For he is convinced that "scientific theories are never fully justifiable or verifiable, but . . . they are nevertheless testable" (p. 44). His rejection of verifiability is a rejection of the positivistic conception of objectivity, a conception that proposes a split between fact and value, between observation and theory. Yet he does not intend to reject objectivity, since "the *objectivity* of scientific statements lies . . . in the fact that they can be *inter-subjectively* tested" (p. 44). Popper is thus able to argue that "theories may correct an 'observational' or 'phenomenal' law which they are supposed to explain (*Objective Knowledge*, p. 204n.).

Defending this conception of science, which characterizes the scientist as a problem-solver, Popper argues that "growth" occurs in science not essentially by accretion but by the revolutionary overthrow of an accepted theory and its replacement by a better one. Consequently, "all that can possibly be 'positive' in our scientific knowledge is positive *only* insofar as certain theories are, at a certain moment of time, preferred to others in the light of our critical discussion. . . . Thus even what may be called 'positive' is so only with respect to negative methods" (*Objective Knowledge*, p. 20). Popper therefore contends that although scientific laws are never conclusively verifiable, they are conclusively falsifiable. He thus conceives the laws of nature as formulated by science "as (conjectural) descriptions of the structural properties of nature—of our world itself" (p. 196). And "we may seek to probe deeper and deeper into the structure of our world or . . . into the properties of the world that are more and more essential, or of greater and greater depth" (p. 196). In effect, scientific theory is to be conceived in the form of deductive systems in which every bit of knowledge appears as an overt, testable assertion. Knowledge results from continuous logical conflict among rival scientific theories, and though it is continuously leading towards a greater adequation of theory with truth, it is essentially provisional.

In sharp contrast to Popper, Kuhn has argued that the whole conception of cumulative, linear, ever-increasing growth of knowledge in science is more or less an illusion, that one cannot characterize the world apart from the theories one holds about it, and that there are no such things as theory-neutral observations and experiments. There is growth, however, in the limited sense that science moves from its primitive condition to maturity. Yet maturity is possible only when a genius proposes a "paradigm," a system of concepts which confers an order on the otherwise chaotic and confused fabric of initial scientific activity.[2] The concept of paradigms is focal to Kuhn's recharacterization of both the concept of scientific knowledge and the status and function of scientific theories. Paradigms are "universally recognized scientific achievements that for a time provide model problems and solution to a community of practitioners" (*Structure of Scientific Revolutions*, p. x). And it is from paradigms that "particular coherent traditions of scientific research" spring, which Kuhn calls "normal science" (p. 10). A paradigm, however, cannot bring under its aegis all of the available facts, since some of them remain recalcitrant to the paradigm. These "fundamental novelties" or "anomalies," as Kuhn calls such facts, produce "tradition-shattering complements to the tradition-bound activity of normal science" (p. 6). "Scientific revolutions," Kuhn argues further, "are inaugurated by a growing sense . . . that an existing paradigm has ceased to function in the exploration of an aspect of nature to which that paradigm itself had previously led the way" (p. 9).

Thus, for Kuhn, "out of date theories are not in principle unscientific because they have been discarded" (*Structure of Scientific Revolutions*, pp. 2–3). Instead, since a paradigm constitutes a puzzle-solving tradition, it can, with or without tests, "prepare the way for its own displacement."[3] Kuhn is able to argue in effect that Popper's "concept of science obscures even the existence of normal science." At least on some occasions, Kuhn asserts, "tests are not requisite to the revolutions through which science advances."[4] He thus joins normal science and scientific revolutions firmly in his concept of the psychology of research, which he characterizes in the following words:

> Scientists . . . never learn concepts, laws, and theories in the abstract and by themselves. Instead, these intellectual tools are from the start encountered in a historically and pedagogically prior unit that displays them with and through their application. A new theory is always announced together with applications to some concrete range of natural phenomena; without them it would not even be a candidate for acceptance. After it has been accepted, those same applications or others accompany the theory into the textbooks from which the future practitioner will learn his trade. . . . The process of learning a theory depends upon the study of applications. . . The student . . . discovers the meaning of terms . . . less from the incomplete though sometimes helpful definitions in his text than by observing and participating in the application of these concepts to problem-solution. [*Structure of Scientific Revolutions*, pp. 46–47]

It might appear that Kuhn's theory, since it is ostensibly a sociology of scientific knowledge, is not really opposed to Popper's, for the latter is concerned primarily with the question of innovation and discovery and hence with the growth of knowledge in science. Nonetheless, Kuhn's ruling assumptions are epistemological in character and imply a theory of knowledge which Popper has condemned as a kind of irrationalism. Popper conceives his logic of scientific discovery in terms of scientific progress, whose conditions it analyzes, and thus it becomes an auxiliary discipline, leading to the institutionalization and acceleration of the process of inquiry as a whole and thus to the progressive adequation of theory with truth (reality). Kuhn conceives his logic of scientific inquiry in terms of paradigms whose conditions it analyzes. It too is an auxiliary discipline, constituting a hermeneutics which promotes a propagation of closed historical consciousnesses (paradigms). For Kuhn there is no such thing as cumulative knowledge in science,[5] whereas for Popper, it is the cumulative knowledge which makes his principle of falsifiability viable; otherwise, conclusive rejection of a theory would not be possible. Kuhn is committed to the coherence and operational validity of each scientific paradigm and thus, almost to an excess, to synchrony. Popper, too, focuses almost exclusively on diachrony, to continuous approximations of theory with truth. History as a dialectical process of continuity marked by a gradual but profound discontinuity is alien to both. Kuhn's is a sociology of the successful models of content in science; in other words, his is a theory of the forms of content. Popper's, on the contrary, is a theory of the content of forms as this content approximates truth more fully than it did before. Each focuses on what the other leaves out. (Kant said that perception without concepts is blind and concepts without perceptions, empty. It would seem to me that both Popper and Kuhn remain excessively committed to one aspect of Kant's dyad and thus suffer limitation from the opposition of each by the other.)

We may disagree with Kuhn that revolution in science follows a long period of normal science and argue instead that both may properly coexist. For when a solution of a puzzle has revolutionary consequences it does not necessarily call in question a great many lower-level theories and practices in science. When the character of normal science itself has undergone fundamental changes, its relationship with previous modes of scientific practice will of course be tenuous. We may also disagree with Kuhn's argument that different scientific theories are self-contained so that they are mutually incommensurate. Yet Kuhn is right in rejecting Popper's contention that they are fully intratranslatable because it involves the unjustified assumption that observational data are neutral and theory-free and equally accessible to all theories.

The above is only part, though an important part, of the complex picture of the nature of scientific inquiry as it is discussed in the current philosophy of science. If we characterize a general popular view of scientific inquiry as a realist conception, basically a Popperian one, it contends that the theories which best conform to observed facts are true and therefore afford us genuine knowledge of how things are. Contrary to this is the skeptical idealist view, for which scientific theories cannot provide knowledge of the world as it is. Because scientific theories involve claims that are not warranted by sense-experience, argues the philosophical skeptic, observation is the proper mode of scientific inquiry. There is also the anarchist-idealist position of P. K. Feyerabend, which begins with some Popperian predicates but ends by rejecting Popper's own position. Feyerabend contends that Popper, though he rejects "the myth of the framework," fails to take into account his own myth. Feyerabend also rejects Kuhn's central thesis that science is an institutional, puzzle-solving activity. In short, this view conceives scientific activity as the activity of autonomous individuals each pursuing tenaciously his own conception of how things are.[6] A modern French scientist, Pierre Duhem, has brought to bear a phenomenological argument on the concept of scientific inquiry. He contends that a theory can never be in principle refuted by an experimental observation; what can be refuted, however, is one or the other subsidiary assumptions the scientist must make in order to bring his theory to observational test.[7]

Notes

INTRODUCTION

1. *Structural Anthropology*, trans. Claire Jacobson and Brooke Grundfest Schoepf (New York: Basic Books, 1963), p. 70.

2. See de Man's *Blindness and Insight: Essays in the Rhetoric of Contemporary Criticism* (New York: Oxford University Press, 1970), p. 8.

3. "Literature and Language: A Commentary," *New Literary History* 4 (Autumn 1974): 184.

4. See, for instance, *Blindness and Insight*, pp. 9, 102–11.

5. "Structure, Sign, and Play in the Discourse of the Human Sciences," in *The Structuralist Controversy: The Languages of Criticism and the Sciences of Man*, ed. Richard Macksey and Eugenio Donato (Baltimore: Johns Hopkins University Press, 1970), p. 265.

6. See for instance de Man's major essay, "The Rhetoric of Blindness: Jacques Derrida's Reading of Rousseau," *Blindness and Insight*, pp. 102–41, where, following Nietzsche, de Man argues for the necessary dependence of interpretation on the text as well as the inescapable element of error in it. It is a measure of the impact of Derrida's thought on recent criticism that Geoffrey Hartman asks the question, "Is it too late, or can our age, like every previous one, protect the concept of art?" (*The Fate of Reading and Other Essays* [Chicago: University of Chicago Press, 1975], p. 107).

7. *The Aims of Interpretation* (Chicago: University of Chicago Press, 1975), p. 74. Hirsch has developed his theory of interpretation in *Validity in Interpretation* (New Haven: Yale University Press, 1967).

8. "Irony as a Principle of Structure," in *Critical Theory since Plato*, ed. Hazard Adams (New York: Harcourt, Brace and Jovanovich, 1971), p. 1045–46. I have chosen the examples of the Lucy poem and the interpretations by Brooks and Bateson from Hirsch, *Validity in Interpretation*, pp. 228–29. I do so partly because Hirsch's selection is a brilliant one, but largely because it has helped me focus my criticism of Hirsch's conception of the logic of inquiry in criticism.

9. *English Poetry: A Critical Introduction*, 2nd ed. (Westport, Conn.: Greenwood, 1978), pp. 33, 80–81.

10. Geoffrey H. Hartman, *Wordsworth's Poetry 1787–1814* (New Haven: Yale University Press, 1964), p. 159. I am indebted to Hartman's reading of

259

Wordsworth, though my reading differs at some points from his. If I do not discuss Hartman's own reading, it is because he interprets all of the Lucy poems together and uses certain terms and concepts that introduce elements which it would take a different and longer treatment to consider. Hartman, for instance, says, "Humanization in the Lucy poems. . . is conceived as a precarious transition from imagination to the philosophic mind" (p. 106). The emphasis on the interplay of metaphor and metonymy in disclosing the turnings of the Wordsworthian consciousness is mine.

11. In a further reading of the Lucy poems, Bateson tries to explain the "sexlessness" of the poems by referring to Coleridge's guess that Wordsworth's sister, Dorothy, was Lucy and that the poem "A slumber did my spirit seal" is an anxiety lyric about Dorothy's future death. See Bateson, *Wordsworth: A Reinterpretation* (London: Longmans, 1956), p. 152; see also pp. 67, 153, 154. Bateson thus asks, "Assuming that Lucy is, in some sense, Dorothy, what is the biographical significance of the Lucy myth?" (p. 153). It is clear, then, that once it is assumed that the poet's life and his poems have an indissoluble bond, it is inevitable for one to assume further that biography and art reflect light on one another.

12. Gerald Graff has recently said, "A continuity of assumptions connects the New Criticism with the more radical skepticism of recent continentally influenced movements . . . practiced in different ways by Bloom, de Man, Barthes, Derrida, J. Hillis Miller, and Hartman." See Graff, *Literature against Itself: Literary Ideas in Modern Society* (Chicago: University of Chicago Press, 1979), p. 145.

13. Thus E. D. Hirsch, because he considers Bateson's approach more objective, finds his reading more probable than that of Brooks. See Hirsch, *Validity in Interpretation*, p. 240. It is Hirsch's contention that the "interpreter's job is to reconstruct a determinate actual meaning" (*Validity in Interpretation*, p. 231). Hirsch, of course, admits that the readings of Brooks and Bateson are incompatible and cannot be reconciled (pp. 229–30). Hirsch's concern, however, is to determine the conditions that would show that one of the interpretations is wrong. I criticize Hirsch's position in chapter 6.

CHAPTER ONE

1. *Aesthetics and Art Theory: An Historical Introduction* (New York: Dutton, 1970), pp. 171–72.

2. "The Unity of Kant's 'Critique of Aesthetic Judgment,'" *British Journal of Aesthetics* 8 (July 1968): 258, 259, 255.

3. For a detailed analysis aimed at Kant's supposed failure to overcome skepticism, see John Fisher and Jeffrey Maitland, "The Subjectivist Turn in Aesthetics: A Critical Analysis of Kant's Theory of Appreciation," *The Review of Metaphysics* 27 (June 1974): 726–51.

4. "Immanuel Kant's Aesthetics and Criticism," in *Discriminations* (New Haven: Yale University Press, 1970), p. 128.

5. *Kant's Critique of Aesthetic Judgment*, trans. James Creed Meredith (Oxford: Clarendon Press, 1911), p. 130. Throughout this chapter, all page refer-

ences in the text are to this edition of the *Critique of Aesthetic Judgment*. For a fuller explanation of Kant's aesthetics, see Donald W. Crawford, *Kant's Aesthetic Theory* (Madison: University of Wisconsin Press, 1974), and Francis J. Coleman, *The Harmony of Reason: A Study in Kant's Aesthetics* (Pittsburgh: University of Pittsburgh Press, 1974).

6. *Philosophy Looks at the Arts*, ed. Joseph Margolis (New York: Scribner, 1962), p. 6.

7. D. W. Gotshalk, "Form and Expression in Kant's Aesthetics," *British Journal of Aesthetics* 7 (July 1967): 250.

8. *The Philosophy of Fine Art*, trans. F. P. B. Osmaston, 3 vols. (London: G. Bell and Sons, 1920), 1:51.

9. Ibid., pp. 154, 78, 67.

10. G. W. F. Hegel, *On Art, Religion, Philosophy: Introductory Lectures to the Realm of Absolute Spirit*, ed. J. Glenn Gray (New York: Harper and Row, 1970), pp. 66–67.

11. *The Philosophy of Fine Art*, 1:11.

12. See Bernard Bosanquet, *Three Lectures on Aesthetics* (London: Macmillan, 1915), pp. 26–29.

13. Ibid., p. 19.

14. Benedetto Croce, *Aesthetic as Science of Expression and General Linguistic*, trans. Douglas Ainslee (London: Macmillan, 1909), pp. 97–100.

15. *Three Lectures on Aesthetics*, pp. 67–70.

16. *Aesthetic as Science*, p. 11.

17. For a full critical account of Croce's theory see Merle E. Brown, *Neo-Idealist Aesthetics: Croce-Gentile-Collingwood* (Detroit: Wayne State University Press, 1966), pp. 17–149. A sympathetic and comprehensive account of Croce's aesthetics and criticism is in G. N. G. Orsini, *Benedetto Croce: Philosopher of Art and Literary Critic* (Carbondale: Southern Illinois University Press, 1961).

CHAPTER TWO

1. Michael H. Mitias, "The Institutional Theory of Artistic Creativity," *British Journal of Aesthetics* 18 (Autumn 1978): 335.

2. See, for instance, Eliseo Vivas, *The Artistic Transaction and Essays on Theory of Literature* (Columbus: Ohio State University Press, 1963), pp. 153–60.

3. "On the Creation of Art," *Journal of Aesthetics and Art Criticism* 23 (Spring 1965): 301.

4. Monroe C. Beardsley and William K. Wimsatt, "The Intentional Fallacy," in Wimsatt, *The Verbal Icon: Studies in the Meaning of Poetry* (Lexington: University of Kentucky Press, 1954), pp. 3–18.

5. For a recent example of the distinction between making and creating, see Jack Glickman, "Creativity in the Arts," *Culture and Art: An Anthology*, ed. Lars Aagaard-Mogensen (Atlantic Highlands, N.J.: Humanities Press, 1976), pp. 130–46.

6. *Creation and Discovery: Essays in Criticism and Aesthetics* (New York: Noonday Press, 1955), pp. 151–52.

7. "Creativity in Art," in *Creativity in the Arts*, ed. Vincent Tomas (Englewood Cliffs, N.J.: Prentice-Hall, 1964), p. 108.

8. Ibid.

9. See Jack Glickman, "Creativity in the Arts," pp. 132–35.

10. *Letters from Joseph Conrad*, ed. E. Garnett (Indianapolis: Bobbs-Merrill Company, 1928), pp. 171–72.

11. "The Creative Process in Art," *British Journal of Aesthetics* 17 (Summer 1977): 230–41.

12. "On the Creation of Art," p. 301.

13. *Artistic Transaction*; the quotes are from pp. 160 and 158.

14. Ibid., pp. 158, 159.

15. Ibid., p. 155.

16. "The Institutional Theory of Artistic Creativity," pp. 334, 336.

17. This is a central theme in part 1 of *Philosophical Investigations*, 3rd ed., trans. G. E. M. Anscombe (New York: Macmillan, 1958).

18. Ibid., see nos. 149, 158, 154, 155.

19. Ibid., no. 153.

20. Ibid., no. 154.

21. "Creative Acts," in *Perspectives in Education, Religion, and the Arts*, ed. Howard E. Kiefer and Milton K. Munitz (Albany: State University of New York Press, 1970), p. 243.

22. For a historical-analytical study of this topic, see Harold Osborne, "Inspiration," *British Journal of Aesthetics* 17 (Summer 1977): 242–53.

23. For a detailed criticism of Glickman's position, see Mitias, "Institutional Theory of Artistic Creativity." Mitias's criticism, however, is vitiated for me since it depends on the theory of the creative process I have criticized here.

24. "Inspiration," pp. 250–51.

25. For a discussion of the testimony of creative artists, see Jerome Stolnitz, *Aesthetics and Philosophy of Art Criticism* (Boston: Houghton Mifflin, 1960) pp. 92–100.

26. "The Intentional Fallacy," p. 7.

27. Thus Haig Khatchadourian's essay on the creative process; see n. 11.

28. See Stolnitz, *Aesthetics and Philosophy of Art Criticism*, pp. 91–92.

29. *Philosophical Investigations*, no. 370.

30. This seems to me to be the point of Joseph Margolis's criticism of Morris Weitz's denial of the condition of artifactuality for art; see Margolis, *The Language of Art and Art Criticism* (Detroit: Wayne State University Press, 1965), p. 40. See also Margolis, "Works of Art as Physically Embodied and Culturally Emergent Entities," *British Journal of Aesthetics* 14 (Summer 1974): 187–96.

CHAPTER THREE

1. A number of major essays on the subject are conveniently collected in *On Literary Intention*, ed. David Newton–de Molina (Edinburgh: University of Edinburgh Press, 1976).

2. "The Intentional Fallacy," in William K. Wimsatt, Jr., *The Verbal Icon*, pp. 3–18. The quotation is from p. 3.

3. I borrow this phrase and concept from W. B. Gallie, *Philosophy and the Historical Understanding* (New York: Schocken Books, 1964), pp. 157–91.

4. A failure to characterize this context has led to confusion in a great deal of discussion on intention. Wimsatt, for instance, has justifiably complained that Frank Cioffi is "largely unaware of the contexts of literary scholarship and criticism which framed" the Wimsatt-Beardsley articles on intention and affective response. Cf. "Genesis: An Argument Resumed," in *Day of the Leopards: Essays in Defense of Poems* (New Haven: Yale University Press, 1976), p. 25, n. 25. Wimsatt is referring to Cioffi, "Intention and Interpretation in Criticism," in *On Literary Intention* ed. Newton–de Molina, pp. 55–73.

5. See his famous "Tradition and the Individual Talent," in *The Sacred Wood: Essays in Poetry and Criticism* (London: Methuen, 1928), pp. 47–59.

6. "The Intentional Fallacy," p. 5. Also see Wimsatt, "Genesis: An Argument Resumed," pp. 11–39, esp. pp. 36–39.

7. Roman Ingarden, too, has argued that where a literary work is ambiguous, it is important to keep to its verbal context since the writer's intentionality is not available for a resolution of the ambiguity. See Ingarden, *The Literary Work of Art: An Investigation of the Borderlines of Ontology, Logic, and Theory of Literature*, trans. George G. Grabowicz (Evanston, Ill.: Northwestern University Press, 1973), pp. 22, 84–91.

8. See, for instance, Monroe C. Beardsley, "On the Creation of Art," p. 301.

9. *The Verbal Icon*, p. 9.

10. Monroe C. Beardsley, *Aesthetics: Problems in the Philosophy of Criticism* (New York: Harcourt, Brace, 1958), p. 29.

11. In *Philosophy and the Historical Understanding*, Gallie develops seven conditions to characterize essentially contested concepts (pp. 161–68), and chooses as his examples the concepts of religion, art, science, democracy, and social justice (pp. 168–82). I do not believe that all of Gallie's seven conditions would apply to the concept of intention. But he would allow intention the status of an essentially contested concept since it is a subordinate concept falling under the concept of art (p. 190).

12. See *The Literary Work of Art*, ch. 8.

13. In this context Gallie's discussion of the concept of art is of some help. See *Philosophy and the Historical Understanding*, pp. 170–78.

14. Thus, for instance, Wimsatt and Brooks write: "In the variation given this philosophy [the expressionist theory of art] by Sainte-Beuve and other men of letters, literature was the expression of personality. In the historical and deterministic critics deriving from Hegel, like Taine, literature was the expression of race, milieu, and moment. The 'extreme impressionists' . . . the later aesthetes, like Pater and Wilde, thought of literature as the 'exquisite expression of delicate and fluctuating sensations or impressions of life.' For all critics and theorists, literature was the expression of something. The norm of expression was the great co-ordinator, harmonizing the toughest and most

scientific research techniques with the softest, most personal and most emotive aesthetic interests." See their *Literary Criticism: A Short History* (New York: Knopf, 1957), pp. 533–34.

15. For a good, brief account of neoclassic criticism see René Wellek, "Neoclassicism and the New Trends of the Time," in his *A History of Modern Criticism: 1750–1950*, 4 vols. (New Haven: Yale University Press, 1955), 1:12–30; see also M. H. Abrams, *The Mirror and the Lamp: Romantic Theory and the Critical Tradition* (New York: Oxford University Press, 1953), pp. 14–21. As I have parenthetically suggested, romanticism is a very complex and at times contradictory body of ideas, and it has drawn rival and competing interpretations. See, for example, Paul de Man, "The Rhetoric of Temporality," in *Interpretation: Theory and Practice*, ed. Charles S. Singleton (Baltimore: Johns Hopkins University Press, 1969), pp. 173–209; see also the essays by Paul de Man, Harold Bloom, and Geoffrey Hartman in *Romanticism: Vistas, Instances, Continuities*, ed. David Thorburn and Geoffrey Hartman (Ithaca, N.Y.: Cornell University Press, 1973); and in *Romanticism and Consciousness: Essays in Criticism*, ed. Harold Bloom (New York: Norton, 1970).

16. "English Romanticism: The Spirit of the Age," in *Romanticism Reconsidered: Selected Papers for the English Institute*, ed. with a foreword by Northrop Frye (New York: Columbia University Press, 1963), p. 57. See also René Wellek, *A History of Modern Criticism*, vol. 2.

17. Abrams, *The Mirror and the Lamp*, p. 22.

18. Abrams, "English Romanticism," p. 62.

19. Hans-Georg Gadamer, *Truth and Method*, trans. Garrett Barden and John Cumming (New York: Seabury, 1975), p. 56.

20. *The Verbal Icon*, pp. 6, 5.

21. *The Use of Poetry and the Use of Criticism* (London: Faber and Faber, 1933), p. 138; see also p. 140.

22. *The Verbal Icon*, p. 7.

23. See *Validity in Interpretation*, ch. 1, and Appendix A and Appendix B.

24. *The Verbal Icon*, p. 5.

25. *The Aims of Interpretation*, p. 91.

26. *Validity in Interpretation*, p. 230. For a good criticism of Hirsch's distinction between meaning and significance see David Couzens Hoy, *The Critical Circle: Literature, History, and Philosophical Hermeneutics* (Berkeley: University of California Press, 1978), pp. 13–24. See also my chapter 6.

27. Ibid., p. 44.

28. Ibid.; the quoted phrases are from pp. 242 and 173.

29. *Charles Dickens: The World of His Novels* (Cambridge, Mass.: Harvard University Press, 1958), p. x.

30. See Georges Poulet, "Criticism and the Experience of Interiority," in *The Structuralist Controversy: The Languages of Criticism and the Sciences of Man*, pp. 56–72. My sentence refers to the discussion that follows Poulet's essay and paraphrases specifically the discussion between Lucien Goldmann and Poulet; see pp. 84–85.

31. Poulet, "Criticism and the Experience of Interiority," p. 72. Poulet, of

course, does not mean that one leaves one's own interiority but rather that one's interiority coincides with another's. For an admirable discussion of Poulet's criticism, see J. Hillis Miller, "Georges Poulet's 'Criticism of Interiority,'" in *The Quest for Imagination: Essays in Twentieth-Century Criticism,* ed. O. B. Hardison, Jr. (Cleveland: The Press of Case Western Reserve University, 1971), pp. 191–224. For a fuller discussion of the Geneva school of criticism, see Sarah Lawall, *Critics of Consciousness: The Existential Structures of Literature* (Cambridge, Mass.: Harvard University Press, 1968), and Robert Magliola, *Phenomenology and Literature: An Introduction* (West Lafayette, Ind.: Purdue University Press, 1977), pp. 19–56.

32. *Truth and Method,* p. 149.

33. Ibid., p. 264.

34. See, for instance, René Wellek, "The New Criticism: Pro and Contra," *Critical Inquiry* 4 (Summer 1978): 611–24. In "A Rejoinder to Gerald Graff," *Critical Inquiry* 5 (Spring 1979): 577, Wellek defends the New Critical theory and practice in terms of Gadamer's notion of a "fusion of horizons."

35. *Day of the Leopards,* p. 202.

36. Gören Hermeren has also argued that "the fundamental issues involved in a stand on intention are nonempirical; they concern normative questions." See his "Intention and Interpretation in Literary Criticism," *New Literary History* 7 (Autumn 1975): 81.

37. See *Kant's Critique of Aesthetic Judgment,* pp. 19–36; see also my Ch. 1.

38. *Truth and Method,* pp. 325–41.

39. This is one of the major concerns in *Philosophical Investigations.*

40. *Zettel,* eds. G. E. M. Anscombe and G. H. von Wright, trans. G. E. M. Anscombe (Berkeley: University of California Press, 1970), par. 112.

41. William Wordsworth, "Preface to the Second Edition of *Lyrical Ballads,*" in *Critical Theory since Plato,* p. 435; Eliot, "Tradition and the Individual Talent," *The Sacred Wood,* p. 58.

42. As a result, my analysis here would change the import of Frank Cioffi's rhetorical question, "Isn't the common authorship of several works a biographical fact?" See "Intention and Interpretation in Criticism," in *On Literary Intention,* p. 68. The antiintentionalist stand (at least that held by Wimsatt and Beardsley) centers on the concept of value of aesthetic objects, a value which is construed to be independent of the connection with the author.

1. In Anglo-American aesthetic discussions, Monroe Beardsley has sought to defend the concept of aesthetic autonomy and to provide a philosophy of criticism; see his *Aesthetics.* For a critical discussion of Beardsley's theories of aesthetic objects and aesthetic experience, see George Dickie, *Art and the Aesthetic: An Institutional Analysis* (Ithaca, N.Y.: Cornell University Press, 1974), chs. 7 and 8.

2. A. C. Bradley, "Poetry for Poetry's Sake," *Oxford Lectures on Poetry* (London: Macmillan, 1909), pp. 3–34; O. K. Bouwsma, "The Expression Theory of

Art," in *Aesthetic and Language,* ed. William Elton (New York: Philosophical Library, 1954), pp. 73–99. Bouwsma says, "The meaning of sentences is translatable, but the 'meaning' of poems, of music, is not" (p. 95).

3. *Coleridge's Shakespearean Criticism,* ed. Thomas Middleton Raysor (Cambridge, Mass.: Harvard University Press, 1930), 1:224.

4. *Verbal Icon,* p. 82. Subsequent citations in this chapter will be in text.

5. Cleanth Brooks, *The Well Wrought Urn* (New York: Reynal and Hitchcock, 1947), pp. 176–96.

6. Stuart Hampshire, "Logic and Appreciation," in *Aesthetics and Language,* pp. 161–69.

7. *Blindness and Insight,* p. 109.

8. See Wimsatt and Beardsley's contention, in "The Intentional Fallacy," that "poetry differs from practical messages which are successful if and only if we correctly infer the intention." See *Verbal Icon,* p. 5.

9. John Crowe Ransom first used these terms and metaphors in *The World's Body* (New York: Scribner's, 1938).

10. Gerald Graff, *Poetic Statement and Critical Dogma* (Evanston, Ill.: Northwestern University Press, 1970), p. 140.

11. Brooks, *Well Wrought Urn,* p. 236.

12. See the discussion by Murray Krieger in *The New Apologists for Poetry* (Minneapolis: University of Minnesota Press, 1956), pp. 64–76; this book provides what is perhaps the fullest critical discussion of the New Criticism. Graff's book, *Poetic Statement and Critical Dogma,* also provides, from a different viewpoint, a sustained criticism of the New Critical theory. The New Criticism, however, is a general designation for the work of a number of critics such as Eliot, Richards, Ransom, Tate, Brooks, Winters, and finally Wimsatt. There are, of course, significant differences among these critics and the term *New Criticism,* often abusively identified as a formalism, does not imply a body of doctrines purged of disagreements or differences among these critics.

13. *Speculations,* ed. Herbert Read (London: Routledge and Kegan Paul, 1924), pp. 134–35.

14. See Krieger, *The New Apologists for Poetry,* pp. 66–78; the quotation from p. 75. Krieger is, of course, trying to develop a systematic theory based on the reflections of the New Critics themselves. See, for instance, Brooks, *Well Wrought Urn,* pp. 3–20; Ransom, *The World's Body,* pp. 111–42; see also Krieger's *Theory of Criticism: A Tradition and Its System* (Baltimore: Johns Hopkins University Press, 1976), chs. 2 and 6.

15. I. A. Richards, *Principles of Literary Criticism* (New York: Harcourt, Brace, 1925), pp. 261–67; see also his *Science and Poetry* (London: K. Paul, Trench, Trubner, 1926), pp. 66–79.

16. See, for instance, A. J. Ayer, *Language, Truth, and Logic* (London: V. Gollancz, 1936).

17. For instance, see Thomas Kuhn, *The Structure of Scientific Revolutions,* 2nd enlarged ed. (Chicago: University of Chicago Press, 1970); Popper, *The Logic of Scientific Discovery.* Despite some basic differences, Popper and Kuhn agree about the "intimate and inevitable entanglement of scientific observa-

tion with scientific theory." Cf. Kuhn, "Logic of Discovery or Psychology of Research?" in *The Philosophy of Karl Popper*, ed. Paul Arthur Schilpp (La Salle, Ill.: Open Court, 1974), 11:798. See also my discussion in Appendix.

18. However, Brooks insufficiently spells out his difference from Richards, though it is implied in his position. See, for instance, his statement of "how the position taken here differs from that taken by Richards." Cf. *Well Wrought Urn*, p. 231.

19. Perhaps the earliest expression of this view in modern thought is in Giambattista Vico, *The New Science of Giambattista Vico*, trans. Thomas Goddard Bergin and Max Harold Fisch (Ithaca, N.Y.: Cornell University Press, 1968).

20. E. D. Hirsch has made this objection in *The Aims of Interpretation*, p. 90.

21. "Logic and Appreciation," in *Aesthetics and Language*, ed. William Elton, p. 169. For a criticism of the uniqueness thesis in aesthetics see Mary Mothersill, " 'Unique' as an Aesthetic Predicate," in *Contemporary Studies in Aesthetics*, ed. Francis J. Coleman (New York: McGraw-Hill, 1968), pp. 193–208.

22. The fullest development of the view that works of art possess a special ontological status is provided by Roman Ingarden, *The Literary Work of Art*. René Wellek's essay, "The Mode of Existence of a Literary Work of Art," in Wellek and Austin Warren, *Theory of Literature*, 3rd ed. (New York: Harcourt, Brace, 1956), pp. 143–57, develops a similar argument. I discuss the ontological question in chapter 6.

23. *Aesthetic*, pp. 144–46, 155.

24. *Principles of Literary Criticism*, pp. 249–52.

25. *Verbal Icon*, p. 50; *Day of the Leopards*, pp. 205–23, 30.

26. Croce, *Aesthetic*, p. 14.

27. Harold Bloom, *The Anxiety of Influence* (New York: Oxford University Press, 1973); and *A Map of Misreading* (New York: Oxford University Press, 1975), esp. pp. 27–40 and 83–105. See also Geoffrey H. Hartman, "Crossing Over: Literary Commentary as Literature," *Comparative Literature* 28 (1976): 257–76. See also my discussion of de Man in chapter 7.

28. *The Sacred Wood*, pp. 47–59.

29. See Croce's "The Breviary of Aesthetic," *Rice Institute Pamphlets* 2 (1915): 223–310. See also his *Aesthetic*, esp. pp. 32–38 and 118–21.

30. See, for instance, Monroe C. Beardsley, "Aesthetic Experience Regained," *Journal of Aesthetics and Art Criticism* 28 (1969): 3–11.

31. See Francis Hutcheson, *An Inquiry into the Original of Our Ideas of Beauty and Virtue* (New York: Garland, 1971); David Hume, "Of the Standard of Taste," *Critical Theory since Plato*, pp. 314–23; and Edmund Burke, *A Philosophical Inquiry into the Origin of Our Ideas of the Sublime and Beautiful* (New York: Columbia University Press, 1958). For an important discussion of eighteenth-century aesthetics, see Jerome Stolnitz, "On the Origins of 'Aesthetic Disinterestedness,'" *Journal of Aesthetics and Art Criticism* 20 (1961): 131–43. For a critical discussion of this tradition of the theory of aesthetic experience, see Dickie, *Art and the Aesthetic*, pp. 53–69.

32. See Stolnitz, *Aesthetics and Philosophy of Art Criticism*, pp. 29–83; Virgil Aldrich, *Philosophy of Art* (Englewood Cliffs, N.J.: Prentice-Hall, 1963), pp. 6–27; and Eliseo Vivas, *Creation and Discovery*, pp. 93–99. Dickie has criticized all three of them though a comparison of Dickie's analysis with my discussion of Vivas's ("A Definition of the Aesthetic Experience," in *Creation and Discovery*, pp. 93–99) will show that my account differs in certain fundamental respects. See Dickie, *Art and the Aesthetic*, pp. 113–46. Dickie is attempting to develop an institutional theory of art, whereas I am concerned with the difficulties that attend definitions of aesthetic experience and their bearing on the problem of interpretation in criticism.

33. See, for instance, Virgil Aldrich, "Back to Aesthetic Experience," *Journal of Aesthetics and Art Criticism* 25 (1966): 363–71; and Joel Kupperman, "Art and Aesthetic Experience," *British Journal of Aesthetics* 15 (Winter 1975): 29–39.

34. *Philosophy of Art*, pp. 19–24. The quoted phrase occurs on p. 21.

35. For instance, Murray Krieger has said that Vivas has provided a definition of aesthetic experience which is necessary for the New Critics to give an adequate theoretical account of the aesthetic object; see *The New Apologists for Poetry*, p. 129.

36. *Creation and Discovery*, p. 93.

37. *The Artistic Transaction*, p. 198.

38. *Creation and Discovery*, p. 97.

39. I should add here that Vivas wrote "A Definition of Aesthetic Experience" in 1937, when his philosophical views were predominantly those of Deweyan naturalism. Vivas puts his "definition" in the context of these views in "A Natural History of the Aesthetic Transaction," written in 1939 and published in *Naturalism and the Human Spirit*, ed. Yervant H. Krikorian (New York: Columbia University Press, 1944), pp. 96–120. His philosophical views underwent a fundamental change, though he says in the first note to his definition essay, "The phenomenological analysis that both it [1939 essay] and this shorter paper undertake seems to me to be valid still." (*Creation and Discovery*, p. 286). Vivas brings his definition into accord with his mature thought later in his longer essay "The Artistic Transaction," dated 1939–62, in his book that bears the same title. In this chapter I concern myself with Vivas's definition in the context of the later expansions of his aesthetic thought.

40. See Vivas's essay "What is a Poem?" in *Creation and Discovery*, esp. p. 74; see also *The Artistic Transaction*, esp. pp. 176, 179, 180, 191.

41. *Creation and Discovery*, p. 95.

42. Ibid., pp. 96, 94.

43. *The Artistic Transaction*, pp. 39, 77.

44. *Creation and Discovery*, p. 94.

45. *The Yale Edition of the Works of Samuel Johnson*, vol. 7, ed. Arthur Sherbo (New Haven: Yale University Press, 1968), pp. 76–77.

46. In somewhat modified versions, this is the position of idealist aesthetics, including the New Criticism.

47. The necessarily broad statement applies, with various modifications,

to the aesthetic and literary theories from Plato and Aristotle to the expressionists in criticism.

48. However, this is precisely what Vivas cannot do. It would require an understanding of the complexity of relations among different contexts of life—a notion which Wittgenstein has subtly and relentlessly explored in *Philosophical Investigations*. Vivas, on the contrary, has attacked Wittgenstein in what I think is a misconstrual of the latter's thought. (See Vivas's attack in *The Artistic Transaction*, pp. 81–88.)

49. Pp. 44–62. For Vivas's criticism of Richards, see *Creation and Discovery*, pp. 209–21.

50. *Creation and Discovery*, p. 97.

51. Ibid., p. 99.

52. *The Artistic Transaction*, pp. 196–98.

53. *Truth and Method*, p. 64. Subsequent references in this chapter will be given in text. For a detailed summary account of Gadamer's critique of modern aesthetics, see Richard E. Palmer, *Hermeneutics: Interpretation Theory in Schleirmacher, Dilthey, Heidegger, and Gadamer* (Evanston, Ill.: Northwestern University Press, 1969), pp. 162–93.

54. In *Modern Dogma and The Rhetoric of Assent* (Chicago: University of Chicago Press, 1974).

55. William K. Wimsatt, *Hateful Contraries: Studies in Literature and Criticism* (Lexington, Ky.: University of Kentucky Press, 1965), p. 48.

CHAPTER FIVE

1. See, for instance, the works of Stanley E. Fish, *Surprised by Sin: The Reader in Paradise Lost*, 2nd ed. (Berkeley: University of California Press, 1971); *Self-Consuming Artifacts: The Experience of Seventeenth-Century Literature* (Berkeley: University of California Press, 1972). Subsequent references to *Self-Consuming Artifacts* will be given in the text throughout this chapter. See also the two books by Wolfgang Iser, *The Implied Reader: Patterns of Communication in Prose Fiction from Bunyan to Beckett* (Baltimore: Johns Hopkins University Press, 1974), and *The Act of Reading: A Theory of Aesthetic Response* (Baltimore: Johns Hopkins University Press, 1978). Iser's work, unlike Fish's, insists on the distinction between literary and ordinary language, and thus suggests a genuine division in the reader-response criticism; see *The Act of Reading*, pp. 60–65. A fuller list of the reader-response critics would have to include, among others, Stephen Booth and Michael Riffaterre.

2. See, for instance, the works of Norman Holland: *The Dynamics of Literary Response* (New York: Oxford University Press, 1968); *Poems in Persons* (New York: W. W. Norton, 1973); and *5 Readers Reading* (New Haven: Yale University Press, 1975). Subsequent references to *Dynamics of Literary Response* will be given in text throughout this chapter. See also David Bleich, *Subjective Criticism* (Baltimore: Johns Hopkins University Press, 1978).

3. Jacques Lacan, *Écrits: A Selection*, trans. Alan Sheridan (London: Tavistock, 1977), and *The Four Fundamental Concepts of Psycho-analysis*, trans. Alan

Sheridan (London: Hogarth Press, 1977). Subsequent references to *Écrits* will be given in text throughout this chapter.

4. See, for instance, *The Standard Edition of the Complete Psychological Works of Sigmund Freud*, trans. James Strachey, Anna Freud, Alix Strachey, and Alan Tyson, ed. James Strachey, 24 vols. (London: Hogarth Press, 1957), esp. vol. 21, *Civilization and Its Discontents*. Throughout this chapter, in-text citations of the *Works of Freud* will refer to this edition.

5. *Beyond the Pleasure Principle*, trans. James Strachey (New York: Bantam, 1959), pp. 38–39.

6. *Works of Freud*, 12:154–56; see also Freud's discussion of transference, 12:99–108.

7. *Dynamics of Literary Response*, p. 307; see also ch. 4, "Form as Defense," pp. 162–90.

8. For a criticism of Holland's systematic rather than exploratory use of psychoanalytic concepts, see Iser, *The Act of Reading*, pp. 39–45.

9. *Works of Freud*, 12:155. I have somewhat modified Freud's idea here because, despite his rigid insistence on technique, he often shows a profound intuitive mastery of the complexity of specific cases.

10. Steven Marcus, *Representations: Essays on Literature and Society* (New York: Random House, 1975), p. 307. For Freud's case history of Dora, see *Works of Freud*, 7:3–122.

11. For a similar criticism from a different viewpoint, see Erich Heller, "The Dismantling of a Marionette Theater; or, Psychology and the Misinterpretation of Literature," *Critical Inquiry* 4 (Spring 1978): 417–32. The scientistic aspirations of psychology are, however, hard to give up. Thus Heinz Kohut, a psychologist, responds to Heller, in an essay that is marked by rear-guard response to the promise of psychology. Kohut nevertheless insists that "depth psychology can for the first time begin, however haltingly and cautiously, to deal with the problems and activities of the whole man." See Kohut, "Psychoanalysis and the Interpretation of Literature: A Correspondence with Erich Heller," *Critical Inquiry* 4 (Spring 1978): 447.

12. Jürgen Habermas, *Knowledge and Human Interests*, trans. Jeremy J. Shapiro (Boston: Beacon Press, 1968), p. 252.

13. For a discussion of this point see George Watson, *The Study of Literature* (London, 1969), pp. 156–71; and Edward Wasiolek, "The Future of Psychoanalytic Criticism," in *The Frontiers of Modern Criticism*, ed. David H. Malone (Los Angeles, Hennessay and Ingalls, 1974), pp. 144–68.

14. See, for instance, the following of his essays: "Unity Identity Text Self," *PMLA* 90 (1975): 813–22; "The New Paradigm: Subjective or Transactive?" *New Literary History* 7 (Winter 1976): 335–46; "Human Identity," *Critical Inquiry* 4 (Spring 1978): 451–69. Holland draws on the concept of identity developed by Heinz Lichtenstein, a number of whose essays are now collected in his *The Dilemma of Human Identity* (New York: J. Aronson, 1977). My argument here is that more recent essays in psychoanalytic criticism do not require or constitute a change in their method of inquiry. They simply continue transposition of psychological concepts to criticism, though they may choose

to employ the latest concepts from psychological investigations. Moreover, Holland's recent emphasis on identity (for instance, *5 Readers Reading*, pp. 113–28) does not differ from his description of the transformational process in *The Dynamics of Literary Response*, chs. 1–6.

15. "Unity Identity Text Self," p. 814.

16. "The New Paradigm," p. 343.

17. "Unity Identity Text Self," p. 816.

18. Norman N. Holland, "Transactive Criticism: Re-Creation Through Identity," *Criticism* 18 (Fall 1976): 334.

19. "Unity Identity Text Self," pp. 816–17.

20. Norman Holland, "Stanley Fish, Stanley Fish," *Genre* 19 (Fall 1977): 439.

21. "Unity Identity Text Self," p. 817.

22. "Human Identity," p. 459.

23. See for instance, Holland's characterization of four interpretations of "Dover Beach," *The Dynamics of Literary Response*, pp. 127–28.

24. *The Dynamics of Literary Response*, chs. 1–6; see also *5 Readers Reading*, pp. 117–23.

25. "Unity Identity Text Self," p. 816. See also *5 Readers Reading*, pp. 130–200.

26. *The Liberal Imagination: Essays on Literature and Society* (New York: Doubleday, 1950), p. 53.

27. For Derrida this would constitute Lacan's logocentricism. See Lacan, "Seminar on 'The Purloined Letter,'" *Yale French Studies* 48 (1972): 38–72; and Derrida's reading of Lacan's reading: "The Purveyor of Truth," *Yale French Studies* 52 (1975): 31–113.

28. "Seminar on 'The Purloined Letter.'"

29. *Lectures and Conversations on Aesthetics, Psychology and Religious Belief,* ed. Cyril Barrett (Berkeley: University of California Press, 1967), p. 51.

30. For two New Critical readings of this poem, see Murray Krieger, *The Play and Place of Criticism* (Baltimore: Johns Hopkins University Press, 1967), pp. 69–75; Alan Roper, *Arnold's Poetic Landscapes* (Baltimore: Johns Hopkins University Press, 1969), pp. 178–82. My brief reading differs from these two because of a desire to account for the experience of the personal that the poem evokes.

31. Gustav Janouch, *Conversations with Kafka*, trans. Goronwy Rees (New York: F. A. Praeger, 1953), p. 35.

32. Thus Heinz Kohut, in a response to Erich Heller, writes (see n. 11) that Heller's critique is based "on an unacceptable text: the paper whose reductionist thesis served you as the supposedly representative example of the misinterpretation of literature by psychoanalysis was not written by a psychoanalyst but by someone in your own field" ("Psychoanalysis and the Interpretation of Literature," p. 434). Kohut, of course, does not pause to reflect that the most formidable figure in his own field, Freud, had serious reservations about the value of psychoanalysis in its scientist aspirations for understanding literature. Moreover, there remain other crucial questions: Which

psychoanalysts, among the many possible contenders, should be considered acceptable? If there are conflicts among psychoanalysts themselves, who would be the adjudicator and how should the victor be denominated? Isn't it possible that someone who has thought deeply about literature and psychoanalysis might be more equipped for psychoanalytic criticism than professional psychoanalysts? If it is, then why should a competent literary critic, whether psychoanalytically inclined or not, not be an appropriate disputant? To grant, in other words, that there be dialogue between psychoanalysis and criticism one also needs to grant that if the dialogue isn't going to lead to mere endless transpositions of concepts from one discipline to another, there should be some grasp of the difficulties in the transaction. Without denying that psychoanalysts can be competent critics of literature, any serious thinking about literature—even for interdisciplinary questions—will need a semiotic, and more specifically literary, competence. To say this is not to imply, however, that one can necessarily arrive at a conclusive set of conditions that designates once and for all the nature of literary competence.

33. *Surprised by Sin*, p. ix. See also his *Self-Consuming Artifacts*, pp. 383–84, 400–410.

34. *Self-Consuming Artifacts*, p. 389. See also his two essays that attack the gap between description and interpretation: "What Is Stylistics and Why Are They Saying Such Terrible Things about It?" in *Approaches to Poetics*, ed. Seymour Chatman (New York: Columbia University Press, 1973), pp. 109–52; and "How Ordinary Is Ordinary Language?" in *Language, Logic and Genre*, ed. Wallace Martin (Lewisberg, Pa.: Bucknell University Press, 1974), pp. 13–27.

35. "Interpreting the *Variorum*," *Critical Inquiry* 2 (Spring 1976): 475.

36. "How Ordinary Is Ordinary Language?" p. 14.

37. *Surprised by Sin*, pp. ix–x.

38. See, for instance, Ingarden, *The Cognition of the Literary Work of Art*, pp. 94–145; Gadamer, *Truth and Method*, pp. 108–14; and as Fish acknowledges, psycholinguists. For the last, see J. M. Schlesinger, *Sentence Structure and the Reading Process* (The Hague: Mouton, 1968).

39. *The Well Wrought Urn*, pp. 3–20, 176–96.

40. "How Ordinary Is Ordinary Language?" p. 15.

41. For an important attempt to articulate and defend the notion of literary competence, see Jonathan Culler, *Structuralist Poetics: Structuralism, Linguistics, and the Study of Literature* (Ithaca, N.Y.: Cornell University Press, 1975), pp. 113–30. See also Culler's criticism of Stanley Fish in his "Stanley Fish and the Righting of the Reader," in *Diacritics* 5 (Spring 1975): 26–31. For other critiques of Fish, see Edward Regis, Jr., "Literature by the Reader: the 'Affective' Theory of Stanley Fish," *College English* 38 (November 1976): 263–80; and Ralph W. Rader, "Fact, Theory and Literary Explanation," *Critical Inquiry* 1 (December 1974): 245–72.

42. *Principles of Literary Criticism*, pp. 44–57.

43. For a critical discussion of Richards, see René Wellek, "On Rereading I. A. Richards," *The Southern Review* 3 (1967): 533–54.

44. *Seven Types of Ambiguity*, 3rd. ed. (Harmondsworth: Penguin, 1961), p. 81.

45. Ibid., p. 94; italics added.

46. *Self-Consuming Artifacts*, pp. 409–10; see also "Interpreting the *Variorum*," pp. 473–85.

47. Empson is certainly far from providing a coherent and fully developed theory of reading. Yet he says that "any contradiction is likely to have some sensible interpretation; and if you think of interpretations which are not sensible, it puts the blame on you." See *Seven Types of Ambiguity*, p. 223.

48. This is a point made by David Couzens Hoy, *The Critical Circle: Literature, History, and Philosophical Hermeneutics*, p. 157.

49. *Principles of Literary Criticism*, pp. 124–31.

50. "Interpreting the *Variorum*," pp. 477, 482.

51. See the example Fish gives in "Interpreting the *Variorum*," pp. 465–77.

52. Stanley Fish, "Normal Circumstances, Literal Language, Direct Speech Acts, the Ordinary, the Everyday, the Obvious, What Goes without Saying, and Other Special Cases," *Critical Inquiry* 4 (1978): 637.

53. "Interpreting the *Variorum*," p. 478.

54. *Truth and Method*, pp. 245–73.

CHAPTER SIX

1. *The Sacred Wood*, p. 59.

2. René Wellek, *A History of Modern Criticism*, 1:1, 2.

3. *Principles of Literary Criticism; Practical Criticism; Science and Poetry; Coleridge on Imagination* (London: K. Paul, Trench, 1934); *The Philosophy of Rhetoric* (New York: Oxford University Press, 1936); with C. K. Ogden, *The Meaning of Meaning* (New York: Harcourt, Brace, 1923); with C. K. Ogden and James Wood, *The Foundations of Aesthetics*, 2nd ed. (New York: Haskell House, 1974).

4. For his attack on the state of critical theories and idealist aesthetics, see *Principles of Literary Criticism*, pp. 5–10 and 11–18, respectively.

5. Ibid., pp. 57–62.

6. Ibid., p. 37.

7. Ibid., pp. 48, 51.

8. This state is called "synaesthesis" in *The Foundations of Aesthetics*, pp. 72–79.

9. *Practical Criticism*, pp. 217–18.

10. See *Principles of Literary Criticism*, p. 110.

11. Ibid., chs. 10, 24, 25.

12. *Anatomy of Criticism* (Princeton, N.J.: Princeton University Press, 1957), pp. 20–28.

13. "On Value-Judgments," *The Stubborn Structure: Essays on Criticism and Society* (Ithaca, N.Y.: Cornell University Press, 1970), p. 69.

14. *Anatomy of Criticism*, p. 7.

15. All quotations are from *Anatomy of Criticism*, pp. 15, 12, 16, 10–11, and 342 respectively.

16. Geoffrey Hartman, *Beyond Formalism*, pp. 38, 39, and 363.

17. *Fearful Symmetry: A Study of William Blake* (Princeton, N.J.: Princeton University Press, 1947), pp. 260–61.

18. "Northrop Frye: The Critical Passion," *Critical Inquiry* 1 (June 1975): 754. Also see Fletcher's earlier essay on Frye, "Utopian History and the Anatomy of Criticism," in *Northrop Frye in Modern Criticism*, ed. Murray Krieger (New York: Columbia University Press, 1966), pp. 31–73.

19. This is a point made by Geoffrey Hartman, *Beyond Formalism*, pp. 39–40.

20. *Anatomy of Criticism*, pp. 341–54.

21. *Validity in Interpretation*; the quotations that follow are from pp. 180, 283, 193, and 172. I should note here that Hirsch's book deals with many issues besides the one I am discussing in this chapter; it is, for instance, an important contribution to the theory of genre which is closely connected with his conception of the logic of inquiry.

22. "Value and Knowledge in the Humanities," in *In Search of Literary Theory*, ed. Morton W. Bloomfield (Ithaca, N.Y.: Cornell University Press, 1972), p. 65. Also reprinted in Hirsch's recent book, *The Aims of Interpretation*.

23. "Three Dimensions of Hermeneutics," *New Literary History* 3 (Winter 1972): 250. Also reprinted in *The Aims of Interpretation*.

24. *Validity in Interpretation*, p. 230.

25. *Truth and Method*, p. 265. For a full discussion of Gadamer's theory see David Couzens Hoy, *The Critical Circle*, pp. 41–72.

26. *Truth and Method*, pp. 346–47.

27. Ibid., pp. 247, 246.

28. Ibid., pp. 261, 265.

29. *The Elizabethan World-Picture* (New York: Macmillan, 1944).

30. For A. C. Bradley, see *Shakespearean Tragedy* (London: Macmillan, 1905); for G. Wilson Knight, see his books, *The Wheel of Fire* (London: Oxford University Press, 1930), and *The Imperial Theme*, 3rd ed. (London: Methuen, 1951); and for W. H. Clemen, see *The Development of Shakespeare's Imagery* (Cambridge, Mass.: Harvard University Press, 1951).

31. See my discussion in the Appendix.

32. Ingarden, *The Literary Work of Art*, pp. 8–9; Wellek and Warren, *Theory of Literature*, p. 186; Aldrich, *Philosophy of Art*, pp. 22, 85.

33. *The Literary Work of Art*, p. 337.

34. Ibid., pp. 373, 336–37. See Wolfgang Iser's criticism of Ingarden's theory in *The Act of Reading*, pp. 170–79.

35. "Works of Art as Physically Embodied and Culturally Emergent Entities"; the quotation is from p. 194.

36. "Rationality and Imagination in Cultural History: A Reply to Booth," *Critical Inquiry* 2 (Spring 1976): 459.

37. This is a recurrent motif of Eliot's early criticism; see for instance his *Selected Essays: 1917–1932* (New York: Harcourt, Brace, 1932), pp. 3–22; and *The Sacred Wood*, pp. vii–xvii and 2–59.

38. *The Sacred Wood*, pp. 96, 47–59, 49.

39. See Matthew Arnold, *Essays in Criticism*, 2nd series (New York: Macmillan, 1924), pp. 1–55. We should note, however, that Arnold did not intend a rigid application of his touchstones: "These few lines, if we have tact and

can use them, are enough even of themselves to keep clear and sound our judgments about poetry, to save us from fallacious estimates of it, to conduct us to a real estimate" (p. 19).

40. Besides Eliot and Gadamer, there are others who have argued that aesthetic criteria are relative, not absolute. See, for instance, M. H. Abrams, "Rationality and Imagination in Cultural History," pp. 447–67, esp. p. 467, where Abrams argues that humanistic inquiry always tries to overcome relativism, though it "can never entirely" do so. For a strong defense of relativism in aesthetic see Joseph Margolis, "Robust Relativism," *Journal of Aesthetics and Art Criticism* 35 (Fall 1976): 37–46.

41. *The Anxiety of Influence*, p. 10.

42. See his *A Map of Misreading*, pp. 27–40 and 83–105.

43. *The Anxiety of Influence*, p. 25.

44. For Eliot's position, see his *Selected Essays*, p. 14. Bloom's is stated in his article, "The Necessity of Misreading," *The Georgia Review* 29 (Summer 1975): 268.

45. *The Anxiety of Influence*, p. 39.

46. *A Map of Misreading*, p. 71.

47. Ibid., p. 80.

48. *The Sacred Wood*, pp. 47–59.

49. Gallie, *Philosophy and the Historical Understanding*, pp. 157–91.

50. Eliot's criticism aspires to a balance between the Christian sense of community and the values of classicism; Bloom derives his critical tools, by his strong "misprision" from Vico, Nietzsche, and the orthodox Freudian theory of defense mechanism. I think Bloom's critical method is excessively schematic and is therefore inadequate to deal with the poetry other than romantic and neoromantic poetry, without considerable distortion. And the distortion that Bloom's practice would involve there would not fall within the purview of his adoption of Nietzsche's concept of "misinterpretation." For a criticism of Bloom see Jerome J. McGann, "Formalism, Savagery and Care; or, The Function of Criticism Once Again" *Critical Inquiry* 2 (1976): 605–30. It is obvious that McGann's criticism of Bloom springs from a decision that is fundamentally opposed to Bloom's. For an admiring but subtly critical response to Bloom, see Geoffrey Hartman, *The Fate of Reading and Other Essays*, pp. 41–56.

51. The attempts in modern analytic aesthetics to propose an institutional theory of art have implications for developing a concept of tradition. See, for instance, Arthur Danto, "The Artworld," *Journal of Philosophy* 61 (October 1964): 571–84; Joseph Margolis, "Works of Art as Physically Embodied and Culturally Emergent Entities"; and George Dickie, *Art and the Aesthetic*, chs. 1 and 7. David Couzens Hoy, *The Critical Circle*, pp. 159–66, discusses Bloom's theory from Gadamer's perspective. The Gadamer quotation is from *Truth and Method*, p. xiv.

52. *Truth and Method*, p. 263.

53. All quotations in this paragraph are from *Truth and Method*, p. 271–73.

54. Ibid., p. 250. Gadamer's remark here has a very strong connection to Eliot's "Tradition and the Individual Talent," especially when Eliot says: "Tra-

dition cannot be inherited, and if you want it you must obtain it by great labour. It involves . . . the historical sense" (*The Sacred Wood*, p. 49).

55. Quotations from *Truth and Method*, pp. 248, 246, 249, 250.

56. This is the objection Frank Lentricchia has raised in his *After the New Criticism* (Chicago: University of Chicago Press, 1980), pp. 153–54.

57. See *Hermeneutik und Dialektic*, vol. 1, ed. R. Bubner et al. (Tübingen: J. C. B. Mohr, 1970), pp. 283–317 (Gadamer) and 78–103 (Habermas) for the debate concerning hermeneutics and the critique of ideology.

58. W. B. Gallie, *Philosophy and the Historical Understanding*, p. 157.

59. See F. R. Leavis, *D. H. Lawrence, Novelist* (London: Chatto and Windus, 1955). For a good discussion of Leavis's criticism see John Casey, *The Language of Criticism* (London: Methuen, 1966), pp. 153–78. In an exchange with René Wellek, Leavis admits that Blake's poetry expresses philosophical ideas, but he refuses to admit that they are either relevant or important to characterize the excellence of his poetry. However, this is precisely the point at which the criticism that follows the Eliot-Leavis mode runs into serious difficulties. It must reject romanticism or risk serious miscomprehension of it because of its refusal to take into account the philosophy that is part of romantic poetry. See René Wellek, "Literary Criticism and Philosophy," and F. R. Leavis, "A Letter," both in *The Importance of Scrutiny: A Quarterly Review, 1932–1948*, ed. Eric Bently (New York: G. W. Stewart, 1948), pp. 23–30, 30–40 respectively.

60. Kuhn, *The Structure of Scientific Revolutions*, pp. 23–32.

61. That they both agree about progress in science is clear in Thomas S. Kuhn, "Logic of Discovery or Psychology of Research?" in *The Philosophy of Karl Popper*, ed. Paul Arthur Schlipp (La Salle, Ill.: Open Court, 1974), 2:805. Also see Kuhn, *The Structure of Scientific Revolutions*, pp. 77–87. For Popper's reply to Kuhn see *The Philosophy of Karl Popper*, ed. Schilpp, 2:1144–48. For the Kuhn quotation, see his *The Structure of Scientific Revolutions*, p. 77; for Popper, see his *Objective Knowledge*, p. 196.

62. Popper, *The Logic of Scientific Discovery*, p. 280.

63. *The Dehumanization of Art and Notes on the Novel*, trans. Helene Weyle (Princeton, N.J.: Princeton University Press, 1948).

64. For a philosophical discussion of these modes of reasoning see John Wisdom, *Paradox and Discovery* (Oxford: Blackwell, 1965) and *Philosophy and Psychoanalysis* (Oxford: Blackwell, 1953).

65. It is in John Stuart Mill's theory of poetry that the romantic theory of self-expression finds its fullest and most extreme expression.

66. *Paradox and Discovery*, p. 137.

CHAPTER SEVEN

1. Among the important essays in de Man's first phase are these three: "Intentional Structure of the Romantic Image," in *Romanticism and Consciousness*, ed. Harold Bloom (New York: Norton, 1970), pp. 65–79; "Symbolic Landscape in Wordsworth and Yeats," in *In Defense of Reading*, ed. Reuben Brower and Richard Poirier (New York: E. P. Dutton, 1962), pp. 22–37; "The Rhetoric of Temporality," in *Interpretation: Theory and Practice*, ed. C. S. Sin-

gleton (Baltimore: Johns Hopkins University Press, 1969), pp. 173–209. For the next two phases, see *Blindness and Insight: Essays in the Rhetoric of Contemporary Criticism* (New York: Oxford University Press, 1971); and *Allegories of Reading: Figural Language in Rousseau, Nietzsche, Rilke, and Proust* (New Haven, Conn.: Yale University Press, 1979). References to "Rhetoric of Temporality," *Blindness and Insight*, and *Allegories of Reading* will be given in the text throughout this chapter.

2. In a very recent work Frank Lentricchia has convincingly shown the influence of Sartre on de Man's essays on romanticism, and exposed many inconsistencies and contradictions throughout de Man's critical work. See Lentricchia, *After the New Criticism*, pp. 283–317. I read Lentricchia's book at the time of preparing the final version of my manuscript for the press. Though Lentricchia seeks to question the epistemological status of de Man's criticism, he does this mainly by giving detailed expository accounts of his work that also bring out the contradictions in it. I am glad to acknowledge the value of Lentricchia's admirably thorough study, though I think the task of showing contradictions is only preliminary to the task of questioning the epistemological status of any critical theory and its practice. The coherence of a theory, for instance, does not make the theory immune to serious criticism, since it could be coherent and yet very narrow, or very broad, or simply vacuous. My own attempt, though not oriented toward proposing an alternative theory because of the nature of my concern in this book, aims at examining the status of de Man's theory and the implications of de Man's mode of theorizing for the theory and practice of criticism.

3. See especially "Symbolic Landscape in Wordsworth and Yeats" and "Intentional Structure of the Romantic Image"; and Lentricchia's discussion of these two essays in *After the New Criticism*, pp. 285–91.

4. See Lentricchia's discussion of de Man in *After the New Criticism*, pp. 292–98.

5. Jean-Paul Sartre, *Search for a Method*, trans. Hazel E. Barnes (New York: Knopf, 1963), pp. 85–166.

6. Paul de Man, "Political Allegory in Rousseau," *Critical Inquiry* 2 (Summer 1976): 674. See also de Man's essay, "The Timid God: A Reading of Rousseau's *Profession de foi du vicaire savoyard*," *Georgia Review* 29 (Fall 1975): 558.

7. "Nietzsche's Theory of Rhetoric," *Symposium* 28 (Spring 1974): 35.

8. Paul de Man, "Semiology and Rhetoric," *Diacritics* 3 (Fall 1973): 30.

9. "Action and Identity in Nietzsche," *Yale French Studies* 52 (Fall 1975): 29.

10. "Genesis and Genealogy in Nietzsche's *The Birth of Tragedy*," *Diacritics* 2 (Winter 1972): 44–53.

11. "The Purloined Ribbon," *Glyph* 1 (1977): 44.

12. "The Epistemology of Metaphor," *Critical Inquiry* 5 (Autumn 1978): 30.

13. "The Epistemology of Metaphor," p. 18.

14. Martin Heidegger, "Holderlin and the Essence of Poetry," in *Existence and Being*, introduction and analysis by Werner Brock (Chicago: Henry Regenery, 1968), pp. 270–91.

15. Jacques Derrida, "Structure, Sign, and Play in the Discourse of the Human Sciences," in *The Structuralist Controversy*, p. 249.

16. *Of Grammatology*, trans. Gayatri Chakravorty Spivak (Baltimore: Johns Hopkins University Press, 1976), p. 49.

17. Jacques Derrida, "Differance," in *Speech and Phenomena and Other Essays on Husserl's Theory of Signs*, trans. David B. Allison (Evanston, Ill.: Northwestern University Press, 1973), pp. 129–60.

18. Ibid., p. 138.

19. Ibid., p. 141.

20. "Structure, Play and Sign in the Discourse of the Human Sciences," in *The Structuralist Controversy*, p. 249.

21. "'Ousia and Grammé': A Note to a Footnote in *Being and Time*," trans. Edward S. Casey, in *Phenomenology in Perspective*, ed. F. J. Smith (The Hague: Nijhoff, 1970), p. 93.

22. "Differance," in *Speech and Phenomena*, p. 153.

23. *Of Grammatology*, pp. 61–62.

24. Ibid., pp. 37, 44.

25. Ferdinand de Saussure, *Course in General Linguistics*, ed. Charles Bally and Albert Sechehaye, in collaboration with Albert Riedlinger; trans. Wade Baskin (New York: McGraw-Hill, 1966).

26. "White Mythology: Metaphor in the Text of Philosophy," *New Literary History* 6 (Autumn 1974): 47.

27. Ibid., p. 44; see also *Of Grammatology*, p. 15: "It is not . . . a matter of inverting the literal meaning and the figurative meaning but of determining the 'literal' meanings of writing as metaphoricity itself."

28. "The Ends of Man," *Language and Human Nature: A French-American Philosophers' Dialogue*, ed. Paul Kurtz (St. Louis, Mo.: W. H. Green, 1971), p. 205.

29. *La Dissémination* (Paris: Editions du Seuil, 1972).

30. Joseph N. Riddel, "From Heidegger to Derrida to Chance: Doubling and (Poetic) Language," *Boundary* 2 4 (Winter 1976): 589.

31. "The Critic as Host," *Critical Inquiry* 3 (Spring 1977): 443; "Stevens' Rock and Criticism as Cure," *Georgia Review* 30 (Spring 1976): 29.

32. Miller, "Stevens' Rock," p. 7.

33. Ibid., pp. 16–26.

34. Miller, "The Critic as Host," pp. 439, 441. Miller is referring here to Wayne Booth's phrase in "M. H. Abrams: Historian as Critic, Critic as Pluralist," *Critical Inquiry* 2 (Spring 1976): 441. The phrase was first cited by Abrams in his "Rationality and Imagination in Cultural History: A Reply to Wayne Booth," p. 458.

35. Miller, "Stevens' Rock and Criticism as Cure," p. 29.

36. Thus M. H. Abrams has said: "If all interpretation is misinterpretation, and if all criticism (like all history) of texts can engage only with a critic's own misinterpretation, why bother to carry on the activities of interpretation and criticism?" "The Deconstructive Angel," *Critical Inquiry* 3 (Spring 1973): 434.

37. "The Deconstructive Angel," p. 428.

38. "Williams' *Spring and All* and the Progress of Poetry," *Daedalus* 99 (Spring 1970): 407.

39. "Theory and Practice: Response to Vincent Leitch," *Critical Inquiry* 6 (Summer 1980): 611.

40. "The Interpretation of *Lord Jim*," in *The Interpretation of Narrative: Theory and Practice*, Harvard English Studies, ed. Morton W. Bloomfield (Cambridge, Mass.: Harvard University Press, 1970), 1:211–28. The quotations are from pp. 211, 213, and 214.

41. Ibid., pp. 215, 211.

42. "The Origin of the Work of Art," in *Poetry, Language, Thought*, trans. Albert Hofstadter (New York: Harper and Row, 1971), pp. 17–87. See also David Couzens Hoy, "Forgetting the Text: Derrida's Critique of Heidegger," *Boundary* 2 8 (Fall 1979): 223–35, for a fine discussion of Derrida's misunderstanding of hermeneutics.

43. *Aesthetic as Science of Expression and General Linguistics*, pp. 146, 150, 144.

44. Hayden White, *Metahistory: The Historical Imagination in Nineteenth-Century Europe* (Baltimore: Johns Hopkins University Press, 1973), p. 390.

45. See E. F. Carritt's criticism of Croce in his *The Theory of Beauty*, 4th ed. (London: Methuen, 1931), pp. 198–202, 291. Carritt's account of Croce is important because without adopting Croce's metaphysics, he is able to give a sympathetic account and defense of Croce's aesthetic theory. For the quotations, see Croce, *Aesthetic*, pp. 13, 14; Richards, Ogden, and Wood, *The Foundations of Aesthetics*, p. 44.

46. Hegel, *The Philosophy of Fine Art*, 1:154: "The beautiful may therefore be defined as the sensuous semblance of the Idea."

47. Miller, "The Critic as Host," p. 447.

48. "Stevens' Rock and Criticism as Cure: II," *Georgia Review* 30 (Summer 1976): 22.

49. *The Portable Nietzsche*, ed. and trans. Walter Kaufmann (New York: Viking, 1967), pp. 46–47.

50. *On the Genealogy of Morals*, trans. Walter Kaufmann (New York: Random House, 1967), p. 45; *The Will to Power*, trans. Walter Kaufmann and R. J. Hollingdale (New York: Random House, 1967), par. 302.

51. Jacques Lacan, *Écrits*, p. 284. See also Roland Barthes, *Critical Essays*, trans. Richard Howard (Evanston, Ill.: Northwestern University Press, 1972), pp. 243–45; Michel Foucault, *The Archeology of Knowledge*, trans. A. N. Sheridan Smith (New York: Harper and Row, 1976), pp. 222–24, and *Language, Counter-Memory, Practice: Selected Essays and Interviews*, trans. Donald F. Bouchard and Sherry Simon (Ithaca, N.Y.: Cornell University Press, 1977), pp. 113–64.

52. See, for instance, Emile Benveniste, *Problems in General Linguistics*, trans. Mary Elizabeth Meek (Coral Gables, Fla.: University of Miami Press, 1971), pp. 195–204 and 223–30.

53. Thus, in "Genesis and Genealogy in Nietzsche's *The Birth of Tragedy*," de Man, for instance, criticizes the readings of Nietzsche by Sarah Kofman and Gilles Deleuze, who privilege the Dionysian as the authority of truth in *The Birth of Tragedy*. De Man criticizes them for failing to question "the logocentric ontology" in Nietzsche's text (p. 48).

54. As Nietzsche put it, "it was as impossible to refute [Socrates for his insistence on divine calling] as to approve of his instinct-disintegrating influ-

ence." See *The Birth of Tragedy* and *The Case of Wagner*, trans. Walter Kaufmann (New York: Random House, 1967), par. 13 in *The Birth of Tragedy*. For a collection of several major poststructuralist essays on Nietzsche, see *The New Nietzsche: Contemporary Styles of Interpretation*, ed. David B. Allison (New York: Dell, 1977). The quotations are from *The Birth of Tragedy*, pars. 13, 23.

55. *Twilight of the Idols, The Anti-Christ*, trans. R. J. Hollingdale (Harmondsworth: Penguin, 1968), par. 43.

56. *The Will to Power*, par. 666.

57. Ibid., pars. 529, 527.

58. Martin Heidegger, *Being and Time*, trans. John Macquarrie and Edward Robinson (New York: Harper and Row, 1962), sec. 32 and *The Question concerning Technology and Other Essays*, trans. William Lovitt (New York: Garland, 1977), pp. 3–35.

59. *Lectures on Poetry*, pp. 3–34.

60. In this context Michel Foucault seems to me important, especially since his work does not permit any simple application to criticism. See, for instance, his books, *The Order of Things: An Archeology of the Human Sciences* (New York: Random House, 1973), and Foucault, *The History of Sexuality*, vol. 1, *An Introduction*, trans. Robert Hurley (New York: Pantheon Books, 1978), esp. pp. 135–59. For two valuable discussions of Foucault, see Hayden White, "Foucault Decoded: Notes from Underground," in his *Tropics of Discourse: Essays in Cultural Criticism* (Baltimore: Johns Hopkins University Press, 1978), pp. 230–60, and Edward W. Said, *Beginnings: Intention and Method* (New York: Basic Books, 1975), pp. 290–311. Among some of the important works in contemporary critical thought are Raymond Williams, *Marxism and Literature* (Oxford: Oxford University Press, 1977); Fredric Jameson, *Marxism and Form* (Princeton, N.J.: Princeton University Press, 1971); Pierre Macherey, *A Theory of Literary Production* (London: Routledge and Kegan Paul, 1978), first published in France in 1966; and the works of Louis Althusser. Important, too, in this context is Frank Kermode's work of the last decade or so, which is a sustained attempt at assimilation, qualification, and rethinking of some of the developments in contemporary cultural thought. To give just two examples, see Kermode, "The Structures of Fiction," in *Velocities of Change: Critical Essays from MLN*, ed. Richard Macksey (Baltimore: Johns Hopkins University Press, 1974), pp. 179–203; and *The Genesis of Secrecy: On the Interpretation of Narrative* (Cambridge, Mass.: Harvard University Press, 1979).

61. Among the important deconstructionist work by Joseph N. Riddel are the following: "Pound and the Decentered Image," *Georgia Review* 29 (Fall 1975): 565–91; and "Decentering the Image: the 'Project' of 'American' Poetics?" in *Textual Strategies: Perspectives in Post-Structuralist Criticism*, ed. Josué V. Harari (Ithaca, N.Y.: Cornell University Press, 1979), pp. 322–58.

CHAPTER EIGHT

1. Stanley Edgar Hyman has attempted to "suggest some possibilities for an integrated and practical methodology that would combine and consolidate the best procedures of modern criticism." See his *The Armed Vision: A Study in*

the Method of Modern Literary Criticism (New York: Knopf, 1948), p. ix. In his "Conclusion: Attempts at Integration," Hyman says, "If we could, hypothetically, construct an ideal modern literary critic out of plastics and light metals, his method would be a practical technique or procedure used by his flesh-and-blood colleagues." Murray Krieger, on the other hand, while trying to defend the fundamental New Critical insights, has sought to ground them in the entire Western humanistic poetics by drawing together the most crucial and compatible claims of that tradition. See, for instance, his most recent book, *Theory of Criticism: A Tradition and Its System*.

2. R. S. Crane, among others, has made this argument in his *The Languages of Criticism and the Structure of Poetry* (Toronto: University of Toronto Press, 1953), esp. pp. 3–38.

3. Monroe Beardsley is perhaps the most representative aesthetician, since he has attempted what is perhaps the most comprehensive and fully developed aesthetic theory. See his *Aesthetics: Problems in the Philosophy of Criticism*.

4. Harold Osborne, *Aesthetics and Criticism* (New York: Philosophical Library, 1955). Osborne's formulation and defense of his theory of configuration, pp. 218–59, follows his critical exposure of the inadequacies of the other theories of art.

5. Some critical theorists, owing to their highly partisan commitments, at times tend to take one of these two positions. Fish, for example, before he proposed his notion of "interpretive communities," would seem to hold that his method of reading shows what every reader does when he reads any piece of language. Bloom, too, to take another example, argues as if the principle of creative anxiety he has developed shows the inescapable condition of artistic creativity. Consequently, for Bloom other concepts are either unimportant or, if important at all, not really at odds with his theory. Now, as I have discussed in chapter 6, the concept of criticism is a disputed concept and allows for a variety of construals. In trying to defend their specific theories, critical theorists find it often necessary to accommodate or criticize other insights. Thus Krieger, in order to save the central New Critical insights as well as the Western humanistic tradition, has attempted a dialectical accommodation of positions sometimes as radically opposed to his as, for instance, Derrida's (see his *Theory of Criticism*, pp. 207–45). Krieger, of course, does not seek to accommodate all the rival insights, but rather by a critical probing of his as well as others' theories he formulates a dialectical theory of criticism that will grant a place of centrality to the Western humanistic tradition.

6. This would seem to be the position of those (for instance, Fish) who argue that each interpretive strategy constitutes any text. This seems to be close to the pluralism of the Chicago Aristotelians but is actually not. For a powerful defense of the latter, one that significantly updates R. S. Crane's, see M. H. Abrams, "What's the Use of Theorizing about the Arts?" in *In Search of Literary Theory*, ed. Morton W. Bloomfield (Ithaca, N.Y.: Cornell University Press, 1972), pp. 3–54.

7. Morris Weitz, *The Opening Mind: A Philosophical Study of Humanistic Concepts* (Chicago: University of Chicago Press, 1977), p. 49.

8. See Weitz, "The Role of Theory in Aesthetics," *Journal of Aesthetics and Art Criticism* 15 (September 1956): 27–35; Kennick, "Does Traditional Aesthetics Rest on a Mistake?" *Mind* 67 (July 1958): 317–34. See also a number of essays that attack the preoccupations of aesthetic theory in *Aesthetics and Language*, ed. William Elton. For a criticism of this position, especially that of Weitz, see Joseph Margolis, *The Language of Art and Art Criticism*, pp. 37–47. On Margolis's view, though most traditional definitions are inadequate, that does not mean that the attempt at definition is therefore fundamentally misguided. For a discussion of Wittgenstein's relevance to criticism, see M. H. Abrams, "A Note on Wittgenstein and Literary Criticism," *ELH* 41 (Winter 1974): 541–54.

9. See M. H. Abrams, "What's the Use of Theorizing about the Arts?" esp. pp. 11–23.

10. *Philosophical Investigations*, no. 664.

11. "The Dreariness of Aesthetics," in *Aesthetics and Language*, pp. 36–55.

12. "Logic and Appreciation," in *Aesthetics and Language*, pp. 161–69.

13. Yet often critics and theorists take their analogies too literally and therefore confuse their thinking. For some good observations on the use and abuse of analogical thinking see M. H. Abrams, *The Mirror and the Lamp*, pp. 34–35.

14. See Culler's qualifications of the value of the linguistic models for criticism in *Structuralist Poetics*, pp. 30–109.

15. "Poetry for Poetry's Sake," *Oxford Lectures on Poetry*, pp. 3–34.

16. *Appreciations, with an Essay on Style* (London: Macmillan, 1889); see "Style," pp. 5–38.

17. *The Blue and Brown Books* (Oxford: Basil Blackwell, 1964), p. 25.

APPENDIX

1. Karl Popper, *The Logic of Scientific Discovery* (New York: Basic Books, 1959), published first in German in 1934; also see his *Conjectures and Refutations: The Growth of Scientific Knowledge* (New York: Basic Books, 1962), and *Objective Knowledge: An Evolutionary Approach* (Oxford: Clarendon Press, 1972). *Logic of Scientific Discovery* and *Objective Knowledge* will be cited in the text hereafter.

2. Kuhn, *The Structure of Scientific Revolutions*. The concept of paradigms is central to Kuhn's concept of scientific inquiry and informs the structure of reasoning in his entire book. *Structure of Scientific Revolutions* will be cited in the text hereafter.

3. Kuhn, "Logic of Discovery or Psychology of Research?" *The Philosophy of Karl Popper*, ed. Paul Arthur Schilpp, 2:805. Also see *The Structure of Scientific Revolutions*, pp. 77–85. For Popper's reply to Kuhn in the Schilpp volume, see pp. 1144–1148.

4. "Logic of Discovery or Psychology of Research?" pp. 806, 805.

5. It is true, however, that Kuhn wishes to soften, if not to avoid altogether, the dismal conclusion of relativism implicit in his concept of para-

digms. He therefore says that "a sort of progress will inevitably characterize the scientific enterprise." Yet, committed to his concept of paradigms, Kuhn avers, "We may have to relinquish the notion, explicit or implicit, that changes of paradigms carry scientists and those who learn from them closer and closer to the truth." See *The Structure of Scientific Inquiry*, p. 170.

6. For an interesting discussion of this point, see P. K. Feyerabend, "Science: The Myth and Its Role in Society," *Inquiry* 18 (Summer 1975): 168–81.

7. Pierre Duhem, *The Aim and Structure of Physical Theory* (Princeton, N.J.: Princeton University Press, 1954).

Index

Index

Hume, David, 91
Husserl, E., 62
Hutcheson, Francis, 17, 91

Idealist aesthetics, 102, 144, 224. *See also* Bosanquet, Bernard; Croce, Benedetto; Hegel, G. W. F.
Identity, concept of, 114
Imagination, 21, 50
Imitation theory of art, 42–44, 243
Ingarden, Roman, 56, 161, 163–64
Intentional fallacy, 56, 59, 124
Intentionalists, 70–72
Interpretive strategies, 133–34
Irony, 6–9, 246; as aesthetic value, 81; and allegory, 208; and reconciliation, 86. *See also* New Criticism

Johnson, Samuel, 58, 99

Keats, John, 60
Kennick, W. E., 46, 242
Khatchadourian, Haig, 42
Kierkegaard, Sören, 237
King Lear (Shakespeare), 94–95
Knight, G. Wilson, 157, 159
Knowledge: in criticism, 181–87; in literature, 147–48, 160–61; in science, 159, 181–87, 255–58
Kuhn, Thomas, 181–82, 186–87, 256–58

Lacan, Jacques, 116–20, 228–29
Language, 75, 154–55, 200; community, 55; Croce on, 223; as figures and tropes, 199–201; literary, 197–99, 203; literary and ordinary, 3, 62, 75–82, 124, 127–28; Nietzsche on, 228–30; and unconscious, 116–19
Leavis, F. R., 180, 192, 252–53
Lévi-Strauss, Claude, 1–2, 234, 239
Linguistics. *See* Signs
Literature: criticism of, meaning in, 198–200; sincerity in, 55–56, 60;

spontaneity in, 55–56, 60
Logical positivism, 79, 159. *See also* Wittgenstein, Ludwig
Logic of Scientific Discovery (Popper), 255
Logocentrism, 219–20, 222
Lord Jim (Conrad), 220–21
"Lucy" (Wordsworth), 6–9

McKeon, Richard, 86
Margolis, Joseph, 164
Marx, Karl, 237
Meaning and significance, 153–54, 158
"The Metamorphosis" (Kafka), 43, 121–22
Metaphor, 119, 217; language as, 233; in "Lucy," 7; poetry as, 77
Methodology. *See* Hermeneutics
Metonymy, 7, 119
Miller, J. Hillis, 64–65, 215, 218–21
Mitias, Michael, 44

Neoclassical criticism, 16, 57–58
Neoclassical theory of poetry, 58
New Criticism: and conceptual stability, 57; de Man on, 205–7; Fish on, 125–33; on language, 78, 81; and uniqueness, 82–84
Nietzsche, Friedrich Wilhelm, 190, 199–201, 228–31, 237
Normal science, 256

Objective Knowledge (Popper), 256
Ontological status: of art objects, 22, 28, 101; of literature, 161–65, 205
"On Value Judgments" (Frye), 149
Organicist doctrine of poetry, 8–9
"The Origin of the Work of Art" (Heidegger), 221
Osborne, Harold, 15, 47
Other, the, 118–19

Paradigm, 256–57
Paraphrase, 126; heresy of, 75, 142, 199

Index